FROM
A BLACK
PERSPECTIVE

Contemporary Black Essays

The evil that is in the world always comes of ignorance, and good intentions may do as much harm as malevolence, if they lack understanding.

Albert Camus

FROM A BLACK PERSPECTIVE

CONTEMPORARY BLACK ESSAYS

edited by

Douglas A. Hughes

Washington State University

Holt, Rinehart and Winston, Inc.

*New York   Chicago   San Francisco
Atlanta   Dallas   Montreal   Toronto*

PREFACE

They began coming to America in the early seventeenth century, long before the great tide of European immigrants. By the middle of the nineteenth century approximately 500,000 black *human beings* had been uprooted from their African homeland and forcefully transported to the Land of the Free and the Home of the Brave. Crushed into fetid, monstrous ships, they came to the New World in chains with brands on their flesh. A half million individual, unique human beings arrived in the United States divested of all property and human dignity, fated to be slaves, to be owned by a man with pale skin. The white man treated the black human beings as exploitable animals and he justified his inhuman attitude and actions by proclaiming, with the sanction of his God and the tacit acceptance of the always silent majority, that white blood is superior to black. Although abused and violated spiritually as well as physically, black men and women survived in America before and after Emancipation. They endured—and had children.

Today the great-grandchildren of those violated men and women are angry and bitter, and some threaten revolution and the destruction of our cities. The bitterness, hatred, and despair are understandable. The freedom and equality repeatedly promised to black Americans for more than a century have never been realized, and for one disconcerting reason: the feeling of white racial superiority, which tolerated slavery and allowed the slaughter of the American Indian, has never been purged from American culture. Like violence, racism—however unintended or unconscious—is as American as cherry pie. Senator Fred Harris, a member of the National Advisory Commission on Civil Disorders, has said that white racism "is the unwillingness of white Americans to accept Negroes as fellow human beings," and it's just that simple.

If Camus is right and evil filters into the world through the pores of human ignorance, then racism, with the dreadful and unnecessary suffering it causes *individual* black children and adults, is curable by ample doses of knowledge and understanding. In spite of black unrest and violence and the so-called white backlash, in spite of the apparently increased polarization of the races, there is now, more than ever, reason to hope for a more harmonious racial climate—if not tomorrow, then the day after tomorrow. Ancient attitudes are being buried and dry souls are blowing away. Young blacks have cast off the ill-fitting image of themselves fashioned for years by the honkey, and are accepting themselves as black beautiful and different from the white man. They look one in the eye and speak of black power as a reality and not a prayer. And for the first time in this nation's history great numbers of young whites are earnestly trying to understand the black man and his condition. Unlike their parents who know the situation but do not understand, that is, who refuse to breathe imagination into lifeless facts, the young often project themselves imaginatively into the black condition, attempting to apprehend the situation from a black man's point of view. This compassion (literally, suffering with) may set the middle-class son or daughter free of the racist inheritance. Although some may become disillusioned and others may occasionally demand that blacks become dark carbon copies of the white model, sensitive white students—the nation's future leaders—give us hope that someday we will accept our creed: "We hold these truths to be self-evident; that all men are created equal."

With the exception of one essay by a white college dean, the nineteen essays collected in *From a Black Perspective* have been written by prominent contemporary black writers and political leaders, both radical and moderate. This book reveals the way it is for the great-grandchildren of American slaves in the seventh decade of the twentieth century and it examines a number of important questions from a black point of view. Aware that some readers may automatically resist the assertions and observations offered in these pages, I would urge students to try to keep an open mind while reading, and in this regard I invoke a thought of that old truth-seeker, Friedrich Nietzsche: "A very popular error: having the courage of one's convictions; rather it is a matter of having the courage for an *attack* on one's convictions!"—or one's prejudices.

Pullman, Washington   D. A. H.
January 1970

CONTENTS

vii

CLAUDE BROWN

The Language of Soul*

CLAUDE BROWN was born in New York City in 1937. He struggled for survival on the streets of Harlem, becoming a clever and experienced juvenile delinquent at an early age. Like many slum kids, Claude Brown appeared headed for a life of petty crime and ultimately prison. Friends and spiritual guardians, however, aided him in rising above his environment and Claude Brown is now finishing a law degree. The shocking, frightening day-to-day life of many blacks trapped in Harlem is recounted by Mr. Brown in his 1965 best-seller, *Manchild in the Promised Land.* This book forcefully answers the ignorant question often asked by whites: "Why don't those niggers just pack up and move out if it's so damn bad?" Commenting on the ghetto in an interview, Mr. Brown said that the best course to follow would be "to burn Harlem to the ground and rebuild it." "The Language of Soul" is a clear, simple essay, with interesting examples, of the black man's language and why it is the way it is. "The Language of Soul . . . is simply an honest vocal portrayal of Black America."

Perhaps the most soulful word in the world is "nigger." Despite
its very definite fundamental meaning (the Negro man), and dis-
regarding the deprecatory connotation of the term, "nigger" has a
multiplicity of nuances when used by soul people. Dictionaries define the term as being synonymous with Negro, and they generally
point out that it is regarded as a vulgar expression. Nevertheless, to
those of chitlins-and-neck-bones background the word nigger is
neither a synonym for Negro nor an obscene expression.

"Nigger" has virtually as many shades of meaning in Colored
English as the demonstrative pronoun "that," prior to application to
a noun. To some Americans of African ancestry (I avoid using the
term Negro whenever feasible, for fear of offending the Brothers X,
a pressure group to be reckoned with), nigger seems preferable to
Negro and has a unique kind of sentiment attached to it. This is
exemplified in the frequent—and perhaps even excessive—usage of
the term to denote either fondness or hostility.

It is probable that numerous transitional niggers and even established ex-soul brothers can—with pangs of nostalgia–reflect upon a
day in the lollipop epoch of lives when an adorable lady named
Mama bemoaned her spouse's fastidiousness with the strictly secu-

lar utterance: "Lord, how can one nigger be so hard to please?" Others are likely to recall a time when that drastically lovable colored woman, who was forever wiping our noses and darning our clothing, bellowed in a moment of exasperation: "Nigger, you gonna be the death o' me." And some of the brethren who have had the precarious fortune to be raised up, wised up, thrown up or simply left alone to get up as best they could, on one of the nation's South Streets or Lenox Avenues, might remember having affectionately referred to a best friend as "My nigger."

The vast majority of "back-door Americans" are apt to agree with Webster—a nigger is simply a Negro or black man. But the really profound contemporary thinkers of this distinguished ethnic group—Dick Gregory, Redd Foxx, Moms Mabley, Slappy White, etc. —are likely to differ with Mr. Webster and define nigger as "something else"—a soulful "something else." The major difference between the nigger and the Negro, who have many traits in common, is that the nigger is the more soulful.

Certain foods, customs and artistic expressions are associated almost solely with the nigger: collard greens, neck bones, hog maws, black-eyed peas, pigs' feet, etc. A nigger has no desire to conceal or disavow any of these favorite dishes or restrain other behavioral practices such as bobbing his head, patting his feet to funky jazz, and shouting and jumping in church. This is not to be construed that all niggers eat chitlins and shout in church, nor that only niggers eat the aforementioned dishes and exhibit this type of behavior. It is to say, however, that the soulful usage of the term nigger implies all of the foregoing and considerably more.

The Language of Soul—or, as it might also be called, Spoken Soul or Colored English—is simply an honest vocal portrayal of black America. The roots of it are more than three hundred years old.

Before the Civil War there were numerous restrictions placed on the speech of slaves. The newly arrived Africans had the problem of learning to speak a new language, but also there were inhibitions placed on the topics of the slaves' conversation by slave masters and overseers. The slaves made up songs to inform one another of, say, the underground railroad's activity. When they sang *Steal Away* they were planning to steal away to the North, not to heaven. Slaves who dared to speak of rebellion or even freedom usually were severely punished. Consequently, Negro slaves were compelled to create a semi-clandestine vernacular in the way that the criminal underworld has historically created words to confound law-enforcement agents. It is said that numerous Negro spirituals were inspired by the hardships of slavery, and that what later became songs were initially moanings and coded cotton-field lyrics. To hear these songs sung today by a talented soul brother or sister or by a group is to be reminded of an historical spiritual bond that cannot be satisfactorily described by the mere spoken word.

The American Negro, for virtually all of his history, has constituted a vastly disproportionate number of the country's illiterates. Illiteracy has a way of showing itself in all attempts at vocal expression by the uneducated. With the aid of colloquialisms, malapropisms, battered and fractured grammar, and a considerable amount of creativity, Colored English, the sound of soul, evolved.

The progress has been cyclical. Often terms that have been discarded from the soul people's vocabulary for one reason or another are reaccepted years later, but usually with completely different meaning. In the Thirties and Forties "stuff" was used to mean vagina. In the middle Fifties it was revived and used to refer to heroin. Why certain expressions are thus reactivated is practically an indeterminable question. But it is not difficult to see why certain terms are dropped from the soul language. Whenever a soul term becomes popular with whites it is common practice for the soul folks to relinquish it. The reasoning is that "if white people can use it, it isn't hip enough for me." To many soul brothers there is just no such creature as a genuinely hip white person. And there is nothing more detrimental to anything hip than to have it fall into the square hands of the hopelessly unhip.

White Americans wrecked the expression "something else." It was bad enough that they couldn't say "sump'n else," but they weren't even able to get out "somethin' else." They had to go around saying *something else* with perfect or nearly perfect enunciation. The white folks invariably fail to perceive the soul sound in soulful terms. They get hung up in diction and grammar, and when they vocalize the expression it's no longer a soulful thing. In fact, it can be asserted that spoken soul is more of a sound than a language. It generally possesses a pronounced lyrical quality which is frequently incompatible to any music other than that ceaseless and relentlessly driving rhythm that flows from poignantly spent lives. Spoken soul has a way of coming out metered without the intention of the speaker to invoke it. There are specific phonetic traits. To the soulless ear the vast majority of these sounds are dismissed as incorrect usage of the English language and, not infrequently, as speech impediments. To those so blessed as to have had bestowed upon them at birth the lifetime gift of soul, these are the most communicative and meaningful sounds ever to fall upon human ears: the familiar "mah" instead of "my," "gonno" for "going to," "yo" for "your." "Ain't" is pronounced "ain'"; "bread" and "bed," "bray-ud" and "bay-ud"; "baby" is never "bay-bee" but "bay-buh"; Sammy Davis Jr. is not "Sammee" but a kind of "Sam-eh"; the same goes for "Ed-deh" Jefferson. No matter how many "man's" you put into your talk, it isn't soulful unless the word has the proper plaintive, nasal "maee-yun."

Spoken soul is distinguished from slang primarily by the fact that the former lends itself easily to conventional English, and the latter is diametrically opposed to adaptations within the realm of conventional English. Police (pronounced po' lice) is a soul term, whereas "The Man" is merely slang for the same thing. Negroes seldom adopt slang terms from the white world and when they do the terms are usually given a different meaning. Such was the case with the term "bag." White racketeers used it in the Thirties to refer to the graft that was paid to the police. For the past five years soul people have used it when referring to a person's vocation, hobby, fancy, etc. And once the appropriate term is given the treatment (soul vocalization) it becomes soulful.

However, borrowings from spoken soul by white men's slang—particularly teen-age slang—are plentiful. Perhaps because soul is probably the most graphic language of modern times, everybody who is excluded from Soulville wants to usurp it, ignoring the formidable fettering to the soul folks that has brought the language about. Consider "uptight," "strung-out," "cop," "boss," "kill 'em," all now widely used outside Soulville. Soul people never question the origin of a slang term; they either dig it and make it a part of their vocabulary or don't and forget it. The expression "uptight," which meant being in financial straits, appeared on the soul scene in the general vicinity of 1953. Junkies were very fond of the word and used it literally to describe what was a perpetual condition with them. The word was pictorial and pointed; therefore it caught on quickly in Soulville across the country. In the early Sixties when "uptight" was on the move, a younger generation of soul people in the black urban communities along the Eastern Seaboard regenerated it with a new meaning: "everything is cool, under control, going my way." At present the term has the former meaning for the older generation and the latter construction for those under thirty years of age.

It is difficult to ascertain if the term "strung-out" was coined by junkies or just applied to them and accepted without protest. Like the term "uptight" in its initial interpretation, "strung-out" aptly described the constant plight of the junkie. "Strung-out" had a connotation of hopeless finality about it. "Uptight" implied a temporary situation and lacked the overwhelming despair of "strung-out."

The term "cop" (meaning "to get"), is an abbreviation of the word "copulation." "Cop," as originally used by soulful teen-agers in the early Fifties, was deciphered to mean sexual coition, nothing more. By 1955 "cop" was being uttered throughout national Soulville as a synonym for the verb "to get," especially in reference to illegal purchases, drugs, pot, hot goods, pistols, etc. ("Man, where can I cop now?") But by 1955 the meaning was all-encompassing. Anything that could be obtained could be "copped."

The word "boss," denoting something extraordinarily good or great, was a redefined term that had been popular in Soulville during the Forties and Fifties as a complimentary remark from one soul brother to another. Later it was replaced by several terms such as "groovy," "tough," "beautiful" and, most recently, "out of sight." This last expression is an outgrowth of the former term "way out," the meaning of which was equivocal. "Way out" had an ad hoc hickish ring to it which made it intolerably unsoulful and consequently it was soon replaced by "out of sight," which is also likely to experience a relatively brief period of popular usage. "Out of sight" is better than "way out," but it has some of the same negative, childish taint of its predecessor.

The expression, "kill 'em," has neither a violent nor a malicious interpretation. It means "good luck," "give 'em hell," or "I'm pulling for you," and originated in Harlem from six to nine years ago.

There are certain classic soul terms which, no matter how often borrowed, remain in the canon and are reactivited every so often, just as standard jazz tunes are continuously experiencing renaissances. Among the classical expressions are: "solid," "cool," "jive" (generally as a noun), "stuff," "thing," "swing" (or "swinging"), "pimp," "dirt," "freak," "heat," "larceny," "busted," "okee doke," "piece," "sheet" (a jail record), "squat," "square," "stash," "lay," "sting," "mire," "gone," "smooth," "joint," "blow," "play," "shot," and there are many more.

Soul language can be heard in practically all communities throughout the country, but for pure, undiluted spoken soul one must go to Soul Street. There are several. Soul is located at Seventh and "T" in Washington, D.C., on One Two Five Street in New York City; on Springfield Avenue in Newark; on South Street in Philadelphia; on Tremont Street in Boston; on Forty-seventh Street in Chicago, on Fillmore in San Francisco, and dozens of similar locations in dozens of other cities.

As increasingly more Negroes desert Soulville for honorary membership in the Establishment clique, they experience a metamorphosis, the repercussions of which have a marked influence on the young and impressionable citizens of Soulville. The expatriates of Soulville are often greatly admired by the youth of Soulville, who emulate the behavior of such expatriates as Nancy Wilson, Ella Fitzgerald, Eartha Kitt, Lena Horne, Diahann Carroll, Billy Daniels, or Leslie Uggams. The result—more often than not—is a trend away from spoken soul among the young soul folks. This abandonment of the soul language is facilitated by the fact that more Negro youngsters than ever are acquiring college educations (which, incidentally, is not the best treatment for the continued good health and growth of soul); integration and television, too, are contributing significantly to the gradual demise of spoken soul.

Perhaps colleges in America should commence to teach a course in spoken soul. It could be entitled the Vocal History of Black America, or simply Spoken Soul. Undoubtedly there would be no difficulty finding teachers. There are literally thousands of these experts throughout the country whose talents lie idle while they await the call to duty.

Meanwhile the picture looks dark for soul. The two extremities in the Negro spectrum—the conservative and the militant—are both trying diligently to relinquish and repudiate whatever vestige they may still possess of soul. The semi-Negro—the soul brother intent on gaining admission to the Establishment even on an honorary basis— is anxiously embracing and assuming conventional English. The other extremity, the Ultra-Blacks, are frantically adopting everything from a Western version of Islam that would shock the Caliph right out of his snugly fitting shintiyan to anything that vaguely hints of that big, beautiful, bountiful black bitch lying in the arms of the Indian and Atlantic Oceans and crowned by the majestic Mediterranean Sea. Whatever the Ultra-Black is after, it's anything but soulful.

KENNETH B. CLARK

The Invisible Wall*

KENNETH B. CLARK was born in 1914 in the Panama Canal Zone. His father remained in Panama as a passenger agent for the United Fruit Company when his mother moved the family to Harlem. Kenneth Clark received his B.A. and M.S. degrees from Howard University and Ph.D. in experimental psychology from Columbia University. In 1942 Professor Clark joined the faculty of City College of New York where he still teaches. He published an important psychological study in 1950 which revealed that segregated education adversely affected white as well as black students. His report was cited by the Supreme Court in its historic decision in 1954 concerning segregated schools. Professor Clark has written many articles and books, including *Prejudice and Your Child* (1955) and *Dark Ghetto: Dilemmas of Social Power* (1965), from which "The Invisible Wall" is reprinted.

ghettos — social, political, educational economic
colonies.

"Ghetto" was the name for the Jewish quarter in sixteenth-century Venice. Later, it came to mean any section of a city to which Jews were confined. America has contributed to the concept of the ghetto the restriction of persons to a special area and the limiting of their freedom of choice on the basis of skin color. The dark ghetto's invisible walls have been erected by the white society, by those who have power, both to confine those who have no power and to perpetuate their powerlessness. The dark ghettos are social, political, educational, and—above all—economic colonies. Their inhabitants are subject peoples, victims of the greed, cruelty, insensitivity, guilt, and fear of their masters.

The objective dimensions of the American urban ghettos are overcrowded and deteriorated housing, high infant mortality, crime, and disease. The subjective dimensions are resentment, hostility, despair, apathy, self-depreciation, and its ironic companion, compensatory grandiose behavior.

The ghetto is ferment, paradox, conflict, and dilemma. Yet within its pervasive pathology exists a surprising human resilience. The ghetto is hope, it is despair, it is churches and bars. It is aspiration for change, and it is apathy. It is vibrancy, it is stagnation. It is courage, and it is defeatism. It is cooperation and concern, and it is suspicion, competitiveness, and rejection. It is the surge toward assimilation, and it is alienation and withdrawal within the protective walls of the ghetto.

The pathologies of the ghetto community perpetuate themselves through cumulative ugliness, deterioration, and isolation and strengthen the Negro's sense of worthlessness, giving testimony to his impotence. Yet the ghetto is not totally isolated. The mass media —radio, television, moving pictures, magazines, and the press— penetrate, indeed, invade the ghetto in continuous and inevitable communication, largely one-way, and project the values and aspirations, the manners and the style of the larger white-dominated society. Those who are required to live in congested and rat-infested homes are aware that others are not so dehumanized. Young people in the ghetto are aware that other young people have been taught to read, that they have been prepared for college, and can compete successfully for white-collar, managerial, and executive jobs. Whatever accommodations they themselves must make to the negative realities which dominate their own lives, they know consciously or unconsciously that their fate is not the common fate of mankind. They tend to regard their predicament as a consequence of personal disability or as an inherent and imposed powerlessness which all Negroes share.

The privileged white community is at great pains to blind itself to conditions of the ghetto, but the residents of the ghetto are not themselves blind to life as it is outside of the ghetto. They observe that others enjoy a better life, and this knowledge brings a conglomerate of hostility, despair, and hope. If the ghetto could be contained totally, the chances of social revolt would be decreased, if not eliminated, but it cannot be contained and the outside world intrudes. The Negro lives in part in the world of television and motion pictures, bombarded by the myths of the American middle class, often believing as literal truth their pictures of luxury and happiness, and yet at the same time confronted by a harsh world of reality where the dreams do not come true or change into nightmares. The discrepancy between the reality and the dream burns into their consciousness. The oppressed can never be sure whether their failures reflect personal inferiority or the fact of color. This persistent and agonizing conflict dominates their lives.

The young people in Harlem, in the Negro ghettos of Chicago, Washington, Cleveland, Detroit, Los Angeles, and other cities, who persist, in spite of obstacles, in seeking an education, who insist upon going to night school and then the day session of a municipal college, whose parents, friends, or teachers encourage and support them demonstrate that a positive resolution of the ghetto's nuclear conflict is possible. But many resolve the conflict negatively—in either a passive or defiant way. Those within the ghetto who are defeated— those who accept the "evidence" of their personal inferiority and impotence, those who express a pervasive sense of personal failure through stagnation and despair, who drop out of school, who depend on marijuana and narcotics—demonstrate a passively negative and self-destructive solution.

The overt delinquent, the acting-out rebel, on the other hand, seeks his salvation in defiant, aggressive, and in the end self-destructive forms. Because the larger society has clearly rejected him, he rejects—or appears to reject—the values, the aspirations, and techniques of that society. His conscious or unconscious argument is that he cannot hope to win meaningful self-esteem through the avenues ordinarily available to more privileged individuals. The avenues have been blocked for him through inadequate education, through job discrimination, and through a system of social and political power which is not responsive to his needs. When a warlord of one of the last of Harlem's active fighting gangs was asked why he did not "go downtown and get a job," he laughed and replied:

> Oh come on. Get off that crap. I make $40 or $50 a day selling marijuana. You want me to go down to the garment district and push one of those trucks through the street and at the end of the week take home $40 or $50 if I'm lucky? They don't have animals doing what you want me to do. There would be some society to protect animals if anybody had them pushing them damn trucks around. I'm better than an animal, but nobody protects me. Go away, mister. I got to look out for myself.

Such rebels are scornful of what they consider the hypocrisy and the dishonesty of the larger society. They point to corruption and criminal behavior among respected middle-class whites. Almost every delinquent or marginal adolescent in a Negro urban ghetto claims to know where and how the corrupt policeman accepts graft from the numbers runners and the pimps and the prostitutes. The close association, collaboration, and at times identity, of criminals and the police is the pattern of day-to-day life in the ghetto as these young people come to know and accept it. Not only do they not respect the police, but they see the police as part of their own total predicament.

Large numbers of other ghetto youth, however, are caught in the paradox of the ghetto unable to resolve their personal conflicts either in positive and socially acceptable forms of adjustment or in direct and assertive antisocial behavior. They are aware of the values and standards of the larger society, but they know that they are not personally equipped to meet its demands. They have neither succumbed totally to pathology nor have they been able to emerge from it. As adults they live out lives they feel helpless to change, in a kind of unstable equilibrium, aware of their plight and yet accepting it. They are the ones who listen to Malcolm X but do not join; who vote Democratic if they bother to register but recognize at the same time that City Hall will do little for them. They are momentarily stimulated by the verbal militance of certain Negro newspaper editors and soapbox orators; they gain vicarious satisfaction through temporary identification with the flamboyance and antiwhite verbal extremisms of charismatic Negro politicians. They send their children to bad public schools reluctantly because they do not have the money for private schools. They are the great potential who could engage in constructive social action or who could become the pawns of the demagogues. They have no inner-determined direction. Whoever develops any movement toward power in the ghetto finally does so through winning the allegiance of this group—the largest in the ghetto—not of the semicriminal and certainly not of the elite and comfortable.

The ferment within Negro communities throughout the nation —hitherto more obvious in certain Southern communities, but beginning to express itself with increasing intensity and even spasmodic ferocity in such Northern urban communities as Chicago, Boston, Philadelphia, Rochester, and New York—suggests that the past cycle, in which personal and community powerlessness reinforces each other, is being supplanted by a more forceful pattern of personal and community action. This is proof that the reservoir of energy was there, ready to be stirred by hope, for effective or even sporadic protest could never have emerged out of total stagnation.

Although the civil rights movement gives Negroes more leverage, enabling many to channel their energies into constructive protest, there is a possibility that these energies could also be diluted into meaningless catharsis. Demonstrations that do not lead to results may become only one more safety valve—as the church has long

been for Negroes—releasing Negro energies without the transformation of society, without any actual change in their relative status.

If mobilized community power and protest do succeed in winning concrete positive changes, Negro self-confidence and pride will
grow, and a new cycle of greater personal and community effectiveness should emerge. But it would not be realistic for the white community to expect protest to subside in the face of gains, for the closer
the Negro community gets to the attainment of its goals—the removal
of the causes and effects of racial exploitation and powerlessness—
the more impatient will Negroes become for total equality. In the
complex turbulence of the Negro ghetto, and consistent with the
affirmative dynamics of the civil rights thrust, success feeds hope
and provides the strength and the motivation for further activity.
This, in turn, makes existing barriers even more intolerable. Acceler-
ated impatience and the lowering of the threshold of frustration
toward remaining inequities, paradoxically increase the chances of
racial tensions and ferment and conflict. Failure would reinforce the
sense of stagnation and despair and establish as fact the sense of
personal and group powerlessness. A truly hopeless group makes no
demands and certainly does not insist upon stark social confrontations.

The summer of 1964 brought violent protests to the ghettos of
America's cities, not in mobilization of effective power, but as an
outpouring of unplanned revolt. The revolts in Harlem were not led
by a mob, for a mob is an uncontrolled social force bent on irrational
destruction. The revolts in Harlem were, rather, a weird social
defiance. Those involved in them were, in general, not the lowest
class of Harlem residents—not primarily looters and semicriminals
—but marginal Negroes who were upwardly mobile, demanding a
higher status than their families had. This was not a race riot in the
sense that mobs of whites were assaulting mobs of Negroes or vice
versa, yet the fact of race was pervasive. The 1964 Harlem riot was
indeed in many respects more frightening than a race riot and the
participants' deliberate mockery more threatening than a mob. Small
groups of young people seemed to take delight in taunting the police,
whose white faces were accentuated by their white helmets: "Here's
a nigger, kill me." Even those Negroes who threw bottles and bricks
from the roofs were not in the grip of a wild abandon, but seemed
deliberately to be prodding the police to behave openly as the bar-
barians that the Negroes felt they actually were. You cannot hear
conversations of a mob, but during the disturbance in Harlem,

groups of young people discussed their plans: "I'll go home and come back tomorrow. Whitey will still be here." "I don't want to be killed tonight; tomorrow will be all right." There was an eerie, surrealistic quality, a silence within the din, punctuated by gunfire and sporadic shattering of glass, a calm within the chaos, a deliberateness within the hysteria. The Negro seemed to feel nothing could happen to him that had not happened already; he behaved as if he had nothing to lose. His was an oddly controlled rage that seemed to say, during those days of social despair, "We have had enough. The only weapon you have is bullets. The only thing you can do is to kill us." Paradoxically, his apparent lawlessness was a protest against lawlessness directed against him. His acts were a desperate assertion of his desire to be treated as a man. He was affirmative up to the point of inviting death; he insisted upon being visible and understood. If this was the only way to relate to society at large, he would die rather than be ignored.

At times of overt social unrest, many white persons who claim to be in favor of civil rights and assert that they are "friends" of the Negro will admonish the Negro not to engage in disruptive and lawless demonstrations lest he incite racism and reverse the progress made in his behalf. These often well-meaning requests may reflect the unconscious condescension of benign prejudices. They demonstrate mistaken assumptions concerning the nature and dynamics of Negro protest. It is argued, for example, that Negroes should "choose" only those techniques, tactics, and demonstrations which do not inconvenience the dominant white society; the oppressed are urged to be concerned about the comfort and sensitivities of those they regard as their oppressors. The implication is that if they do not, middle-class whites will use their own power to retaliate against all Negroes. Negroes are increasingly reminded of the sting of the "white backlash." Many middle-class Negroes as well as whites accept these arguments and behave accordingly. Yet the threat is not new. The struggle of those with power to deny power to those who have none is age-old, and accommodation and appeasement have not resolved it. The "white backlash" is a new name for an old phenomenon, white resistance to the acceptance of the Negro as a human being. As the Negro demands such status—as he develops more and more effective techniques to obtain it, and as these techniques come closer to success—the resistance to his demands rises in intensity and alarm. The forms it takes vary from the overt and barbaric murders and bombings to the more subtle innuendo of irritation and disparagement.

Many whites also assume that a governing group of Negro leaders chooses tactics for the Negro masses. Yet leaders of the stature and responsibility of Roy Wilkins and Whitney M. Young, Jr., James Farmer or Martin Luther King cannot impose tactics upon the masses of marginal Negroes, who are not disciplined members of any group. And the masses of Negroes do not "choose" tactics at all. They respond to the pressures of their lives and react spontaneously to incidents which trigger explosions or demonstrations. When a bewildered white liberal asks why, in the face of the passage of the Civil Rights Bill of 1964, "they" still revolt—and not in the dignified, respectable nonviolent way of the earlier student sitins— he betrays his own alienation from the Negroes whose cause he espouses. The Civil Rights Act was so long coming it served merely to remind many Negroes of their continued rejected and second-class status. Even well-meaning whites continue to see and talk of Negroes as "they," clearly differentiated from "we," the "outgroup" from the "ingroup." As long as this alienation remains, the masses of whites will be irritated and inconvenienced by any meaningful activity by Negroes to change their status. No real revolt can be convenient for the privileged; no real revolt can be contained within comfortable bounds or be made respectable.

In the face of the growing unrest, careful, thoughtful, and realistic planning becomes starkly imperative. Some whites would react to renewed protest by warning Negroes not to go too far too fast, not to alienate the white liberals who have, even if often timidly, supported them. To others, less well-intentioned, Negro unrest is but confirmation of their own prejudice: Negroes are, after all, behaving as the uncivilized do. But unrest *is* a characteristic of civilization, and to fight against oppression—even unwisely—is a sign that men have begun to hope. As studies on social disasters have demonstrated, people who feel there is no escape submit to their fate; it is those who see an exit sign and an open door who struggle to reach it.

Furthermore, energies devoted to a struggle for constructive social change are clearly not simultaneously available for antisocial and self-destructive patterns of behavior. In those communities such as Montgomery, Alabama, where Negroes mobilized themselves for sustained protest against prevailing racial injustice, *the incidence of antisocial behavior and delinquency decreased almost to a vanishing point during the period of protest.*

The Negro cannot any longer feel, if he ever did, that he should have to prove himself "worthy" in order to gain his full freedom— the rights guaranteed to all other American citizens, including those most recently naturalized. The Negro cannot be asked to prove that he "deserves" the rights and responsibilities of democracy, nor can he be told that others must first be persuaded "in heart and mind" to accept him. Such tests and trials by fire are not applied to others. To impose them on the Negro is racist condescension. It is to assume that the Negro is a special type of human being who must pass a special test before admission to a tenuous status worthy of governmental protection. It is to place upon the Negro a peculiar burden reflecting and exploiting his powerlessness, and it is, paradoxically, to deny him the essential human rights of frailty and imperfection. The experience of inferior racial status has not transformed the Negro into a super human being. To demand that he demonstrate virtues not ordinarily found in more privileged people, before he may enjoy the benefits of democracy, is not only irrational and inconsistent but gratuitously cruel. And above all it is evidence that the invisible wall is opaque from outside in.

No one ought to expect the transition from a system of injustice to a system of social justice to occur without personal and social trauma for the Negro as well as the white. The intensification of conflict and resistance inherent in the immediacy of the Negro's demands, and the dramatic methods which he is now using to attain his goals, understandably obscure some of the more profound human problems involved in progressing from a racially segregated to a nonsegregated society. But, when the cries of anguish of all the segregationists have subsided, as they will eventually, the Negro will be confronted with his own inner anxieties, conflicts, and challenges as he dares to move into a society of open competition. It will then be clear that though the problems of adjusting to change are difficult for whites, in even more insidious ways they are quite painful for Negroes. The invisible walls of a segregated society are not only damaging but protective in a debilitating way. There is considerable psychological safety in the ghetto; there one lives among one's own and does not risk rejection among strangers. One first becomes aware of the psychological damage of such "safety" when the walls of the ghetto are breached and the Negro ventures out into the repressive, frightening white world. Some Negroes prefer to stay in the ghetto, particularly those who have developed seemingly effective defenses to protect themselves against hurt, those who fear for their children, and those who have profited from the less competitive segregated society. Other Negroes, particularly the young, are militant in their efforts to crash the remaining barriers of race. But even among this group it is not always easy to tell who is totally committed and willing to assume the risks and who is only talking militance. Most Negroes take the first steps into an integrated society tentatively and torn with conflict. To be the first Negro who is offered a job in a company brings a sense of triumph but also the dread of failure. To be the "show" Negro, the symbol of a new-found policy of racial democracy in an educational institution, private industry, or governmental agency, imposes demands for personal restraint, balance, and stability of character rare among any group of mere human beings. For a Negro to be offered friendship and to find himself unable to accept it fully, to find that he is himself in the grip of hitherto unrealized racial prejudice—or, more precisely racial anger—is to look into the hidden recesses of his own mind. A person—or a race—who has been forced to be ashamed of his identity cannot easily accept himself simply as a human being and surrender either the supportive group identification or hostility toward those who have rejected him.

The newly emerging Negro—the assertive, militant, defiant, self-affirming Negro seeking his identity—will probably at first seem a caricature, a person who wears the mask of race with its fixed artificial expression. No more than the white bigot who succumbs to his passion of hatred and fear, or the white "liberal" who struggles to reconcile his affirmation of racial justice with his visceral racism, has the Negro escaped domination of his own individuality by the role of race. Only when the need to play such a role is no longer urgent will the individual Negro and white feel free to be merely themselves, without defenses.

JAMES BALDWIN

Fifth Avenue, Uptown: A Letter From Harlem*

JAMES BALDWIN, one of America's most gifted contemporary novelists, was born in 1924, the oldest of nine children, in New York City. He was reared in Harlem, about which he has often written with understanding and compassion. He lived in Paris for nearly ten years, where he wrote his first two novels, *Go Tell It on the Mountain* (1952) and *Giovanni's Room* (1956). In 1962 Mr. Baldwin published his third novel, *Another Country,* and in 1963 his *The Fire Next Time,* two open letters on the relationship of blacks and whites in America, became a best-seller. He has published two books of his essays, *Notes of a Native Son* (1955) and *Nobody Knows My Name* (1961), from which the following essay is reprinted. "Fifth Avenue, Uptown" describes the life and squalor at the Harlem ghetto end of the elegant, impressive avenue which runs north and south through Manhattan. This essay discusses how and why the black man is oppressed in Harlem. "It is a terrible, an inexorable, law," writes Mr. Baldwin, "that one cannot deny the humanity of another without diminishing one's own: in the face of one's victim, one sees oneself."

There is a housing project standing now where the house in which we grew up once stood, and one of those stunted city trees is snarling where our doorway used to be. This is on the rehabilitated side of the avenue. The other side of the avenue—for progress takes time—has not been rehabilitated yet and it looks exactly as it looked in the days when we sat with our noses pressed against the window-pane, longing to be allowed to go "across the street." The grocery store which gave us credit is still there, and there can be no doubt that it is still giving credit. The people in the project certainly need it—far more, indeed, than they ever needed the project. The last time I passed by, the Jewish proprietor was still standing among his shelves, looking sadder and heavier but scarcely any older. Farther down the block stands the shoe-repair store in which our shoes were repaired until reparation became impossible and in which, then, we bought all our "new" ones. The Negro proprietor is still in the window, head down, working at the leather.

These two, I imagine, could tell a long tale if they would (perhaps they would be glad to if they could), having watched so many, for so long, struggling in the fishhooks, the barbed wire, of this avenue.

The avenue is elsewhere the renowned and elegant Fifth. The

area I am describing, which, in today's gang parlance, would be called "the turf," is bounded by Lenox Avenue on the west, the Harlem River on the east, 135th Street on the north, and 130th Street on the south. We never lived beyond these boundaries; this is where we grew up. Walking along 145th Street—for example—familiar as it is, and similar, does not have the same impact because I do not know any of the people on the block. But when I turn east on 131st Street and Lenox Avenue, there is first a soda-pop joint, then a shoe-shine "parlor," then a grocery store, then a dry cleaners', then the houses. All along the street there are people who watched me grow up, people who grew up with me, people I watched grow up along with my brothers and sisters; and, sometimes in my arms, some-times underfoot, sometimes at my shoulder—or on it—their children, a riot, a forest of children, who include my nieces and nephews.

When we reach the end of this long block, we find ourselves on wide, filthy, hostile Fifth Avenue, facing that project which hangs over the avenue like a monument to the folly, and the cowardice, of good intentions. All along the block, for anyone who knows it, are immense human gaps, like craters. These gaps are not created merely by those who have moved away, inevitably into some other ghetto; or by those who have risen, almost always into a greater capacity for self-loathing and self-delusion; or yet by those who, by whatever means—War II, the Korean war, a policeman's gun or billy, a gang war, a brawl, madness, an overdose of heroin, or, simply, unnatural exhaustion—are dead. I am talking about those who are left, and I am talking principally about the young. What are they doing? Well, some, a minority, are fanatical churchgoers, mem-bers of the more extreme of the Holy Roller sects. Many, many more are "moslems," by affiliation or sympathy, that is to say that they are united by nothing more—and nothing less—than a hatred of the white world and all its works. They are present, for example, at every Buy Black street-corner meeting—meetings in which the speaker urges his hearers to cease trading with white men and estab-lish a separate economy. Neither the speaker nor his hearers can possibly do this, of course, since Negroes do not own General Motors or RCA or the A & P, nor, indeed, do they own more than a wholly insufficient fraction of anything else in Harlem (those who *do* own anything are more interested in their profits than in their fellows). But these meetings nevertheless keep alive in the participators a certain pride of bitterness without which, however futile this bitter-ness may be, they could scarecly remain alive at all. Many have given up. They stay home and watch the TV screen, living on the earnings of their parents, cousins, brothers, or uncles, and only leave the house to go to the movies or to the nearest bar. "How're you making it?" one may ask, running into them along the block, or in the bar. "Oh, I'm TV-ing it"; with the saddest, sweetest, most shame-faced of smiles, and from a great distance. This distance one is compelled to respect; anyone who has traveled so far will not easily be dragged again into the world. There are further retreats, of course, than the TV screen or the bar. There are those who are simply sitting on their stoops, "stoned," animated for a moment only, and hide-ously, by the approach of someone who may lend them the money for a "fix." Or by the approach of someone from whom they can purchase it, one of the shrewd ones, on the way to prison or just coming out.

And the others, who have avoided all of these deaths, get up in the morning and go downtown to meet "the man." They work in the white man's world all day and come home in the evening to this fetid block. They struggle to instill in their children some private sense of honor or dignity which will help the child to survive. This means, of course, that they must struggle, stolidly, incessantly, to keep this sense alive in themselves, in spite of the insults, the indifference, and the cruelty they are certain to encounter in their working day. They patiently browbeat the landlord into fixing the heat, the plaster, the plumbing; this demands prodigious patience; nor is patience usually enough. In trying to make their hovels habitable, they are perpetually throwing good money after bad. Such frustration, so long endured, is driving many strong admirable men and women whose only crime is color to the very gates of paranoia.

One remembers them from another time—playing handball in the playground, going to church, wondering if they were going to be promoted at school. One remembers them going off to war—gladly, to escape this block. One remembers their return. Perhaps one re-members their wedding day. And one sees where the girl is now—vainly looking for salvation from some other embittered, trussed, and struggling boy—and sees the all-but-abandoned children in the streets.

Now I am perfectly aware that there are other slums in which white men are fighting for their lives, and mainly losing. I know that blood is also flowing through those streets and that the human dam-age there is incalculable. People are continually pointing out to me the wretchedness of white people in order to console me for the wretchedness of blacks. But an itemized account of the American failure does not console me and it should not console anyone else. That hundreds of thousands of white people are living, in effect, no better than the "niggers" is not a fact to be regarded with complacency. The social and moral bankruptcy suggested by this fact is of the bitterest, most terrifying kind.

The people, however, who believe that this democratic anguish has some consoling value are always pointing out that So-and-So, white, and So-and-So, black, rose from the slums into the big time. The existence—the public existence—of, say, Frank Sinatra and Sammy Davis, Jr. proves to them that America is still the land of opportunity and that inequalities vanish before the determined will. It proves nothing of the sort. The determined will is rare—at the moment, in this country, it is unspeakably rare—and the inequalities suffered by the many are in no way justified by the rise of a few. A few have always risen—in every country, every era, and in the teeth of regimes which can by no stretch of the imagination be thought of as free. Not all of these people, it is worth remembering, left the world better than they found it. The determined will is rare, but it is not invariably benevolent. Furthermore, the American equation of success with the big times reveals an awful disrespect for human life and human achievement. This equation has placed our cities among the most dangerous in the world and has placed our youth among the most empty and most bewildered. The situation of our youth is not mysterious. Children have never been very good at listening to their elders, but they have never failed to imitate them. They must, they have no other models. That is exactly what our children are doing. They are imitating our immorality, our disrespect for the pain of others.

All other slum dwellers, when the bank account permits it, can move out of the slum and vanish altogether from the eye of persecution. No Negro in this country has ever made that much money and it will be a long time before any Negro does. The Negroes in Harlem, who have no money, spend what they have on such gimcracks as they are sold. These include "wider" TV screens, more "faithful" hi-fi sets, more "powerful" cars, all of which, of course, are obsolete long before they are paid for. Anyone who has ever struggled with poverty knows how extremely expensive it is to be poor; and if one is a member of a captive population, economically speaking, one's feet have simply been placed on the treadmill forever. One is victimized, economically, in a thousand ways—rent, for example, or car insurance. Go shopping one day in Harlem—for anything—and compare Harlem prices and quality with those downtown.

The people who have managed to get off this block have only got as far as a more respectable ghetto. This respectable ghetto does not even have the advantages of the disreputable one—friends, neighbors, a familiar church, and friendly tradesmen; and it is not, moreover, in the nature of any ghetto to remain respectable long. Every Sunday, people who have left the block take the lonely ride back, dragging their increasingly discontented children with them. They spend the day talking, not always with words, about the trouble they've seen and the trouble—one must watch their eyes as they watch their children—they are only too likely to see. For children do not like ghettos. It takes them nearly no time to discover exactly why they are there.

The projects in Harlem are hated. They are hated almost as much as policemen, and this is saying a great deal. And they are hated for the same reason: both reveal, unbearably, the real attitude of the white world, no matter how many liberal speeches are made, no matter how many lofty editorials are written, no matter how many civil-rights commissions are set up.

The projects are hideous, of course, there being a law, apparently respected throughout the world, that popular housing shall be as cheerless as a prison. They are lumped all over Harlem, colorless, bleak, high, and revolting. The wide windows look out on Harlem's invincible and indescribable squalor: the Park Avenue railroad tracks, around which, about forty years ago, the present dark community began; the unrehabilitated houses, bowed down, it would seem, under the great weight of frustration and bitterness they contain; the dark, the ominous schoolhouses from which the child may emerge maimed, blinded, hooked, or enraged for life; and the churches, churches, block upon block of churches, niched in the walls like cannon in the walls of a fortress. Even if the administration of the projects were not so insanely humiliating (for example: one must report raises in salary to the management, which will then eat up the profit by raising one's rent; the management has the right to know who is staying in your apartment; the management can ask you to leave, at their discretion), the projects would still be hated because they are an insult to the meanest intelligence.

Harlem got is first private project, Riverton*—which is now, naturally, a slum—about twelve years ago because at that time Negroes were not allowed to live in Stuyvesant Town. Harlem watched Riverton go up, therefore, in the most violent bitterness of spirit, and hated it long before the builders arrived. They began hating it at about the time people began moving out of their condemned houses to make room for this additional proof of how thoroughly the white world despised them. And they had scarcely moved in, naturally, before they began smashing windows, defacing walls, urinating in the elevators, and fornicating in the playgrounds. Liberals, both white and black, were appalled at the spectacle. I was appalled by the liberal innocence—or cynicism, which comes out in practice as much the same thing. Other people were delighted to be able to point to proof positive that nothing could be done to better the lot of the colored people. They were, and are, right in one respect: that nothing can be done as long as they are treated like colored people. The people in Harlem know they are living there because white people do not think they are good enough to live anywhere else. No amount of "improvement" can sweeten this fact. Whatever money is now being earmarked to improve this, or any other ghetto, might as well be burnt. A ghetto can be improved in one way only: out of existence.

Similarly, the only way to police a ghetto is to be oppressive. None of the Police Comissioner's men, even with the best will in the world, have any way of understanding the lives led by the people they swagger about in twos and threes controlling. Their very presence is an insult, and it would be, even if they spent their entire day feeding gumdrops to children. They represent the force of the white world, and that world's real intentions are, simply, for that world's criminal profit and ease, to keep the black man corraled up here, in his place. The badge, the gun in the holster, and the swinging club make vivid what will happen should his rebellion become

*The inhabitants of Riverton were much embittered by this description; they have, apparently, forgotten how their project came into being; and have repeatedly informed me that I cannot possibly be referring to Riverton, but to another housing project which is directly across the street. It is quite clear, I think, that I have no interest in accusing any individuals or families of the depredations herein described: but neither can I deny the evidence of my own eyes. Nor do I blame anyone in Harlem for making the best of a dreadful bargain. But anyone who lives in Harlem and imagines that he has *not* struck this bargain, or that what he takes to be his status (in whose eyes?) protects him against the common pain, demoralization, and danger, is simply self deluded.

overt. Rare, indeed, is the Harlem citizen, from the most circumspect church member to the most shiftless adolescent, who does not have a long tale to tell of police incompetence, injustice, or brutality. I myself have witnessed and endured it more than once. The businessmen and racketeers also have a story. And so do the prostitutes. (And this is not, perhaps, the place to discuss Harlem's very complex attitude toward black policemen, nor the reasons, according to Harlem, that they are nearly all downtown.)

It is hard, on the other hand, to blame the policeman, blank, good-natured, thoughtless, and insuperably innocent, for being such a perfect representative of the people he serves. He, too, believes in good intentions and is astounded and offended when they are not taken for the deed. He has never, himself, done anything for which to be hated—which of us has?—and yet he is facing, daily and nightly, people who would gladly see him dead, and he knows it. There is no way for him not to know it: there are few things under heaven more unnerving than the silent, accumulating contempt and hatred of a people. He moves through Harlem, therefore, like an occupying soldier in a bitterly hostile country; which is precisely what, and where, he is, and is the reason he walks in twos and threes. And he is not the only one who knows why he is always in company: the people who are watching him know why, too. Any street meeting, sacred or secular, which he and his colleagues uneasily cover has as its explicit or implicit burden the cruelty and injustice of the white domination. And these days, of course, in terms increasingly vivid and jubilant, it speaks of the end of that domination. The white policeman standing on a Harlem street corner finds himself at the very center of the revolution now occurring in the world. He is not prepared for it—naturally, nobody is—and, what is possibly much more to the point, he is exposed, as few white people are, to the anguish of the black people around him. Even if he is gifted with the merest mustard grain of imagination, something must seep in. He cannot avoid observing that some of the children, in spite of their color, remind him of children he has known and loved, perhaps even of his own children. He knows that he certainly does not want *his* children living this way. He can retreat from his uneasiness in only one direction: into a callousness which very shortly becomes second nature. He becomes more callous, the population becomes more hostile, the situation grows more tense, and the police force is increased. One day, to everyone's astonishment, someone drops a match in the powder keg and everything blows up. Before the dust has settled or the blood congealed, editorials, speeches, and civil-rights commissions are loud in the land, demanding to know what happened. What happened is that Negroes want to be treated like men.

Negroes want to be treated like men: a perfectly straightforward statement, containing only seven words. People who have mastered Kant, Hegel, Shakespeare, Marx, Freud, and the Bible find this statement utterly impenetrable. The idea seems to threaten profound, barely conscious assumptions. A kind of panic paralyzes their features, as though they found themselves trapped on the edge of a steep place. I once tried to describe to a very well-known American intellectual the conditions among Negroes in the South. My recital disturbed him and made him indignant; and he asked me in perfect innocence, "Why don't all the Negroes in the South move North?" I tried to explain what *has* happened, unfailingly, whenever a significant body of Negroes move North. They do not escape Jim Crow: they merely encounter another, not-less-deadly variety. They do not move to Chicago, they move to the South Side; they do not move to New York, they move to Harlem. The pressure within the ghetto causes the ghetto walls to expand and this expansion is always violent. White people hold the line as long as they can, and in as many ways as they can, from verbal intimidation to physical violence. But inevitably the border which has divided the ghetto from the rest of the world falls into the hands of the ghetto. The white people fall back bitterly before the black horde; the landlords make a tidy profit by raising the rent, chopping up the rooms, and all but dispensing with the upkeep; and what has once been a neighborhood turns into a "turf." This is precisely what happened when the Puerto Ricans arrived in their thousands—and the bitterness thus caused is, as I write, being fought out all up and down those streets.

Northerners indulge in an extremely dangerous luxury. They seem to feel that because they fought on the right side during the Civil War, and won, they have earned the right merely to deplore what is going on in the South, without taking any responsibility for it; and that they can ignore what is happening in Northern cities because what is happening in Little Rock or Birmingham is worse. Well, in the first place, it is not possible for anyone who has not endured both to know which is "worse." I know Negroes who prefer the South and white Southerners, because "At least there, you haven't got to play any guessing games!" The guessing games referred to have driven more than one Negro into the narcotics ward, the madhouse, or the river. I know another Negro, a man very dear to me, who says, with conviction and with truth, "The spirit of the South is the spirit of America." He was born in the North and did his military training in the South. He did not, as far as I can gather, find the South "worse"; he found it, if anything, all too familiar. In the second place, though, even if Birmingham *is* worse, no doubt Johannesburg, South Africa, beats it by several miles, and Buchenwald was one of the worst things that ever happened in the entire history of the world. The world has never lacked for horrifying examples; but I do not believe that these examples are meant to be used as justification for our own crimes. This perpetual justification empties the heart of all human feeling. The emptier our hearts become, the greater will be our crimes. Thirdly, the South is not merely an embarrassingly backward region, but a part of this country, and what happens there concerns every one of us.

As far as the color problem is concerned, there is but one great difference between the Southern white and the Northerner: the Southerner remembers, historically and in his own psyche, a kind of Eden in which he loved black people and they loved him. Historically, the flaming sword laid across this Eden is the Civil War. Personally, it is the Southerner's sexual coming of age, when, without any warning, unbreakable taboos are set up between himself and his past. Everything, thereafter, is permitted him except the love he remembers and has never ceased to need. The resulting, indescribable torment affects every Southern mind and is the basis of the Southern hysteria.

None of this is true for the Northerner. Negroes represent nothing to him personally, except, perhaps, the dangers of carnality. He never sees Negroes. Southerners see them all the time. Northerners never think about them whereas Southerners are never really thinking of anything else. Negroes are, therefore, ignored in the North and are under surveillance in the South, and suffer hideously in both places. Neither the Southerner nor the Northerner is able to look on the Negro simply as a man. It seems to be indispensable to the national self-esteem that the Negro be considered either as a kind of ward (in which case we are told how many Negreos, comparatively, bought Cadillacs last year and how few, comparatively, were lynched), or as a victim (in which case we are promised that he will never vote in our assemblies or go to school with our kids). They are two sides of the same coin and the South will not change—*cannot* change—until the North changes. The country will not change until it re-examines itself and discovers what it really means by freedom. In the meantime, generations keep being born, bitterness is increased by incompetence, pride, and folly, and the world shrinks around us.

It is a terrible, an inexorable, law that one cannot deny the humanity of another without diminishing one's own: in the face of one's victim, one sees oneself. Walk through the streets of Harlem and see what we, this nation, have become.

NATHAN HARE

Brainwashing of Black Men's Minds*

NATHAN HARE, who lived on a sharecropper's farm near Slick, Oklahoma, as a boy, earned his Ph.D. in sociology from the University of Chicago and is now a professor at San Francisco State College. He has published essays in *Saturday Review, The Saturday Evening Post, Crime and Delinquency,* and *Negro History Bulletin* and is the author of *The Black Anglo Saxons.* In the following essay Professor Hare reminds the reader how the white man has sought to undermine the black man's self-image and to keep blacks ignorant for centuries.

---

*"Brainwashing of Black Men's Minds," by Nathan Hare. *Liberator,* Vol. 6, No. 9. Copyright © 1966 by Liberator.

As a boy I used to hear old folks laughing and talking about the way white folks tricked Negroes to America as slaves with stories of a land where creeks were overflowing with molasses and flapjacks grew on trees. While hardly anybody seemed really taken in by that myth, it did have, as most jokes have of necessity, a certain tone of truth: that the Negro in America has been everlastingly misled, tricked and brainwashed by the ruling race of whites.

It seems certain, as recorded history bears out, that white conquerors supplemented more deadly weaponry by falling back on ideological warfare in confrontations with other races in the lands they "explored." Guns were used, as in Hawaii, for example, but not guns alone. Explorers, trailed by missionaries and other warriors, first sought to convert "natives" to the Christian religion. Then, failing to "save" the pagan chief, they merely proceeded to convert a "commoner" and provide him guns with which to overthrow the chief. This well-known tactic of divide-and-rule is proving just as efficient to this day. "Why" is still the question.

Africans in the know have finally come to realize that: "Once we had only the land. The white man came and brought us the Bible. Now we have the Bible, and they have the land." To accomplish this piracy—and retain the loot indefinitely—it was of course necessary to control the minds and bodies of the subjugated blacks. Indeed, control over the body is one basic means of manipulating thought. This was accomplished even more successfully in the case of American blacks, compared to Africans, because of the fact that brainwashing is best implemented by removing the subject from his normal setting, severing his social relations and identities ordinarily sustained only by regular interaction with family, friends and "significant others." Communication is then restricted—in the case of the Negro slave, it was virtually destroyed—and the "stripping process," the process of self-mortification (the destruction of identity and self-esteem) is then almost a matter of course.

Not only were slaves cut off from contacts and lifelines of old, they were restricted in their social relations with one another (sold apart as well from their families on the whims of their "masters") and forbidden to congregate without the presence of a white "overseer." Even after they were permitted to enter the confines (pun intended) of Christendom, pastors of Negro churches such as First Baptist in Petersburg, Virginia, seat of a violent slave uprising, were at first typically white. Ritualistic deference (such as keeping eyes downcast in the presence of whites, addressing them as "Mr.", "Sir" or "Suh," and other means described in Bertram Doyle's *Racial Etiquette in the South)* also aided in undermining the slave's self-respect and stimulating his glorification of the white man's world which in turn made him more inclined to bow down to the Great White Society.

A University of Chicago history professor, Stanley Elkins, in a book called *Slavery,* has likened the practices and consequences of the slave plantation to the Nazi concentration camp. This fits in with the basic principles of brainwashing in the setting of "total institutions" (prisons, asylums, concentration and POW camps) set forth by University of California sociologist Erving Goffman in the book, *Asylum.* The slave plantation was a total institution in that a large number of persons were restricted against their will to an institution which demanded total loyalty and was presided over and regimented by an "all-powerful" staff, and "master."

Even the language of white America has exhibited a built-in force destructive of the black man's self-image. Blacks were taught to worship a god who was always painted white, and then, to sing that they wanted to "be more and more like Jesus" who would be "riding six white horses when He comes." While the color white symbolized purity (Negroes may be found singing in church houses, even today, that they are going to be "washed white as snow in the blood of the lamb"), black stood—stands now—for evil and derogatory referents. You "blackball" a person from your club; an employee is "blacklisted"; phony magic is "black magic"; illegal commerce comprises a "black market"; you are in a "dark mood" or "blackhearted" on "Black Thursday"; especially if you are behind the eight-ball, which of course is painted black in pool. If a chartreuse cat or a polka-dot cat crosses your trail, it is no cause for alarm, but if a black cat crosses your trail, you are doomed to bad luck. We refer here only to the cat that purrs. Admittedly women may be in trouble when some black cats cross their trails.

It seems no accident, in any case, that a romance word for "black"—"Negro" (capitalized only in the past four decades)—was attached to a group which, owing to the white man's sexual drives and his Christian manipulation of the sexual and familial relations of his slaves, soon became a *potpourri* of colors and racial derivations. The word "black" was used by the English to describe a free man of color while a "Negro" was used to designate a black slave. Naturally, the word "Negro" eventually assumed a connotation of low esteem regardless of, but not exclusively independent of, the color or biological characteristics of the individual to whom the appellation was applied. This allowed some Negroes of "fair" features to "pass" (also a word for the act of death, just as a Negro who passed was called a "harp"—which he was going to play when he got to Heaven). Confusion arose requiring laws fixing a white person's race as Negro if it was known that he had even the remotest bit of black ancestry. Today's experts still stammer in their efforts to clarify the concept: *Webster's Collegiate Dictionary* finally winds up declaring a Negro anyone with "more or less Negro blood" and the 1960 Bureau of the Census instructions directed interviewers to classify as Negro any descendant of a black man, or a black man and any other race, *unless the Negro is regarded as an Indian in the community!* This was a concession to the white-Negro-Indians of the Carolinas and Oklahoma where I have known Negro women of the Aunt Jemima variety to wear a wig (long before it was the fashion), marry an Indian, fry their offsprings' hair, and send them to a white or/and Indian school, except when the children were bounced back as a bit too black.

The standard of beauty, so essential to a group's self-image, also was derogatory to the Negro. Not only were mulatto descendants of white masters given special privileges and higher status among slaves, all beauty queens and men of power were visibly white. Even today, "Miss Washington, D.C.," where Negroes are in the majority, for example, is likely to live in the suburbs, in Fairfax, Virginia or Silver Spring, Maryland, and, regardless of her residence, she is certain to be white.

On top of all of the foregoing, there has been a massive effort, deliberate and persistent in speed, to keep the black man in ignorance. During the early days of slavery, it was illegal to teach, aid or abet a black slave to learn to read, for fear he might find out how he was being treated. Books, newspapers, periodicals and other media of information have consistently been published or controlled, in almost every case, by white men. The King James' version of the Bible, the only book many Negroes ever read, also plays down the black man; for example, "black but (nevertheless) comely." Negro worshippers are exhorted to tuck in their whimpering tails and conform to white society by such tidbits as: "The meek shall inherit the earth," "Thou shalt not covet thy neighbor's goods . . .," "We'll all be one when we get over yonder" and "To him who hath shall be given, and to him who hath not, *even that which he thinks he hath,* shall be taken away."

Most other books, too, including those on the Negro—especially those promoted and accepted in the United States—are not only published but also generally written by white men. Thus the Negro is led to depend on the white man to tell him what to think even about himself! During Negro History Week last February (known as "Brotherhood Week" now that we are "integrated"), I happened to notice in the lobby of Howard University's Founder's Library a set of twelve books on display as "books about the Negro." I knew, because of my special interest in literature on the race issue, the names of eleven of the authors. All were white. I walked over to the circulation desk and asked the black gentleman behind it: "How about a book about the Negro by a Negro?" He laughed and thought the matter one big joke.

Children (learning to read on white Dicks and Janes) internalize the hatred of black men early in life. Although some black Anglo-Saxon Negroes will claim that they never knew there was a difference made between whites and Negroes until they were going on seventeen or had "got grown." Only a moment ago, even as I was writing this article, I learned that a black schoolteacher in Washington, D.C.'s summer school program got mad at a white teacher and called her a "black Jew!" With teachers like that, our children don't have a chance.

I once sat on a churchhouse step and watched a band of boys about ten years old stand beside their bicycles on the sidewalk and swap black epithets for thirty minutes by the clock. "You black as tar; can't get to heaven on an electric wire." "You so black your mama had to throw a sheet over your head so sleep could slip up on you." Thus they grow up to look down on their own kind and idolize, mimic and conform to white standards of behavior.

Consequently, the black man's passive approval of the control of media of communication by white men in this mass society makes it virtually impossible for a black leader to emerge except through the white press. Accordingly, aspirants as well as established "spokesmen" for the Negro must slant their strategy toward capturing the spotlight of the white press.

W. E. B. DuBois, for example, had to contend in his day with white promotion of Booker T. Washington, now widely known as an Uncle Tom. DuBois sought to persuade Negroes to do half-a-century ago—though he later realized his error—what the NAACP eventually did, but, by that time, still fifty years ahead of his time and having fallen into disrepute with the white establishment, was not even invited to the NAACP's fiftieth anniversary, according to newspaper reports. Schools fail to carry his name, in spite of his legendary attributes as a scholar, just as E. Franklin Frazier, in spite of his acceptance by the white sociological establishment, has been overlooked. Instead, acceptable Negroes such as Booker T., Ralph Bunche, George Washington Carver, Charles Johnson and Marian Anderson, along with Abraham Lincoln and Franklin D. Roosevelt, are symbols for the Nation's black schoolchildren. Although Rev. King is not a name for a school—to my knowledge yet while he lives—he eventually will join his brethren as a white-groomed Negro leader, as indicated by the plethora of prizes and honorary degrees already bestowed upon his crown.

Conversely, all the pretense of not understanding "Black Power" (a simple phrase) is merely an effort to whitewash the tardy awakening of black men in America and deter them from any attempt to acquire or utilize power to their own advantage.

White theorists have disseminated a number of false theories readily gobbled up and parroted by hoodwinked Negroes. One is that the Negro should not be bitter, whereas Anna Freud, in *Ego and the Mechanisms of Defense*, suggests that it is natural to be bitter in a bitter situation. For instance, if somebody sticks a pin in a portion of your anatomy and you do not yell out, then something is wrong with you or that portion of your anatomy. Another erroneous theory, geared to keeping Negroes conformist, is that Negroes are hopelessly outnumbered in America and must act to gain white sympathy, to "change white hearts and souls." This led to the assimilationist craze now increasingly apparent on the part of the Negro's "civil rights" movement before SNCC and CORE sought to put some sense into the movement. LBJ, in a recent effort to scare rioting Negroes, made a big ado about the Negro comprising only ten per cent of the population (actually he comprises at least eleven per cent, according to the Government's own figures) but white boys never get their facts straight about the Negro. The truth is that, regardless of their numbers, white men rule—two per cent in South Africa or Jamaica, forty per cent in Washington, D.C. or Mississippi or ninety-nine per cent in Maine or Montana. It is a mental attitude—not numbers. What excuse, then, had black men in Rhodesia (who grumbled privately when Smith took over but grinned and cowardly tucked their tails whenever a white person passed by for fear he might overhear them)? Outnumbering whites twenty-three to one, they could have taken each white man—one each grabbing a finger, ten others a toe, one the head and two whatever portion pleased them—and pulled him apart.

But, of course, black men are supposed to be non-violent in conflict with whites, while violent in his behalf and with one another. The non-violent hypocrisy has been perhaps the most ridiculous and appalling farce ever perpetrated upon and swallowed by a supposedly sane group of human beings. Only recently have black people begun showing signs of shedding this preposterous shackle.

It is amusing to watch the media's effort to commit the Afro-American to the Vietnam fiasco. While Afros virtually never make the daily press in a laudatory manner—not to mention the front page—they frequently find themselves turning up there now in uniform, holding up some wounded white "buddy," eating chicken, turkey or goose on Thanksgiving Day, or saving a Bible from perspiration and harm by wearing it under the band around their helmets. It is enough to cause a man to hang his head in shame.

Even on the home front, news about the Afro is slanted and sorted to suit the white power structure's purposes. William Worthy, for example, foreign correspondent for the *Afro-American* newspaper, was gagged by white newspapers when he ran afoul of then-Attorney-General Robert Kennedy's great white liberal graces after going to Cuba, and reporting that Castro was solving the race problem exported there by United States-dominated industry. William Worthy was believed to be the first newsman to test the right to go abroad, write home the news, and come home again—and though the white press is forever crying crocodile tears over "freedom of the press"—the press fell curiously silent in this case. So much so, that some brainwashed Negro students in a class of mine, during a discussion on mass communications, insisted that the United States has a free press. Yet, when I placed the name of William Worthy on the board—at a time when his case was current—along with five multiple-choice descriptions of his identity, only six in a class of twenty-four were able to choose the correct answer.

These students were, in the full sense of the word, pathetically "miseducated," in the manner described by Carter G. Woodson, in his *The Miseducation of the Negro.* They, like most Negroes, are merely products of generations of the most efficient and gigantic system of brainwashing the world has ever known. Thus, while they once merely chanted desires of being "more and more like Jesus," they now typically long and struggle to be more and more like "whitey" as a group. No doubt their brains, at least, at last have been *"washed white as snow. . . ."*

NATHAN WRIGHT, JR.

Knowing the Beauty
of What We Are*

DR. NATHAN WRIGHT, JR., a longtime civil rights leader, is Executive
Director of the Department of Urban Work of the Episcopal Diocese
of Newark, New Jersey. He is also a lecturer in urban sociology at
New York City Community College and the author of several books
on sociology and religion. Dr. Wright holds five college degrees,
including a doctorate in education from Harvard University. In
"Knowing the Beauty of What We Are," he discusses the need for
blacks to shake off the self-hatred which is "the black side of the
racism that permeates the nation." Blacks must learn to accept
themselves for what they are.

---

*From the book LET'S WORK TOGETHER by Nathan Wright, Jr. Copy-
right © 1968 by Nathan Wright, Jr. Published by Hawthorn Books, Inc.

One of my most unforgettable experiences as a young altar boy at St. Andrew's Church in Cincinnati occurred after the 11:00 service one Sunday morning. It was Father Oxley's custom to greet his parishioners and visitors at the main door of the church as they left. The altar boys took turns making themselves handy near the door.

On this particular Sunday, a proud-looking white woman had visited the church. Father Oxley, noting her British accent, asked where her home was. "I am visiting here from England," was her pleasant answer. His handsome dark West Indian face came alive with delight. "I am a Britisher, too," he said. "I was born in Trinidad." His affirmation of a kind of patriotic kinship was received with devastating scorn. "You are *not* a Britisher!" the visitor replied with fierce contempt. "You are a British *subject*."

That experience was one of many that drove into my consciousness, during my early years, how low in esteem and power black people are. The abrupt change to brusque unkindliness by one who had only an instant before appeared to be a thoroughly gracious lady, however, gave me particular pause. Just what kind of graciousness could be so deeply lacking in grace? That specific instance of gratuitous belittlement before his parishioners of a man who, in my young eyes, deserved great respect haunted me for years. It brought into focus for me the need for black people to deal far more effectively than we had done before with the issues of group respect and power—and I have wrestled with the issues ever since.

In this chapter, we shall examine some aspects of growing black self-awareness and self-respect. In the next chapter, we shall examine some current promising approaches to the long-standing struggle for black group status and power. In Chapter 8, we shall discuss how the growth of black self-awareness and the development of black group power may serve as vital ingredients in the reordering of our presently fractured national and global society.

It is only one of countless strange occurrences of history that a black man in his mid-twenties, already branded by many as a wild and reckless militant, should raise and bring into focus for the benefit of our nation and the world the two most basic needs in all our personal and community lives: first, the need to come to terms with oneself, to discover the beauty of what one essentially is, and, second, the need for power to fulfill individual promise. Black power —the most creative social concept of the present century—thus is designed only incidentally, although most immediately, to encourage black people to discover their own identities and to create *for themselves* group power. All of us must come to terms with who we are. Some people in the insurance business claim that more than 90 per cent of automobile accidents are related to identity problems. Many social scientists believe that our soaring incidence of mental disease and our mounting divorce and delinquency rates—along with obvious aspects of our foreign relations and other unresolved domestic social problems—also attest to the serious identity crisis that we collectively face.

It is good, then, that black people at least are beginning a process that should be entered upon by the nation as a whole: the sometimes awkward struggle for self-awareness.

"PRUNES AND PRISMS"

My mother was a beautiful woman of golden-brown complexion, and she carried herself with great dignity. Both as a schoolteacher and as a mother she exercised great care of those for whose upbringing she felt responsible. She went to her reward when I was twelve.

I am told that among the Samoans there is a legend about creation that squares with my own early perceptions of reality. The story is that, when God sought to create man in his own image, he first shaped the clay and then baked it. The first clay was a bit too light. He tried again, and the second clay was darker than the ideal. On the third attempt the clay came out a rich golden brown in the exact image of the Creator. He looked upon this precise model of himself and smiled!

Among black people there are all shades; some are light, some are golden brown, and some are deep brown. But my mother's complexion, in my early conception of reality, was perfect, the best that the Creator could give to man or woman.

My twin brother and I are somewhat darker than our parents were. Our two sisters, Lina and Lydia, are quite fair, what was referred to as *marrone*. In our household there were thus all the colors that make up our race. Our parents were eager that we come to see ourselves in a positive way and to accept our heritage as good. Yet somehow I came to feel that, although my mother's rich golden-brown complexion was the most beautiful that God had made, it was still necessary to improve upon His work. Thick lips, for instance, had to be kept pulled in tight lest they appear too large.

Mom, like many other mothers of that period, would have us stand before a mirror and go through the exercise of saying "prunes and prisms" while pulling our lips in gently. Madam A'Lelia Walker, who invented the hot hair-straightening comb, was also a kind of patron saint in our household. Our parents dressed us somewhat lavishly. We were scrubbed and brushed and pressed, and our arms and legs were oiled so that the ashen or rusty look that dark skin often develops in cold weather would take on a satiny luster. We were taught to be proud but also to be as much like the white ideal as our black selves could be. Like so many "refined" white Americans who try to emulate the English, we either could not or would not accept ourselves for what we were. We were not even conscious of our self-depreciation.

The story here is in a sense a tragic one, but it represents a well-nigh universal experience among black people brought up in the United States. At the same time that we have striven for pride in what we have been, what we are, and what we yet may be, we have taken as our unacknowledged but universal model the ideal white American. Ludicrous evidence of this split are the occasional black men who, having spent all their lives in a black American world, speak with a Cockney accent.

We have sought, albeit unconsciously, to be carbon copies of what we could not and should not be in fact. What seems especially unfortunate is that we have sought to purchase stock in a value system that tends—despite its ethical component—to give a higher priority to material things than to human values. We have largely copied rather than creatively adapted these values, often taking form without substance, a tendency that has compounded our tragedy. But it must be made absolutely clear that *our efforts to be like white people, even emulating their disdain for blackness, have, ironically, served our survival.*

Unconscious black self-hatred is the black side of the racism that permeates the nation. It is self-destructive insofar as it works to make black people "acceptable" and worthwhile to the larger society at the price of diminishing black identity, integrity, and self-respect.

The effects of this tragic ambivalence, however, touch the lives of all Americans, for those who will destroy themselves are not meticulous in setting limits on what else they will destroy. Black people, in their perilously benighted condition, cannot afford any longer to seek to be what they are not. Nor can the nation encourage such self-hatred or sit idly by as its corrosive effects day by day endanger the nation's future.

Furthermore, it should be clear to all in the United States today that fulfillment can come to the nation as a whole *only* when it comes to every member of the nation. Black people cannot offer the nation their very best at the same time that they hate themselves and devote their energies to being other than what they are. Self-discovery and self-awareness are necessary gateways to maturity and fulfillment. The immaturity that pervades our nation is of a piece with—and partly rooted in—the failure, however understandable historically, of black America to come into its own.

For this reason, every American should rejoice at what our black young people especially are seeking to do, as they add their concerted efforts to the struggle that generations before them have fought with varying degrees of effectiveness. They are seeking to end the negative aspects of the "prunes and prisms" days and to promote in new ways what is called "black consciousness" and "black pride." They see consciousness of group identity as part of the development of power for black people to relate to others *as they choose* with dignity and command.

These young people recognize the validity of Alexis de Tocqueville's observation that much of the genius of America was that here

men with common perceptions of their plight would seek one another out. United this way, they were no longer impotent or isolated
men but "a power seen from afar." The perception of our common
condition as black people is perhaps the basic ingredient of black
consciousness. It is the foundation stone for group power.

1 black experience

BEING "FOR REAL"

Black consciousness, as Mrs. Rowena Rand of Washington,
D.C., puts it, is essentially the capacity for knowing who and what
we are. One proud black lady at an "urban affairs" meeting at Quin-
nipiac College in Hamden, Connecticut, explained that being black
simply means being "for real." Noting that some white people cannot understand black people's "soul talk," the lady explained,
"You've got to be 'for real' to read us."

The August 1967 issue of *Redbook* contained an article by Jean
Smith, a former S.N.C.C. volunteer with the Mississippi Freedom
Democratic Party, now married and living in Greenville, Mississippi.
The article was entitled "I Learned to Feel Black." Mrs. Smith's story
typifies the spirit of self-discovery, of being "for real," that growing
numbers of black young people are experiencing. It is a story worth
examining carefully either in *Redbook* or in the excellent collection
of basic essays, *The Black Power Revolt,* edited by Floyd B. Barbour.
Jean Smith's story is one of rebirth, of growth into a new and liberating self-awareness, which is, after all, the only life pattern that
can bring personal and collective fulfillment.

Jean Smith was an idealistic freedom worker in the early 1960s,
when to be a member of S.N.C.C. was still regarded by the public
generally as representative of American idealism at its best. She
writes:

> When I left Washington, D.C. [where she was a student at
> Howard University], in 1963 to go South with S.N.C.C., you knew
> me. Now, four years later, I am a different person.
>
> Essentially the difference is that I became consciously black.
> I came to understand that there wasn't room enough in the society
> for the mass of black people, that the majority of Americans are
> acting either in unbearably bad faith or in tragic ignorance when
> they project to their children the image of an American society
> where all men are free and equal. (*The Black Power Revolt,* p. 209)

The bulk of Mrs. Smith's article is a moving recapitulation of her disillusioning experience with the Mississippi Freedom Democratic Party. She speaks of her own stubborn idealism and of her resistance to recognizing that the freedom movement did not and could not, under circumstances prevailing in the black and white communities, win the freedom that it sought. "I had invested so much of myself in the fight," she writes, "that I didn't want to admit that it came to so little."

"The best way to understand," the article continues, "is to look at what the Negro people who cast their lot with the Movement believed." Here is the heart of her presentation:

> The crux of the matter is that they believed that there was a link between representation in government and making that government work for you. What they—and I—discovered was that, for some people, this link does not exist. For most black people, voting has not much more benefit than the exercise of walking to the polls. Why is this the case? Because the link between voting and partaking of the benefits of society exists at the pleasure of society. The society must be willing to respond to the legitimate needs of the people; only then can the channels for the expression of these needs, such channels as voting, be meaningfully employed.
>
> A dramatic example is glaringly visible today on the national scene. In January of 1967, when Adam Clayton Powell was barred from his seat in the House of Representatives, he was prevented from acting for his Harlem constituents, the people of the 18th Congressional District of the State of New York, who had elected him. When he was stripped of his chairmanship of the House Education and Labor Committee, he was stripped of the power effectively to represent the Negro people, a power it had taken him 22 years to build. He was prevented from representing these people because the majority of Congress, which in this instance speaks for the larger society, does not want him. It is as simple as that.
>
> Our effort in the South to enter the society through the use of the vote came to an anticlimax because we had been lied to. We had worked feverishly to qualify under objective standards for our rights, only to learn that these rights are arbitrarily conferred by those in power. In the end, we learned that there are a thousand ways for a people who are weaker than the rest to be "kept in their place," appeals to good conscience notwithstanding. There are simple mechanisms, like last-minute changes in election laws and altering the boundaries of election districts. And there are subtler means,

such as making bank loans to the "leaders" of a poverty-stricken community so that they can never afford to disagree with you; such as busing newly eligible voters off to Florida to pick fruit. (pp. 211–12)

It was through such experiences that the Jean Smiths—the youthful idealists who had the greatest faith in possibilities for achieving good for all through the existing order of relationships— lost their hope. Or, as Boston's Byron Rushing puts it, they died to their old awarenesses that they might be reborn.

Jean Smith now finds herself with a new orientation, away from excessive or needless dependence among black people and toward both black initiative for the entire nation's good and a new kind of cooperative alliance—based on mutual maturity—with white people. In the remainder of this chapter, we shall examine Jean Smith's seven precepts for black group self-awareness as I have extracted them from her own story. They are representative in a sense of the new synthesis of what black America has sought through the years to achieve.

NEW PRINCIPLES

Our young people today are reminding us of precepts that date back among our people to Benjamin Banneker and Henry Garnet and can be traced down through Marcus Garvey and Walter White to the present.

Benjamin Banneker (1731–1806) was an astronomer and surveyor, one of a team of three men who set out the boundaries of Washington, D.C. Banneker, like Henry Garnet, a Presbyterian minister who lived a generation later, was a militant advocate of both black pride and development of black potential for the nation's growth. Marcus Garvey and Walter White were black elder statesmen during my youth. Although each had a unique program, they were united in their conviction that black people must share an awareness of the prophetic role that they can and should play in the world.

1. *Growth comes from within*. The long-standing conviction that only through prior self-development can personal and corporate fulfillment be achieved is restated in Jean Smith's youthful yet wise words. She writes, capturing for today the spirit of our black forebears, as follows:

> Negroes must turn away from the preachings, assertions and principles of the larger society and must turn inward to find the means whereby black people can lead full, meaningful lives. We must become conscious that our blackness calls for another set of principles, principles on whose validity we can depend because they come from our own experiences. (p. 217)

Growth can be stimulated by externals, but it occurs only in accordance with inner needs. By learning who we are and by becoming our best selves we also learn to relate to others. Our purpose is to develop *the capacity* to cooperate or to combine our interests with those of others, whether or not the capacity is used. Maturity is achieved when people are in a position to engage in equitable interrelationships. Our focus then must be upon the use of our own experiences as the foundation for our own growth.

Everyone in America should insist that black people develop themselves to enrich the nation's common life. An African proverb has it that "The day of weaning is the day of birth." We must become ourselves *as black people* before we can hope to relate with integrity to others and so make our unique and invaluable contribution to a good life in which we and all others may share. Indeed, the search for inner resources is part of the universal process of growth that black Americans, in a strategic way, may encourage in all of us.

"Should we not be color blind?" is a question that every black American is asked sooner or later. While recognizing the good will of the questioner, we must answer unequivocally "no!" Not "in spite of our blackness" but "in and through" our own precious—and, for most of us, rediscovered—black integrity we must join equally in a common humanity.

The regenerative possibilities in what Vincent Harding of Atlanta's Spellman College calls "the gift of blackness" must be added to our common values. We shall look at this gift more closely in Chapter 8. It is enough at this point to underscore the fact that black people must temporarily put preponderant emphasis upon the too long neglected task of looking inward. Our immaturity—and the immaturity of the nation as a whole—can be overcome in large measure as we become far more self-aware. This growth involves controlling—or, better, casting off—our unconscious self-hatred and *looking within far more appreciatively.*

2. *Black consciousness does not exclude integration.* It simply does not require integration as an absolute end. Integration (or, more accurately, "desegregation," which subordinates *social* inte-

gration) is only a means to achieve freedom and fulfillment for all.
Jean Smith writes:

> I think the fight for integration must continue because we derive
> some benefits from it. It means better living conditions for a few
> of us, a few more yearly incomes above the poverty level. It means
> that we can feel more like men and women because we've insisted
> on the rights that society says are ours. (pp. 217–18)

There are only limited dividends from some forms of "integration," not because integration is not good, but partly because, to be
effective, it requires equitable power relations first. The staff of the
N.A.A.C.P. Legal Defense Fund thus views black self-awareness as
basic to the accomplishment of its purpose. Gustav Heningburg of
the Fund staff believes that, although our commitment to most forms
of integration must not slacken, our emphasis upon black consciousness must greatly increase. "Low self-esteem and an apologetic view
of what we are worth as black people," he says, "are primary hin-
drances in what the Legal Defense Fund of the N.A.A.C.P. seeks to
do."

Similarly, H. Naylor Fitzhugh, black vice-president of Pepsi-
Cola, complains that in his work with business and industrial leaders our own black low estimates of our due place in America's life
are a major cause of the failure of these leaders to respond. "Black
people need to have their integration into business programmed and
spelled out more clearly, in qualitative and quantitative, step-by-step
terms, with some accompanying time table, if it is to be meaningful,"
Fitzhugh explains. "But the problem is," he continues, "that black
people must take more initiative in this effort. To date, we have not
commanded sufficient resources to begin to do this in a remotely adequate way." Those of us already in the white business structures
must band and work together more effectively to add our contributions to those of the valiant professional civil rights leaders—in
order to take the initiative in realistic programming for this kind of
integration. Perhaps our rather naïve efforts to become "integrated"
at too superficial a level have impeded such efforts "in the past."

3. *Achievement of black self-awareness can be facilitated by
white cooperation.* Jean Smith writes:

> Obviously, we need access to the capital and to the intellectual
> resources of the larger society. We need to know how to build
> lathes and how to market products. We need to know the ins and

outs of prevailing political forms and to have access to the body
of scientific knowledge. . . . (p. 217)

Black self-awareness involves using white people creatively instead
of being misused by white people. An Urban League executive noted
how he had pounded so hard for years at the doors of white-con-
trolled industry only to discover that he was "successful" in having
the door opened only sufficiently to fill industry's needs. This limited gain is typical of the sad experiences of the past—and the present—for us all. For we have not closed what the National Urban
League calls "the unclosing gap" between white and black Americans.

Jean Smith mentions our need of capital from the larger society.
It has long been recognized that this capital is ours by right of
"equity and restitution," which is what the black abolitionist David
Walker meant when he wrote in 1829, "America is more our country,
than it is the whites'—we have enriched it with our *blood* and *tears*."
The Ford and Carnegie Foundations—along with other agencies for
urban and educational development—should place development and
research capital in the hands of black men of competence. Indeed,
these foundations, if they are to achieve their stated purposes of
educational and urban regeneration, should have black men at their
helms. White people should be accepting—as they must come to do
in the future—urgently needed black ideas on our educational and
urban problems.

The black community must come to see that its basic problem is
a communal one. All elements of the black community must work
together and develop a common picture of the *one basic problem*
that is associated with their shared low status as black people. Then
leadership representative of the black community as a whole should
command and control the resources necessary to accomplish goals
determined in shared and responsible assessment.

Our black young people often ask: "Shall I go on to college?
Shall I go to a white college or a black one?" All in our society,
young and old alike, need the benefits of continuing education. For
black people especially it is necessary for survival. In any educational enterprise we must acquire and develop *tools* and be careful
not to acquire the *agenda* of those who teach. With this distinction
in mind, the most important consideration is that black people, by
whatever reasonable means are available, acquire the necessary
tools.

Perhaps the greatest cooperative service that white people can render for our mutual benefit would be financial assistance of thoughtful black people–from all walks of life—who seek to develop new educational models and new prescriptions for urban rehabilitation. White technicians have failed partly because they are equipped only to execute what the architects design, and so far the right architects have not had the opportunity to design.

SELF-DEVELOPMENT

Black self-awareness involves not only new relationships with white people but also new dedication to the long-neglected task of self-development.

4. *Only on the basis of black group purpose or black consciousness can black institutional life be built.* Jean Smith puts it this way:

> We have to build a broad-based black consciousness so that we can begin to depend on one another for economic, political and social support. We have to build our own businesses to put money into the development of the Negro community, businesses to establish foundations to support our own new educational and social ventures. We have to make our politicians more responsible to us so that either they improve our communities or they go. Living, growing communities must be built to replace our strife-ridden ghettos. The problems of illiteracy and the inability to communicate must be tackled. (p. 217)

In August 1967 I had one of the richest experiences of my life. It was the opportunity to meet the Messenger, the Honorable Elijah Muhammad. My host in Chicago on that particular visit was William Meyer, Vice-President of the Combined Insurance Company of America. Mr. Muhammad learned that I was in his city and invited me to tea. He also graciously welcomed my white host, of whose responsibility for my visit to Chicago he was informed, and for approximately an hour the Messenger shared something of the richness of his thoughts and emotions with us. I have never heard expressed more beautifully the need for black people to know the innate and unrealized beauty of their being and to discover the priceless benefits of simply becoming what they are designed or "called" to be. In essence, here is what the Messenger said to us:

We must be self-reliant. Those who are beggars will forever be treated with disrespect.

Development cannot be an individual enterprise. It must be shared by those who share our condition of common oppression.

Black people must know that they are a peculiar people, in the Old Testament sense, set in the world to share in its redemption. [This role is, in fact, the historical role of oppressed minorities. One has only to read Arnold Toynbee, Martin Luther King, W. E. B. Du Bois, Pitirim Sorokin, Reinhold Niebuhr, Frantz Fanon, and Paul Tillich in this regard.]

All people must own and control land to have identity. The earth is a source and symbol of one's past, present, and future destiny.

Personal pride is a product of group pride. We must develop group pride. We must be proud of ourselves as a race. If we are not for ourselves, who then can—or even should—be for us?

We must never waste our precious energy hating others. We must show our care for human life by our willingness to defend it.

A world where violence and the denial of human values is affirmed must be regenerated by the initiative of black men who know more than do any others the self-defeating nature of such a world.

We must, in every way possible, set new standards of justice, beauty, and truth.

Black men must learn that a basic purpose of life is to cooperate freely with our family first and then with all others.

As we as black people change, so will our world.

In all my life, I never expected to have a direct confrontation with such an oracle. But I found myself that day sitting before a prophet who uttered the clear and simple truths needed for our redemption. Can we afford, good brothers, to miss his saving message? If the whirlwind and the fire spoke divine truth in the days of old, can we deny the mysteries of truth's operation in our day where new truth somehow must be proclaimed—and heard?

5. *Power is needed to deal with others with dignity and effectiveness.* Jean Smith writes:

Our immediate objective must be the strengthening of the black community instead of the apparently unattainable goal of diffusion of all black people into the main stream of American life. We have to become so strong that we can depend on one another to meet our needs and so that we'll be able to deal with white people as we choose to, not as we are obliged to. (p. 217)

Why have our Jewish brothers been able to survive and to act as creatively as they have done in every society of which they have been a part? Because, first of all, they have been deeply aware of themselves as a people and a worthy people. Maulana Ron Karenga, whom some theologians have called "the nation's new systematic theologian," remarks that the Jews have integrated several key ingredients of their culture in a way that few other groups have done. Black people, he argues, must seek to integrate (and to develop) all the elements that constitute a culture. He lists "the seven criteria for culture":

> mythology
> history
> social organization
> political organization
> economic organization
> creative motif
> ethos

criteria for culture

The key is "integration," the integration of all that we as a people are. It should serve as a more than ample basis for our future survival and self-fulfillment.

MOVING AHEAD

Recently, I had the opportunity to review a mass of literature selected at random from the young so-called "black pride" and "black power" advocates. I must admit that even I was surprised at what I read. Like most black people in America, I tended to believe that a significant number of the new generation wanted out of the American enterprise altogether, although I thought the number was probably exaggerated. I found, however, scarely a trace of this attitude, even among avowed Marxist thinkers. What I read was a composite manifesto, calling upon black people to cease trying to adopt strange and unproductive ways and to begin to shape the future in ways that are appropriate to their own needs. What I read might best be summed up in the next precept for self-awareness.

6. *Black consciousness is at present the best contribution to the whole country's growth into maturity.* According to Jean Smith:

> I think that after the black community has become strong enough, the rules of the game will change; society may decide to join hands with us on equal terms. It may even decide to join hands with us to build a country where all of us, white and black, can live. (p. 218)

Recently I met at breakfast in Washington, D.C., with a group of undersecretaries from several Cabinet departments and the chief administrators of approximately a dozen Federal agencies. They had read my books and wanted to hear more about the necessity for new definitions of practically all problems relating to black people if we are to have tangible results from our efforts to solve them. One of those present asked me to define the difference between myself and other black leaders. It gave me the opportunity to say what I have learned and what all of us must join in saying: that all black brothers working for freedom mutually reinforce one another. Just as Malcolm X made the N.A.A.C.P. and the Urban League seem "more respectable" and paved the way for Dr. King's international acclaim, any one of us who is "heard" today owes a debt to those who have provided the bafflement that enables us to speak up to clarify and help others to "understand."

Brothers, black brothers everywhere, our freedom and the nation's growth depend upon our development as a group into a kind of maturity based upon self-awareness and upon working together in unity. Even now, we may begin to be heard—and possibly even heeded—if we are conscious of our common condition and our common need for growth for our own and the nation's larger good.

Moving out of old ways is never easy, for change inevitably brings uncertainty. Yet change we must. The younger generation, which is redefining freedom on the basis of historical and immediate black experience, is deeply aware of this fact. This awareness is apparent in the last of the seven precepts that I have extracted from Jean Smith's autobiographical sketch.

7. *Change from old ways is painful but nonetheless good for all.* Mrs. Smith writes:

The call for black consciousness is at first painfully hard to answer. It's hard to start all over again and establish new principles and modes of operation. For we have struggled vainly for so long, trying to approximate white culture! Our artists, our scientists, our leaders, have been respected by us only after they have been "legitimized" by the white world. . . . We face a prodigious task. We've danced to the tune so long; and now it becomes necessary to stop and gather our senses, to stop and listen to the tune and decide which of its elements warrant our response. (p. 218)

Not long ago I had lunch with one of the eminent black scientists of the world. He was "open" to the concept of black power and to the need for black group awareness. I suggested to him that more than openness was needed. The younger generation has issued a call. It is up to those of us with ears to hear, eyes to see, lips to speak, and hearts and hands to work to respond to this call and to strive in unity to reveal the good in our common black heritage. He seemed unmoved. I hope that he was not.

Omar Abu Ahmed serves along with C. Sumner Stone, Isaiah Robinson, Baulana Karenga, and me as members of the Committee on Continuation for the 1968 National Conference on Black Power. Omar Ahmed, a second-generation Muslim, has perhaps more than any other individual impressed upon me the need for developing— for the benefit of the entire world—new modes of operational harmony. We need not be in agreement on many specific issues as long as we work harmoniously for what we recognize as our common good. First, however, *we must be aware that we have a deeply urgent common need.* When we have this awareness we shall have taken the first important step in developing *black* awareness.

It's exhilarating to know—or to rediscover—just who and what you are. It was good to hear Bishop John Bright tell his people in Bermuda several years ago that the future would belong to them if they fulfilled their unique destiny as black people. The people had sung the stirring African Methodist Episcopal hymn, "The Church Is Moving On." Bishop Bright told his people to continue the great tradition of the pioneers of African Methodism, to set their own priorities, to do their own thinking, and to become leaders of a new world and not followers in a world destined to decay and pass away. There is a scripture verse of which I was reminded by his words;

it calls forth some of the beauty that is our heritage as black people. It speaks to us as in a parable.

> How beautiful upon the mountains are the feet of him who brings good tidings, who proclaims peace. . . .
> Your watchmen shall lift up their voices; with one voice they shall rejoice; they shall see eye to eye, when the great day comes at last!

Shortly before Freida de Knight, food and fashion editor for *Ebony,* died, I suggested to her that she set a new tone for the food and fashion world by emphasizing African motifs and African-made materials. She was open to the idea, and some small but significant beginnings have since been made by Mrs. John Johnson. On every hand, we must become contributors and leaders and pace setters rather than the passive recipients and followers of others' cultures and customs.

There was a moment of reawakening in our own household when we were offered some reproductions of famous works of art and could not decide easily upon using them. Our oldest daughter Lydia, founding president of the Black Students Association at Upsala College, settled the matter by suggesting the obvious. "The most beautiful thing that we could do to brighten our house would be to do something a bit different, which we have already begun to do." Her mother inquired just what that might be. Lydia said: "We can enlarge our black art collection. We already have African carvings. We can add some black American and black African paintings." We are in the process of doing so, beginning with a cultural motif executed by our son Nathan III, who is an art student in New York City.

More and more each day, I find now a wonderful time to be alive, as I see black people being turned on and turning others on. Victor Solomon of Harlem CORE and Preston Wilcox of I.S. 202 in Harlem are typical heralds of a wonderful new day. I spent a morning with them recently at a meeting held, under the leadership of Harry Bright and Dr. Oscar Lee, by the National Conference of Christians and Jews; it was entitled "Black Power: A Positive Force." They underscored for me and for many others who were present that the beauty of realized and integrated black experience may serve the entire nation's good. But first we must begin to become self-aware.

Whenever I see a black youngster—or a black man or woman, —with a "natural" hairdo, I recognize that he or she is seeking greater self-awareness. Whatever the path, we must all keep in mind that the end is necessary and glorious. It means that black people are coming to recognize that, as with all men, if they are to be their best, they must be truly themselves.

BLACK IS GLORIOUS

Rosaline Harris from Pennsylvania wrote "The Retarded Tree" at the age of sixteen:

> They planted in my mind the seed of despair
> They told me my Black face was ugly and so was my kinky hair
> They said no matter how hard I tried, I'd be a slave until I died
> But I was determined to be free
> To have my taste of liberty
> So I followed them up the down stairs
> Bleached my skin and straightened my hair
> They said I was dumb and needed an education, so I tried that too
> Later I found I had been a Black Princess in a white man's zoo
> All of my life I pursued untruth
> Following after the white man with futile proof of his . . . truths
> Now I'm old, my children are grown
> Possessing sweet dreams of their own
> They have gone a little further than I
> Talking about something called Black pride
> They say Black skin is beautiful and so is kinky hair
> They say trying to be white just ain't gettin' nowhere
> I am old but I know that pride is "our" need
> For they have planted in our mind the "retarded seed," of "despair-ity"

Barbara Buckner Wright, our second daughter, wrote the following poem, which is entitled "Black," in 1967, when she was seventeen:

> I am a Negro———
>   And I am ashamed.
> Chemicals in my hair to make it other than what it is,
> Bleaches on my skin to make it more . . . non-black,

Cosmetics on my face to be like the "other"
Why must I try to be other than what I am?

The French say they are French,
                         from France,
The Irish say they are Irish,
                         from Ireland,
The Italians say they are Italian,
                         from Italy,
And I say I am Negro————
                         from where?

Is there a Negro land?
The French, Irish, Italians all have a culture and heritage.
What is My land? Where are My people? My Culture? My heritage?
I am a Negro————
        And I am ashamed.
Who GAVE me this name?
"Slaves and dogs are named by their masters . . . Free men name
        themselves" *
Must I be other than what I am?

I am Black. This is a source of pride.
My hair is short and finely curled.
My skin is deep-hued, from brown to black.
My eyes are large, open to the world.
My lips are thick, giving resonance to my words.
My nose is broad to breathe freely the air.
My heritage is my experience in America . . . although not of it;
Free from pretense; open to truth
Seeking freedom that all life may be free

I am Black. America has cause to be proud.

Arthur Earley writes of the new spirit abroad among our black
young people. He admonishes those of us who are older to heed
their words of warning and supplication. He reports, "The most
spectacular phenomenon extant in Black America today is the en-
thusiastic and inspiring preoccupation of our black youth with the

*Maulana Ron Karenga in The Quotable Karenga (1967)

development of black pride and self-determination among the black community."

In his position paper entitled "The Emerging Black Community," prepared for a retreat at Radnor, Pennsylvania, in January 1968, Mr. Earley lamented that so many older people, both black and white, are separated from young people by a "generation gap." This gap, he believes, must be closed. The burden rests chiefly upon the older and ostensibly more sober and reflective adults to bridge the gap of suspicion, distrust, and misunderstanding. This effort is of the greatest urgency, for in fact "the future of Black America is in the hands of our black youth."

To those who sometimes criticize our youth for not having a positive program, Arthur Earley replies on two levels. He believes, first, that young people are saying a number of positive things and, second, that they are asking for help from all others in the black community, working together. In fact, the latter point respresents a new stance, seeking a broad response in terms of self-development and self-determination from the entire black community. It is not the traditional appeal for a chiefly personal response or one from a few appointed leaders who may then speak to the consciences of white people. New words, even if they fulfill in a glorious way old desires, are sometimes painful to hear. Our young people therefore must add a thoughtful and appreciative patience to their firm and unwavering insistence that "new occasions teach new duties."

Mr. Earley describes the positive message that black youth, using its own language forms, is attempting to communicate to us all:

> An examination of the slogans of our black youth will, if understood, reveal a blueprint by which the entire black community could be melded into the most powerful ethnic group in America; to wit:
>
> *"Black Power"*—cultural, economic and political development.
> *"Think Black"*—loyalty and dedication to advancing the cause of Black America.
> *"Black Is Best"*—absolute confidence in our ability to function as complete humans in any given situation and under all circumstances.
> *"Black Is Beautiful"*—shameless appreciation for all that the black man was, is, and hopes to be.
> *"Self-determination"*—at all times, the captains of our fate.
> *"Separatism"*—integration will only fragment the community

and destroy its power potential. Stay together and become strong together. Only then can the yoke of 400 years of servitude be cast off.

The analysis can be as endless as the slogans.

Mr. Earley spells out in practical detail what he sees as the programmatic aspects of the message of our black youth, including bloc voting, refusing to be bound by party labels in elections, indoctrination of the black family "in the principles and ideologies of active self-determination," black cultural and historical awareness, black economic development, black control of urban rebuilding, and redirection along constructive lines of the activity of black gangs. More important, he insists that older trained leadership must pool its skills and resources as never before to respond to the call of black youth for aid.

There is also sober advice for our more mature black brothers and sisters:

> These suggestions are necessarily broad. They would certainly require close examination, and may in the end prove valueless. But, whatever goals may be developed, the black youth must be totally and uncompromisingly involved. It is their energy, their inventiveness, their dedication which must be harnessed. They are begging for responsible leadership. They want direction—goals. They recognize the social dynamic that exists today, and they know the role they must play. It is incumbent upon the black professional, the black intelligentsia, the black parent, the black worker to insure the black youth full enjoyment of their role in this social dynamic. They need us—we need them. Together.

"A little child shall lead them," a sacred book records. This prophecy may well be fulfilled in our time. How can we be other than grateful to the tens of thousands of young Jean Smiths and to "our Jean" in particular? Although I do not recall having ever met her personally, I feel that she is one of my own. Don't you?

Knowing the rich beauty of what we are is a continuous process and not a static fact. As with all voyages of discovery, there will be dead ends and retreats. But they are part of growth. We as black people must be willing to accept our rediscovered way of life, if we are to do our unique and far more substantial part in helping to lead our nation and our world.

JOHN OLIVER KILLENS

Explanation of the "Black Psyche"*

J OHN KILLENS was born in Macon, Georgia, in 1916. He attended a number of schools, including Howard and Columbia Universities. Now a teacher of creative writing at the New School for Social Research in New York, Mr. Killens is the author of two novels, *Youngblood* (1954) and *And Then We Heard the Thunder* (1963). "Explanation of the 'Black Psyche,' " reprinted from his *Black Man's Burden* (1965), examines the very real differences between black and white attitudes in America. The black man *is* different from the white man, and Mr. Killens is speaking for more than himself when he writes, "My fight is not to be a white man in a black skin, but to inject some black blood, some black intelligence into the pallid main stream of American life. . . ."

When I was a boy in Macon, Georgia, one of the greatest compli-
ments a benevolent white man could give a Negro was usually
found in the obituary column of the local newspaper: "He was a black
man, but he had a white heart." And the burden of every black man
was supposedly just a little easier to bear that day. It was a time
when many of us black folk laughed at the antics of Amos 'n' Andy
and wept copious tears at a ridiculous movie, very aptly titled
"Imitation of Life." Most of us looked at life through the eyes of
white America.

The great fictional and filmic masterpieces on the American
racial theme usually fell into two categories. One theme dealt with
the utter heartbreak of the mulatto, who rejected his black blood
and was in turn rejected by his white blood. A variation of this
theme was the shattering experience of "passing." The other theme
was the "Uncle Tom," or what I like to call the "Gunga Din," theme.
This one also had many variations, but over all there was the image
created by that great apologist for colonialism, Rudyard Kipling,
of a man who—

> . . . For all 'is dirty 'ide
> 'E was white, clear white, inside
>   When 'e went to tend the wounded under fire!

With some "additional dialogue" by Hollywood, dear old "white inside" Gunga was a marvelous figment of Western man's wistful imagination, the personification of his wish fulfillment. Gunga was a water boy for the British regiment and, in the movie, finally blew the bugle against his own people. And how "whiter" inside could a "noble savage" be?

I am waging a quiet little campaign at the moment to substitute the term "Gunga Din" for that much maligned character "Uncle Tom," in designating the contemporary water boys who still blow the bugles for ol' Massa, better known these days as "Mister Charlie." For, although Mrs. Stowe's beloved "Uncle Tom" was indeed an Uncle Tom, as we understand the term today, he, nevertheless, in the final confrontation, chose death rather than blow the bugle against his people.

Variations of the Gunga Din theme were seen in a rash of movie epics like "Gone With the Wind" and "Virginia" and "Kentucky," etc., ad infinitum, ad nauseam, always played magnificently with tongue in cheek by such stalwarts as Hattie McDaniel and Louise Beavers. In the great emotional scene the black mammy was usually in the big house, weeping and moaning over little pure-white-as-the-driven-snow Missy Anne, who had just sneezed, while mammy's own young 'un was dying of double pneumonia, unattended down in the cabins. All in all, the slaves were presented as carefree and contented in their idyllic degradation. If the black man *really* believed in this romantic version of American slavery, he would have long since wasted away, pining for those good old happy-go-lucky days of bondage.

Last year I did considerable research on that bygone utopian era, and I got a very different picture, slightly less romantic. I found that the slaves were so happy that most of the plantation owners could not afford the astronomical rates of fire insurance. Those rapturous slaves were setting fire to the cotton patches, burning down the plantations, every day the good Lord sent them. They organized countless insurrections, killed their masters, poisoned their mistresses, put spiders in the bighouse soup. They demonstrated their contentment in most peculiar ways.

I shall never forget an evening I spent in a movie house in Hollywood, watching a closed-circuit television broadcast of the first Patterson-Johansson fight, and the great shame I felt for my white countrymen that night, as they began to smell a possible victory for the white foreigner over the black American. Forgotten entirely was the fact that soft-hearted Floyd Patterson was a fellow-countryman. Color superseded patriotism. As I sat there hearing shouted exhortations like, "Kill the nigger!," I felt that Patterson and I were aliens in a strange and hostile country, and Ingemar was home amongst his people.

In fairness to my countrymen in the closed circuits of America that night, their reactions were not intellectual, not even willful. They were spontaneous, not unlike a conditioned reflex. This ecstasy at the sudden emergence of a new white hope came from the metaphoric guts of them; from their hearts, their souls, their bellies. This was their white insides reacting.

It has been rationalized to me that this incident had no racial implications at all, that these rabid Johansson fans were merely in the Old American tradition of rooting for the underdog. Well, I was also rooting for the underdog, and I knew that, win or lose, the underdog in America was Floyd Patterson, Harry Belafonte, Emmett Till, Rosa Parks, Meredith, Poitier, the black American me. The words, "Kill the nigger!" could not possibly have come screaming from my throat, subconsciously, unconsciously or otherwise.

Just as surely as East is East and West is West, there is a "black" psyche in America and there is a "white" one, and the sooner we face up to this social and cultural reality, the sooner the twain shall meet. Our emotional chemistry is different from yours in many instances. Your joy is very often our anger and your despair our fervent hope. Most of us came here in chains and most of you came here to escape your chains. Your freedom was our slavery, and therein lies the bitter difference in the way we look at life.

You created the myth of the faithful slave, but we know that the "loyal slave" is a contradiction in terms. We understand, though, that the master must always make himself believe in the undying love of his slave. That is why white America put words in the black man's mouth and bade him sing—improbable lyrics like

All de darkeys am a-weepin'
Massa's in de cold, cold ground.

But my great-grandmother told me differently. "We wept all right, honey! Great God Almighty! We cried for joy and shouted hallelujah," when old master got the cold, cold ground that was coming to him.

In order to justify slavery in a courageous new world which

was sprouting slogans of freedom and equality and brotherhood, the enslavers, through their propagandists, had to create the fiction that the enslaved people were subhuman and undeserving of human rights and sympathies. The first job was to convince the outside world of the inherent inferiority of the enslaved. The second job was to convince the American people. And the third job, which was the cruelest hoax of all, was to convince the slaves themselves that they deserved to be slaves.

The propagandists for American slavery (the creative writers of the time) tackled these tasks with alacrity and a great measure of success, the effects of which still remain with us today, a hundred years after the Emancipation Proclamation, almost 200 years after the Declaration of Independence. Thus, the Negro was invented and the American Revolution thwarted. Knock on any door in Harlem. Ask any black man or woman in Alabama or Mississippi: Was 1776 for real?

Ironically enough, the fathers of our magnificent Revolution, Washington and Jefferson, themselves owned hundreds of human chattels and even though the great Thomas Jefferson made many speeches against the peculiar institution, he was never able to convince himself to the extent of manumitting his own slaves during his own lifetime.

Surely the great irony of the situation did not escape my ancestors back in the days of the Revolution. And now, today, it does not escape their great-great-grandchildren. When we black folk hear one of our white leaders use the phrase, "the free world," even though the same white leader may very well be the Governor of the state of Mississippi or Alabama, or any other state, for that matter, we—as the slaves of Washington and Jefferson must have done—stare at him incredulously and cannot believe our ears. And we wonder how this word "freedom" can have such vastly different meanings, such conflicting connotations.

But the time has come for you (white America) and me (black America) to work this thing out once and for all, to examine and evaluate the differences between us and the differences inside of us. Time is swiftly running out, and a new dialogue is indispensable. It is so long overdue it is almost half past midnight.

My fight is not to be a white man in a black skin, but to inject some black blood, some black intelligence into the pallid main stream of American life, culturally, socially, psychologically, philosophically. This is the truer deeper meaning of the Negro revolt, which is not yet a revolution—to get America ready for the middle of the 20th century, which is already magnificently here.

This new epoch has caught our country (yours and mine) napping in a sweet nostalgia of the good old days. Our country slumbers in a world of yesteryears, before Africa and Asia got up off their knees and threw off the black man's burden; the good old days when you threw pennies to the "natives" and there were gunboats in the China Sea and Big Stick Policies and Monroe Doctrines and "Old Coasters" from the U.K. sipped their gin-and-tonics in Accra and Lagos and talked about the "natives," as they basked in their roles of Great White Fathers in that best of all possible worlds.

That world is gone forever, and black and brown men everywhere are glad, deep in their hearts, but most Western men are chagrined, which is the understatement of the century. This is why the world is becoming much too much for Western men, even for most of you liberal Western men, even you radical Western men, whoever you are, and wherever.

But the world is becoming more and more to my liking, to my taste and in my image. It gladdens my heart to see black and brown men and women come with dignity to the United Nations in affirmation of the manhood and the self-hood of the entire human race.

The American Negro, then, is an Anglo-Saxon invention, a role the Anglo-Saxon gentlemen invented for the black man to play in his drama known euphemistically as the American Way of Life. It began as an economic expedient, frankly, because you wanted somebody to work for nothing. It is still that, but now it is much more than that. It has become a way of life within a way of life, socially, economically, psychologically, philosophically.

But now, in the middle of the 20th century, I, the Negro, am refusing to be your "nigrah" any longer. Even some of us "favored," "talented," "unusual" ones are refusing to be your educated, sophisticated, split-leveled "nigrahs" any longer. We refuse to look at ourselves through the eyes of white America.

We are not fighting for the right to be like you. We respect ourselves too much for that. When we fight for freedom, we mean freedom for us to be black, or brown, and you to be white and yet live together in a free and equal society. This is the only way that integration can mean dignity for both of us.

I, for one, am growing weary of those well-meaning white liberals who are forever telling me they don't know what color I am. The very fact that they single me out at the cocktail party and gratuitously make me the beneficiary of their blessed assurances gives the lie to their pronouncements.

My fight is not *for* racial sameness but for racial equality and *against* racial prejudice and discrimination. I work for the day when my people will be free of the racist pressures to be *white like you;* a day when "good hair" and "high yaller" and bleaching cream and hair-straighteners will be obsolete. What a tiresome place America would be if freedom meant we all had to think alike and be the same color and wear the same gray flannel suit!

If relationships are to improve between us Americans, black and white and otherwise, if the country is to be saved, we will have to face up to the fact that differences do exist between us. All men react to life through man-made symbols. Even our symbolic reactions are different from yours. To give a few examples:

In the center of a little Southern town near the border of Mississippi, there is a water tower atop which is a large white cross, illumined at night with a lovely (awesome to Negroes) neoned brightness. It can be seen for many miles away. To most white Americans who see it for the first time it is a beacon light that symbolizes the Cross upon which Jesus died, and it gives them a warm feeling in the face and shoulders. But the same view puts an angry knot in the black man's belly. To him it symbolizes the very, very "Christian" K.K.K.

To the average white man, a courthouse, even in Mississippi, is a place where justice is dispensed. To me, the black man, it is a place where justice is dispensed—with.

Even our white hero symbols are different from yours. You give us moody Abraham Lincoln, but many of us prefer John Brown, whom most of you hold in contempt and regard as a fanatic; meaning, of course, that the firm dedication of any white man to the freedom of the black man is *prima facie* evidence of perversion and insanity.

You look upon these times as the Atomic Age, the Space Age, the Cold War era. But I believe that when the history of these times is written, it will not be so important who reached the moon first or who made the largest bomb. I believe the great significance will be that this was the century when most of mankind achieved freedom and human dignity. For me, this is the Freedom Century.

So now it is time for you to understand us, because it is becoming increasingly hazardous for you not to. Dangerous for both of us. As Richard Wright said in his "Twelve Million Black Voices," voices you chose not to heed: "Each day when you see us black folk upon the dusty land of your farms or upon the hard pavement of your city streets, you usually take us for granted and think you know us, but our history is far stranger than you suspect, and we are not what we seem."

The Rev. Ralph Abernathy of Montgomery placed the question humorously when he said that the new Negro of Montgomery had stopped laughing when he wasn't tickled and scratching when he didn't itch.

In a word we are bringing down the curtain on this role you cast us in, and we will no longer be a party to our own degradation. We have become unbelievers, no longer believing in the absolute superiority of the white man's juju. You have never practiced what you preached. Why would we want to be like you? We have caught you in too many lies. You proud defenders of the chastity of womanhood, you champions of racial purity, you are, if I may coin a phrase, "the last of the great miscegenators."

Yes, we are different from you and we are not invisible men, Ralph Ellison notwithstanding. We are the most visible of Americans. We are both Americans and Negroes. Other Americans, for the most part, excepting Puerto Ricans and Mexicans, are just Americans. But we are more than just Americans, not because of our color but because of how America exploited our color. We are different, not because we willed it, but because America set us apart from the rest of the community for special exploitation. And so we are special, with extraspecial insights.

In the summer and fall of 1961 I traveled in a Land Rover 12,000 miles through Africa. I talked to people in the cities, on the farms, in the villages. I talked with workers, farmers, artists, market women, ministers of state, politicians, teachers, and the same question was asked me everywhere I went, with variations: "How can we believe your country's professions of goodwill to us, with whom they have not lived, when they deny human dignity to you who come from us and have lived with them for centuries and helped to build their great civilization?"

It is a question America has to answer to the entire New World of Africa and Asia. The only way we Americans, black and white, can answer this question affirmatively is to make freedom and democracy work *here* and *now*. Just as most Negroes still believe that the ultimate solution for us is in America, I am firmly convinced that the ultimate salvation of America is in the Negro.

The Negro loves America enough to criticize her fundamentally. Most of white America simply can't be bothered. Ironically enough, in the middle of the 20th century, the Negro is the new white hope. To live castrated in a great white harem and yet somehow maintain his black manhood and his humanity—this is the essence of the new man created out of the Negro Invention. History may render the verdict that this was the greatest legacy handed to the New World by the West.

Western man wrote *his* history as if it were the history of the entire human race. I hope that colored men all over the world have watched Western man too long to commit the fatal folly of writing history with a colored pencil. For there is great wisdom in the old Ghana proverb, which says "No one rules forever on the throne of time."

We black folk have learned many lessons during our sojourn in this place. One of them is the truth of another Ghana proverb that says: "Only a fool points to his heritage with his left hand." We are becoming prouder and prouder of our heritage in America and Africa. And we know the profound difference between pride and arrogance; the difference, if you will, between James Meredith and Ross Barnett, both of Mississippi. . . . Yes, we black people stand ready, eager, willing and able to make our contribution to the culture of the world. Our dialogue will not be protest but *affirmation* of the human dignity of all people everywhere.

I know there are white folk who want America to be the land of the free and the home of the brave, but there are far too few of them, and most of them are seldom brave. And I, too, cherish old John Brown and Garrison and William Moore. Let the winter patriots increase their ranks. Let those who truly love America join the valiant Negro Revolt and save the beloved country.

STOKELY CARMICHAEL

Power and Racism*

STOKELY CARMICHAEL, the originator of the often misunderstood slogan "black power," until recently was the head of the Student Non-Violent Coordinating Committee (SNCC). During the mid-Sixties he rose to prominence by appealing unashamedly to the more militant and aggressive black men, declaring that black men must obtain political and economic power over their own lives. "Power and Racism" is an attempt to justify the militancy of the young black leaders and their efforts to gain political power for the black community. In his essay Mr. Carmichael explains precisely what black power means and why blacks must act for themselves without leaning on white liberals. And he says, "Black people do not want to 'take over' this country. They don't want to 'get whitey'; they just want to get him off their backs, as the saying goes."

*First appeared as "What We Want" in *The New York Review of Books*, September 22, 1966. Reprinted by permission of the Student National Coordinating Committee.

One of the tragedies of the struggle against racism is that up to
now there has been no national organization which could speak
to the growing militancy of young black people in the urban ghetto.
There has been only a civil rights movement, whose tone of voice
was adapted to an audience of liberal whites. It served as a sort
of buffer zone between them and angry young blacks. None of its
so-called leaders could go into a rioting community and be listened
to. In a sense, I blame ourselves—together with the mass media—
for what has happened in Watts, Harlem, Chicago, Cleveland,
Omaha. Each time the people in those cities saw Martin Luther
King get slapped, they became angry; when they saw four little
black girls bombed to death, they were angrier; and when nothing
happened, they were steaming. We had nothing to offer that they
could see, except to go out and be beaten again. We helped to build
their frustration.

For too many years, black Americans marched and had their
heads broken and got shot. They were saying to the country, "Look,
you guys are supposed to be nice guys and we are only going to do
what we are supposed to do—why do you beat us up, why don't
you give us what we ask, why don't you straighten yourselves out?"
After years of this, we are at almost the same point—because we

demonstrated from a position of weakness. We cannot be expected any longer to march and have our heads broken in order to say to whites: come on, you're nice guys. For you are not nice guys. We have found you out.

An organization which claims to speak for the needs of a community—as does the Student Nonviolent Coordinating Committee—must speak in the tone of that community, not as somebody else's buffer zone. This is the significance of black power as a slogan. For once, black people are going to use the words they want to use—not just the words whites want to hear. And they will do this no matter how often the press tries to stop the use of the slogan by equating it with racism or separatism.

An organization which claims to be working for the needs of a community—as SNCC does—must work to provide that community with a position of strength from which to make its voice heard. This is the significance of black power beyond the slogan.

Black power can be clearly defined for those who do not attach the fears of white America to their questions about it. We should begin with the basic fact that black Americans have two problems: they are poor and they are black. All other problems arise from this two-sided reality: lack of education, the so-called apathy of black men. Any program to end racism must address itself to that double reality.

Almost from its beginning, SNCC sought to address itself to both conditions with a program aimed at winning political power for impoverished Southern blacks. We had to begin with politics because black Americans are a propertyless people in a country where property is valued above all. We had to work for power, because this country does not function by morality, love, and nonviolence, but by power. Thus we determined to win political power, with the idea of moving on from there into activity that would have economic effects. With power, the masses could *make or participate in making* the decisions which govern their destinies, and thus create basic change in their day-to-day lives.

But if political power seemed to be the key to self-determination, it was also obvious that the key had been thrown down a deep well many years earlier. Disenfranchisement, maintained by racist terror, made it impossible to talk about organizing for political power in 1960. The right to vote had to be won, and SNCC workers devoted their energies to this from 1961 to 1965. They set up voter registration drives in the Deep South. They created pressure for the vote by holding mock elections in Mississippi in 1963 and by helping to establish the Mississippi Freedom Democratic Party (MFDP) in 1964. That struggle was eased, though not won, with the passage of the 1965 Voting Rights Act. SNCC workers could then address themselves to the question: "Who can we vote for, to have our needs met—how do we make our vote meaningful?"

SNCC had already gone to Atlantic City for recognition of the Mississippi Freedom Democratic Party by the Democratic convention and been rejected; it had gone with the MFDP to Washington for recognition by Congress and been rejected. In Arkansas, SNCC helped thirty Negroes to run for School Board elections; all but one were defeated, and there was evidence of fraud and intimidation sufficient to cause their defeat. In Atlanta, Julian Bond ran for the state legislature and was elected—twice—and unseated—twice. In several states, black farmers ran in elections for agricultural committees which make crucial decisions concerning land use, loans, etc. Although they won places on a number of committees, they never gained the majorities needed to control them.

All of the efforts were attempts to win black power. Then, in Alabama, the opportunity came to see how blacks could be organized on an independent party basis. An unusual Alabama law provides that any group of citizens can nominate candidates for county office and, if they win 20 per cent of the vote, may be recognized as a county political party. The same then applies on a state level. SNCC went to organize in several counties such as Lowndes, where black people—who form 80 per cent of the population and have an average annual income of $943—felt they could accomplish nothing within the framework of the Alabama Democratic Party because of its racism and because the qualifying fee for this year's elections was raised from $50 to $500 in order to prevent most Negroes from becoming candidates. On May 3, five new county "freedom organizations" convened and nominated candidates for the offices of sheriff, tax assessor, members of the school boards. These men and women are up for election in November—if they live until then. Their ballot symbol is the black panther: a bold, beautiful animal, representing the strength and dignity of black demands today. A man needs a black panther on his side when he and his family must endure—as hundreds of Alabamians have endured—loss of job, eviction, starvation, and sometimes death, for political activity. He may also need a gun and SNCC reaffirms the right of black men everywhere to defend themselves when threatened or attacked. As for initiating the use of violence, we hope that such programs as ours will make that unnecessary; but it is not for us to tell black communities whether they can or cannot use any particular form of action to resolve their problems. Responsibility for the use of violence by black men, whether in self-defense or initiated by them, lies with the white community.

This is the specific historical experience from which SNCC's call for "black power" emerged on the Mississippi march last July. But the concept of "black power" is not a recent or isolated phenomenon: It has grown out of the ferment of agitation and activity by different people and organizations in many black communities over the years. Our last year of work in Alabama added a new concrete possibility. In Lowndes county, for example, black power will mean that if a Negro is elected sheriff, he can end police brutality. If a black man is elected tax assessor, he can collect and channel funds for the building of better roads and schools serving black people— thus advancing the move from political power into the economic arena. In such areas as Lowndes, where black men have a majority, they will attempt to use it to exercise control. This is what they seek: control. Where Negroes lack a majority, black power means proper representation and sharing of control. It means the creation of power bases from which black people can work to change state-wide or nationwide patterns of oppression through pressure from strength—instead of weakness. Politically, black power means what it has always meant to SNCC: the coming-together of black people to elect representatives and *to force those representatives to speak to their needs.* It does not mean merely putting black faces into office. A man or woman who is black and from the slums cannot be automatically expected to speak to the needs of black people. Most of the black politicians we see around the country today are not what SNCC means by black power. The power must be that of a community, and emanate from there.

SNCC today is working in both North and South on programs of voter registration and independent political organizing. In some places, such as Alabama, Los Angeles, New York, Philadelphia, and New Jersey, independent organizing under the black panther symbol is in progress. The creation of a national "black panther party" must come about; it will take time to build, and it is much too early to predict its success. We have no infallible master plan and we make no claim to exclusive knowledge of how to end racism; different groups will work in their own different ways. SNCC cannot spell out the full logistics of self-determination but it can address itself to the problem by helping black communities define their needs, realize their strength, and go into action along a variety of lines which they must choose for themselves. Without knowing all the answers, it can address itself to the basic problem of poverty; to the fact that in Lowndes County, 86 white families own 90 per cent of the land. What are black people in that county going to do for jobs, where are they going to get money? There must be reallocation of land, of money.

Ultimately, the economic foundations of this country must be shaken if black people are to control their lives. The colonies of the United States—and this includes the black ghettoes within its borders, north and south—must be liberated. For a century this nation has been like an octopus of exploitation, its tentacles stretching from Mississippi and Harlem to South America, the Middle East, southern Africa, and Vietnam; the form of exploitation varies from area to area but the essential result has been the same—a powerful few have been maintained and enriched at the expense of the poor and voiceless colored masses. This pattern must be broken. As its grip loosens here and there around the world, the hopes of black Americans become more realistic. For racism to die, a totally different America must be born.

This is what the white society does not wish to face; this is why that society prefers to talk about integration. But integration speaks not at all to the problem of poverty, only to the problem of blackness. Integration today means the man who "makes it," leaving his black brothers behind in the ghetto as fast as his new sports car will take him. It has no relevance to the Harlem wino or to the cottonpicker making three dollars a day. As a lady I know in Alabama once said, "the food that Ralph Bunche eats doesn't fill my stomach."

Integration, moreover, speaks to the problem of blackness in a despicable way. As a goal, it has been based on complete acceptance of the fact that in order to have a decent house or education, blacks must move into a white neighborhood or send their children to a white school. This reinforces, among both black and white, the idea that "white" is automatically better and "black" is by definition inferior. This is why integration is a subterfuge for the maintenance

*Over power
on both
sides*

*—integration
becomes
relevant.*

of white supremacy. It allows the nation to focus on a handful of Southern children who get into white schools, at great price, and to ignore the 94 per cent who are left behind in unimproved all-black schools. Such situations will not change until black people have power—to control their own school boards, in this case. Then Negroes become equal in a way that means something, and integration ceases to be a one-way street. Then integration doesn't mean draining skills and energies from the ghetto into white neighborhoods; then it can mean white people moving from Beverly Hills into Watts, white people joining the Lowndes County Freedom Organization. Then integration becomes relevant.

Last April, before the furor over black power, Christopher Jencks wrote in a *New Republic* article on white Mississippi's manipulation of the anti-poverty program:

> The war on poverty has been predicated on the notion that there is such a thing as *a community* which can be defined geographically and mobilized for a collective effort to help the poor. This theory has no relationship to reality in the Deep South. In every Mississippi county there are *two* communities. Despite all the pious platitudes of the moderates on both sides, these two communities habitually see their interests in terms of conflict rather than cooperation. Only when the Negro community can muster enough political, economic and professional strength to compete on somewhat equal terms, will Negroes believe in the possibility of true cooperation and whites accept its necessity. En route to integration, the Negro community needs to develop greater independence—a chance to run its own affairs and not cave in whenever "the man" barks. . . . Or so it seems to me, and to most of the knowledgeable people with whom I talked in Mississippi. To OEO, this judgment may sound like black nationalism. . . .

Mr. Jencks, a white reporter, perceived the reason why America's anti-poverty program has been a sick farce in both North and South. In the South, it is clearly racism which prevents the poor from running their own programs; in the North, it more often seems to be politicking and bureaucracy. But the results are not so different: In the North, non-whites make up 42 per cent of all families in metropolitan "poverty areas" and only 6 per cent of families in areas classified as not poor. SNCC has been working with local residents in Arkansas, Alabama, and Mississippi to achieve control by the poor of the program and its funds; it has also been working with groups in the North, and the struggle is no less difficult. Behind it all is a federal government which cares far more about winning the war on the Vietnamese than the war on poverty; which has put the poverty program in the hands of self-serving politicians and bureaucrats rather than the poor themselves; which is unwilling to curb the misuse of white power but quick to condemn black power.

To most whites, black power seems to mean that the Mau Mau are coming to the suburbs at night. The Mau Mau are coming, and whites must stop them. Articles appear about plots to "get Whitey," creating an atmosphere in which "law and order must be maintained." Once again, responsibility is shifted from the oppressor to the oppressed. Other whites chide, "Don't forget—you're only 10 per cent of the population; if you get too smart, we'll wipe you out." If they are liberals, they complain, "what about me?—don't you want my help any more?" These are people supposedly concerned about black Americans, but today they think first of themselves, of their feelings of rejection. Or they admonish, "you can't get anywhere without coalitions," without considering the problems of coalition with whom?; on what terms? (coalescing from weakness can mean absorption, betrayal); when? Or they accuse us of "polarizing the races" by our calls for black unity, when the true responsibility for polarization lies with whites who will not accept their responsibility as the majority power for making the democratic process work.

White America will not face the problem of color, the reality of it. The well-intended say: "We're all human, everybody is really decent, we must forget color." But color cannot be "forgotten" until its weight is recognized and dealt with. White America will not acknowledge that the ways in which this country sees itself are contradicted by being black—and always have been. Whereas most of the people who settled this country came here for freedom or for economic opportunity, blacks were brought here to be slaves. When the Lowndes County Freedom Organization chose the black panther as its symbol, it was christened by the press "the Black Panther Party"—but the Alabama Democratic Party, whose symbol is a rooster, has never been called the White Cock Party. No one ever talked about "white power" because power in this country *is* white. All this adds up to more than merely identifying a group phenomenon by some catchy name or adjective. The furor over that black panther reveals the problems that white America has with color and sex; the furor over "black power" reveals how deep racism runs and the great fear which is attached to it.

Whites will not see that I, for example, as a person oppressed because of my blackness, have common cause with other blacks who are oppressed because of blackness. This is not to say that there are no white people who see things as I do, but that it is black people I must speak to first. It must be the oppressed to whom SNCC addresses itself primarily, not to friends from the oppressing group.

From birth, black people are told a set of lies about themselves. We are told that we are lazy—yet I drive through the Delta area of Mississippi and watch black people picking cotton in the hot sun for fourteen hours. We are told, "if you work hard you'll succeed"— but if that were true, black people would own this country. We are oppressed because we are black—not because we are ignorant, not because we are lazy, not because we're stupid-(and got good rhythm), but because we're black.

I remember that when I was a boy, I used to go to see Tarzan movies on Saturday. White Tarzan used to beat up the black natives. I would sit there yelling, "Kill the beasts, kill the savages, kill 'em!" I was saying: Kill me. It was as if a Jewish boy watched Nazis taking Jews off to concentration camps and cheered them on. Today, I want the chief to beat hell out of Tarzan and send him back to Europe. But it takes time to become free of the lies and their shaming effect on black minds. It takes time to reject the most important lie: that black people inherently can't do the same things white people can do, unless white people help them.

The need for psychological equality is the reason why SNCC today believes that blacks must organize in the black community. Only black people can convey the revolutionary idea that black people are able to do things themselves. Only they can help create in the community an aroused and continuing black consciousness that will provide the basis for political strength. In the past, white allies have furthered white supremacy without the whites involved realizing it—or wanting it, I think. Black people must do things for themselves; they must get poverty money they will control and spend themselves, they must conduct tutorial programs themselves so that black children can identify with black people. This is one reason Africa has such importance: The reality of black men ruling their own nations gives blacks elsewhere a sense of possibility, of power, which they do not now have.

This does not mean we don't welcome help, or friends. But we want the right to decide whether anyone is, in fact, our friend. In the past, black Americans have been almost the only people whom everybody and his momma could jump up and call their friends. We have been tokens, symbols, objects—as I was in high school to many young whites, who liked having "a Negro friend." We want to decide who is our friend, and we will not accept someone who comes to us and says: "If you do X, Y, and Z, then I'll help you." We will not be told whom we should choose as allies. We will not be isolated from any group or nation except by our own choice. We cannot have the oppressors telling the oppressed how to rid themselves of the oppressor.

I have said that most liberal whites react to "black power" with the question, What about me?, rather than saying: Tell me what you want me to do and I'll see if I can do it. There are answers to the right question. One of the most disturbing things about almost all white supporters of the movement has been that they are afraid to go into their own communities—which is where the racism exists— and work to get rid of it. They want to run from Berkeley to tell us what to do in Mississippi; let them look instead at Berkeley. They admonish blacks to be nonviolent; let them preach nonviolence in the white community. They come to teach me Negro history; let them go to the suburbs and open up freedom schools for whites. Let them work to stop America's racist foreign policy; let them press this government to cease supporting the economy of South Africa.

There is a vital job to be done among poor whites. We hope to see, eventually, a coalition between poor blacks and poor whites. That is the only coalition which seems acceptable to us, and we see such a coalition as the major internal instrument of change in American society. SNCC has tried several times to organize poor whites; we are trying again now, with an initial training program in Tennessee. It is purely academic today to talk about bringing poor blacks and whites together, but the job of creating a poor-white power bloc must be attempted. The main responsibility for it falls upon whites. Black and white can work together in the white community where possible; it is not possible, however, to go into a poor Southern town and talk about integration. Poor whites everywhere are becoming more hostile—not less—partly because they see the nation's attention focused on black poverty and nobody coming to them. Too many young middle-class Americans, like some sort of Pepsi generation, have wanted to come alive through the black community; they've wanted to be where the action is—and the action has been in the black community.

Black people do not want to "take over" this country. They don't want to "get whitey"; they just want to get him off their backs, as the saying goes. It was for example the exploitation by Jewish landlords and merchants which first created black resentment toward Jews—not Judaism. The white man is irrelevant to blacks, except as an oppressive force. Blacks want to be in his place, yes, but not in order to terrorize and lynch and starve him. They want to be in his place because that is where a decent life can be had.

But our vision is not merely of a society in which all black men have enough to buy the good things of life. When we urge that black money go into black pockets, we mean the communal pocket. We want to see money go back into the community and used to benefit it. We want to see the cooperative concept applied in business and banking. We want to see black ghetto residents demand that an exploiting landlord or storekeeper sell them, at minimal cost, a building or a shop that they will own and improve cooperatively; they can back their demand with a rent strike, or a boycott, and a community so unified behind them that no one else will move into the building or buy at the store. The society we seek to build among black people, then, is not a capitalist one. It is a society in which the spirit of community and humanistic love prevail. The word love is suspect; black expectations of what it might produce have been betrayed too often. But those were expectations of a response from the white community, which failed us. The love we seek to encourage is within the black community, the only American community where men call each other "brother" when they meet. We can build a community of love only where we have the ability and power to do so: among blacks.

As for white America, perhaps it can stop crying out against "black supremacy," "black nationalism," "racism in reverse," and begin facing reality. The reality is that this nation, from top to bottom, is racist; that racism is not primarily a problem of "human relations" but of an exploitation maintained—either actively or through silence—by the society as a whole. Camus and Sartre have asked, can a man condemn himself? Can whites, particularly liberal whites, condemn themselves? Can they stop blaming us, and blame their own system? Are they capable of the shame which might become a revolutionary emotion?

We have found that they usually cannot condemn themselves, and so we have done it. But the rebuilding of this society, if at all possible, is basically the responsibility of whites—not blacks. We won't fight to save the present society, in Vietnam or anywhere else. We are just going to work, in the way *we* see fit, and on goals *we* define, not for civil rights but for all our human rights.

LOUIS E. LOMAX

The Black Muslims*

L OUIS E. LOMAX was born in Valdosta, Georgia, in 1922. He was
graduated from Paine College in Augusta, Georgia, and, after some
graduate work, became an assistant professor of philosophy at
Georgia State College (Savannah). From education he shifted to
journalism, becoming a feature writer for the Chicago *American*. Mr.
Lomax moved New York City in 1958 and was the first black man to
appear on television as a newsman. He has written articles for
Harper's, The New Republic, The Nation, and other periodicals and
is the author of *The Reluctant African* (1960) and *The Negro Revolt*
(1962), from which "The Black Muslims" is taken. The essay explains
the background and purpose of the Black Muslims. Although much
has happened since the essay was written in 1962—Malcolm X
withdrew from the organization and was later murdered—the
Muslims have not changed and they remain a potent force in the
black community.

The extreme form of the Negro's revolt against his plight can be seen in the rise of the Honorable Elijah Muhammad, whose followers are known as the Nation of Islam or the Black Muslims.[1] Oddly enough, I may well have been somewhat responsible for the group's growth. But this is the way of publicity in America; it is impossible to conduct a public discussion of a group's activity without moving some people to go out and join that group.

It all started—for me, that is—on a Saturday night back in 1958. I was walking through Harlem with a fellow writer and friend, Robert Maynard, and his wife, Elizabeth. Bob is Negro, Liz is white. We paused to listen to a Harlem street corner orator rave and rant about the "condition of my people." I was fairly new in New York at the time and was struck by the inverse racism in everything the speaker said. I knew full well that if some white speaker had taken to a street corner platform to say similar things about Negroes there would have been hell to pay and I would gladly be among those who

---

[1]The term "Black Muslim" was coined by Dr. Eric Lincoln while he was preparing his Ph.D. dissertation on the followers of Muhammad. They do not use the term when speaking of themselves. They call themselves "Muslims." However, they do not object to the term employed by Lincoln.

dished it out. Yet—and this is what struck me—there the man stood, on a street corner in mid-Harlem, an American flag waving conspicuously (the speaker explained that "this damn flag is here not because I respect it or believe in it but because this is the only way I can hold a public meeting and not be put in jail").

"Now gather round," the speaker said. "I want to tell you about the white man."

"Say on, brother," some sister yelled from the crowd.

"Did you ever—hear me now—did you ever know a white man to do anything right?"

The crowd roared with scornful laughter.

"Hell, no," a man screamed out. "Right ain't in them!"

"Tell them about it," a woman joined in.

"Now listen," the speaker said. "I want you to understand how the white man, particularly the Jew, keeps you in the economic locks. Am I right or wrong?"

"You right," the crowd shot back.

"Now, now, now," the speaker stammered for emphasis, "this is the way it is. You get up early every morning with roaches and rats running round your bed. Is that right?"

"That's right."

"You stumble over to your child's bed to make sure the rats ain't done bit his ears off. Is that right?"

"That's right."

"Then you make it through falling plaster to a leaky water closet to wash your face."

"Yes, sir . . . that's it, that's it."

"You finally get the sleep out of your eyes and put on some clothes that are just about worn out but you ain't finished paying for them yet."

"Say on, brother. The white man ought to be killed!"

"Then, then, then—hear me now—then you go down in the subway and make it down to the garment district to meet the man. Am I right or wrong?"

"You right!"

"And this is where the economic lock come in; you go downtown to work for Mr. Eisenberg."

"Yeah!"

"You work all day, eight hours a day, five days a week for forty-four dollars."

"That's right."

"And while you making forty-four dollars, Mr. Eisenberg is watching you sweat and grunt and he makes forty-four hundred dollars. Am I right or wrong?"

"You right; great God, you right!"

"Say on."

"Tell it like it is."

"Oh, don't worry, brother, I'm going to tell it just like it is; I'm going to bring it right down front so everybody can smell it!"

"Now—and watch this—you work all day for Mr. Eisenberg, you come back up here to Harlem and buy your clothes from Mr. Gosenberg.

"Yeah."

"You buy your jewelry from Mr. Goldberg."

"Yes."

"You pay rent to Mr. Fineberg."

"Yes."

"You get borrowed money from a finance company headed by Mr. Weinberg."

"Yes, tell it."

"Now what you don't know is that Mr. Eisenberg and Mr. Gosenberg and Mr. Fineberg and Mr. Goldberg and Mr. Weinberg is all cousins. They got you working for nothing, and then they take back the little nothing you make before you can get home with it. That's how they got you in the economic locks!"

And with this the crowd breaks with wild, pained laughter.

I did not grow up around all this, and I was shocked by it. My shock was translated into anger when one of the Negro men in the crowd came over and insulted Bob for being with a white woman. He told us to move on. I wanted to stay and have it out, but Bob, by then used to such things, said no.

I went home that night and filed a feature story entitled "Harlem, Saturday Night" to the Afro-American newspaper. I was their United Nations correspondent at the time but I felt I had a better story in Harlem than I had down on the East River.

I never forgot what I saw and felt that night. And when, over a year later, I joined Mike Wallace's TV news staff, I asked and received permission to do a TV documentary on Harlem's street corner speakers. After a few hours of moving around in Harlem I discovered that the street corner speakers represented several African nationalist organizations. These organizations were composed of Negroes who deny everything American, think of themselves as

Africans, and who view themselves as the real champions for African freedom in the United States. The more I probed these nationalist organizations, the more I heard about a group called the "Muslims." At first, like most Americans, I took the Muslims to be none other than followers of the Islamic faith in America. The evidence, however, began to indicate that they were a good deal more than that. I went digging for the Muslims and, after much secret negotiation and meetings in restaurants, I finally obtained information which resulted in a two-hour-long TV documentary called *The Hate That Hate Produced*.

The documentary opened with a recording made during a morality play given by the Black Muslims. The play, called *The Trial*, depicts the white man being tried by the remainder of the world for his crimes against black peoples. The prosecutor summed up his case with these words:

> I charge the white man with being the greatest liar on earth. I charge the white man with being the greatest drunkard on earth. I charge the white man with being the greatest swine-eater on earth. Yet the Bible forbids it. I charge the white man with being the greatest gambler on earth. I charge the white man, ladies and gentlemen of the jury, with being the greatest murderer on earth. I charge the white man with being the greatest peace-breaker on earth. I charge the white man with being the greatest adulterer on earth. I charge the white man with being the greatest robber on earth. I charge the white man with being the greatest deceiver on earth. I charge the white man with being the greatest troublemaker on earth. So therefore, ladies and gentlemen of the jury, I ask you, bring back a verdict of guilty as charged.

The jury brought in a verdict of guilty and the applause of the audience was so thunderous it drowned out the judge's voice as he sentenced the white man to death.

This play was staged before huge audiences all over the non-South, including two appearances at New York's Carnegie Hall, and it tells a good deal about the nature and purpose of the Black Muslims. The Muslims use a good deal of the paraphernalia of the traditional religion of Islam but they add a few innovations of their own. When Mike Wallace and I first broke the story of the Muslims they were denied by orthodox Moslems. However, the denial was retracted and since then the exact relationship between the followers of Muhammad and orthodox Islam has been a moot question.

The driving force in the Black Muslim movement—they now claim a membership of over a quarter of a million[2]—is one Elijah Muhammad, a sixty-year-old American Negro who was born Elijah Poole and spent his early life as a Baptist minister. Muhammad is a strikingly unimpressive man; he is small, five feet five, and speaks with a disturbing lisp. It is difficult to believe that he is the moving spirit behind a religion that is now being taught in fifty schools across the nation. Yet when Muhammad speaks the audience sits entranced for from four to five hours while he delivers a most amazing doctrine. And it is during the mass rallies where Mr. Muhammad speaks that the Muslims can best be studied.

Their withdrawal from America is almost complete. They speak of themselves as a "nation," indicating that they are not of the American body politic; they do not vote nor do they participate in political affairs. The Muslim women keep their heads covered at all times; they wear the long, flowing, white skirts one associates with Islam. They have their own stores, supermarkets, barbershops, department stores and fish markets.

Minister Malcolm X, a brilliant man and an ex-convict, is Muhammad's chief lieutenant. Wherever Mr. Muhammad speaks, Minister Malcolm X sets the stage with an introduction. This is how Malcolm X introduced Mr. Muhammad during a recent Black Muslim rally in Washington, D.C.'s Uline Arena:

MINISTER X: Everyone who is here today realizes that we are now living in the fulfillment of prophecy. We have come to hear and to see the greatest and wisest and most fearless black man in America today. In the Church, we used to sing the song "Good News, the Chariot Is Coming." Is that right or wrong?
AUDIENCE: Right!
MINISTER X: But what we must bear in mind is that what's good news to one person is bad news to another. While you sit here today, knowing that you have come to hear good news, you must realize in advance that what might be good news for you might be bad news for somebody else. What's good news for the sheep might be bad news for the wolves.

The "good news" for the black man, according to Minister X, is that he is on the verge of recapturing his position as ruler of the

---

[2]Experts on the Black Muslims say the membership does not exceed 100,000.

universe. The "bad news" for the white man is that his wicked reign will soon be over.

Then Muhammad spoke. This was his central theme:

"The Christian religion has failed. Your leaders of that religion have failed. Now the government of America has failed you. You have no justice coming from no one. It is written that you are like sheep among wolves . . . every wolf taking a bite at you. You want justice; you want freedom; you want equality . . . but get none. . . .

"The only thing for you to do is separate from the white man and have some land of your own."

Elijah Muhammad is aging, his health is bad and he bought a home in Arizona late in 1961 in order to live in a dry climate. Much of his work, and all his speaking engagements, are being carried on by Minister Malcolm X, whom many feel will one day be the leader of the movement. Malcolm X is a tall, lanky, light-brown-skinned man with an almost innate mastery of mass psychology. He served a prison term for robbery; now he is changed. He will not smoke, drink or even eat in a restaurant that houses a bar. He says the change came when he heard Mr. Muhammad speak and he lost his shame about being colored. During an extensive interview, Malcolm X gave me this outline of the Black Muslim's faith:

> LOMAX: Mr. Elijah Muhammad teaches . . . that his faith . . . that the Islamic faith is for the black man and that the black man is good. He also uses the Old Testament instance of the serpent in Adam and Eve and the Garden of Eden, and he sets up the proposition that this is the great battle between good and evil, and he uses the word devils.
>
> MINISTER X: Yes.
>
> LOMAX: He uses it almost interchangeably and synonymous with the word snake. Well, what does he mean there?
>
> MINISTER X: Well, number one, he teaches us that there never was a real serpent.
>
> LOMAX: It was not a real serpent?
>
> MINISTER X: . . . that went into the Garden.
>
> LOMAX: What was it?
>
> MINISTER X: But, as you know, the Bible was written in symbols and parables, and this serpent or snake is a symbol that's used to hide the real identity of the one whom that actually was.
>
> LOMAX: Well, who was it?
>
> MINISTER X: The white man.

LOMAX: I want to call your attention, Minister Malcolm, to one paragraph in this column [written by the Honorable Elijah Muhammad]. He said, and I quote him, "The only people born of Allah are the black nation, of whom the so-called American Negroes are descendants."

MINISTER X: Yes.

LOMAX: Now is this your standard teaching?

MINISTER X: Yes. He teaches us that the black man by nature is divine.

LOMAX: Now, does this mean that the white man by nature is evil?

MINISTER X: By nature, he is other than divine.

LOMAX: Well, now, does this mean he is evil? Can he do good?

MINISTER X: By nature he is evil.

LOMAX: He cannot do good?

MINISTER X: History is best qualified to reward all research and we don't have any historic example where we have found that they collectively as a people have done good.

LOMAX: Minister Malcolm, you know, in Chicago, and in Detroit, you have universities of Islam, do you not?

MINISTER X: Yes, sir, in Detroit and Chicago.

LOMAX: And you take your parishioners—you take children from the kindergarten ages and you train them right through high school, is that true?

MINISTER X: Yes, sir, from the age of four, I think, upward.

LOMAX: And you have a certified parochial school operating in Chicago.

MINISTER X: In Chicago . . .

LOMAX: And in Detroit . . .

MINISTER X: And in Detroit . . .

LOMAX: And kids come to your school in lieu of going to what we would call regular day school?

MINISTER X: Yes, sir, many.

LOMAX: What do you teach them there?

MINISTER X: We teach them the same things that they would be taught ordinarily in school, minus the Little Black Sambo story and the things that were taught to you and me when we were coming up to breed that inferiority complex in us.

LOMAX: Do you teach them what you have just said to me—that the white man is the symbol of evil?

MINISTER X: You can go to any little Muslim child and ask them where is hell and who is the devil, and he wouldn't tell you that hell is down in the ground or that the devil is something invisible that you can't see. He'll tell you that hell is right where he has been catching it and he'll tell you the one who is responsible for him having received this hell is the devil.

LOMAX: And he would say that the devil is the white man?

MINISTER X: Yes.

LOMAX: Can a white man join your temple?

MINISTER X: None has ever joined.

LOMAX: If one came up and attempted to join, would he be allowed to come in and be taught?

MINISTER X: No, sir.

LOMAX: Why not?

MINISTER X: Well, that's one of the reasons why most people think that Mr. Muhammad teaches hate, but if there is a rattlesnake in the field who has been biting your brothers and your sisters, then you go and tell them that that's a rattlesnake and all of the harm that's ever come to them has come to them from that particular source. Well, then, that rattler will think that the warner is teaching hate. He'll go back and tell the other snakes that this man is teaching hate . . . this man is teaching hate . . . but it's not hate . . . it's just that when you study people who have been harmed and discover the source of their injury—the source of all their defects, and you begin to point out that source, it's not that you hate the source, but your love for your people is so intense—so great—that you must let them know what is wrong with them, what is the cause of their ills. And this is one of the basic factors, I believe, involved, when the propaganda is put out that Mr. Muhammad teaches hate. He teaches black people to love each other, and our love for each other is so strong, we don't have any room left in our hearts.

It is clear, then, that we are witnessing the first home-grown American Negro religion. In essence, Muhammad is saying this: God and black are one, therefore all blacks are divine; the opposite of black is evil, therefore all white men are evil. Then he extends his argument: The world's black men are divine, therefore unified. The weakest link in the black brotherhood is the so-called American Negro, who is all mixed up with the white man. The return of black men to power, then, is waiting upon the American Negro to come out from among the white men and be separated—not segregated.

To accomplish this Muhammad demands "some states" where the Negro can set up his own nation. (A group of us offered Muhammad Mississippi; he turned it down.)

Muhammad's demand for a separate state, like his Islamic trappings, are not taken too seriously. Most people are convinced that he doesn't really mean this; and we are convinced that most of his followers are not culturally able to execute the alliance with traditional Islam that the spokesman for the movement would have one believe. These—the separate state and the Islamic trappings—are not the arresting things. There are matters raised by Muhammad, however, that demand, and have received, serious attention from sober Negroes.

First, Muhammad's indictment of Christianity has forced thoughtful Negro preachers into an almost impossible position. I have talked this over with scores of Negro clergymen, and, almost to a man, they agree that Muhammad has deeply shaken the Negro Christian community. Muhammad's recital of how the Christian faith—"By their fruits ye shall know them"—has failed the Negro has slunk deeper into the hearts of the Negro masses than Negro clergymen will admit publicly. But, and as a direct result of what Muhammad has said, Negro clergymen are scurrying around for new Sunday school picture cards, religious literature that pictures God and Christ, if not black, at least resembling a Negro. I know of one Negro minister, a Harvard graduate at that, who has delivered several sermons on the question of Christ's physical appearance. "And his hair was like lamb's wool." This, the minister says, is the only physical description of Jesus. Then he tells his middle-class Negro congregation that his, the minister's hair, looks more like lamb's wool than do Norman Vincent Peale's forelocks.

And although they are bitter ideological enemies, there is only a thin line between Muhammad and Martin Luther King. King, of course, will have none of Muhammad's blanket indictment of the white man; nor will King abide black supremacy notions. But both King and Muhammad are saying that the purpose of a religion is to explain life for the people who adopt or create it and that the function of a gospel is to speak to the frustrations of a people. Muhammad's gospel as a whole will not be accepted by the Negro. But—and this is the important thing—no gospel that fails to answer Muhammad's criticism of Christianity will be accepted either.

In the process of indicting Christianity and criticizing Negro leaders who seek "integration," Muhammad, largely through the spellbinding work of Malcolm X, has caused thousands of the Negro masses to become race-conscious in a way they never were before. It is the rise of Muhammad that has caused Jackie Robinson to realize that Negro leadership organizations are not reaching the Negro masses. William Berry, executive secretary of the Chicago Urban League, readily confesses: "Hell, these Muslims make more sense to the Negro on the street than I do!"

It is quite a pageant to see hundreds of Negro women, formerly Baptists, Methodists and what have you, marching into Washington's Uline Arena, draped in white, their heads covered, to hear Elijah speak. Their withdrawal is fairly complete. They have no more faith in the white man or in the American dream. They don't condemn the white man for they feel he is incapable of doing good. Their chant, like that of the early Jew, is, "How can we sing the Lord's song in a strange land?"

And police brutality, particularly in New York, has helped the Black Muslim movement. Two years ago, several policemen, all of them white, shot their way into a Muslim home on Long Island. They were under the mistaken impression that a fugitive was hiding there. The policemen terrorized one man, several children and two pregnant women. The Muslims retaliated with milk bottles, sticks and stones. Of course, they were all arrested for assaulting policemen. But an all-white jury set them free. Then there is the case of Johnson Hinton, a Muslim who happened to be on a Harlem street when a fight broke out. White policemen waded in swinging their clubs. Hinton fell to the ground, his head split open. He was hospitalized and five hundred Muslim men threw a cordon around the hospital and all but started a race riot. A steel plate was put in Hinton's head, and he recovered. He was acquitted of any wrongdoing. Then came the lawsuit. The jury awarded Hinton $75,000; then, rather than go through endless appeals, the City settled for $70,000.

It is no accident that the Black Muslims do a land-office recruiting job in the nation's prisons. These jails are jammed with Negroes who, even though guilty, have known the bitter taste of police brutality and short-shrift justice. To them, the Muslims present a deadly argument and the prisoners have responded by the hundreds. Just recently the Black Muslims went to court and won the right to practice their faith inside New York State prisons; in California prisons the Muslims presented such a challenge that state officials had to make special arrangements to accommodate them and their faith.

And it is just here, in their work with Negro criminals, that the

Muslims have won the respect of Negro and white social workers. Their rehabilitation program is nothing short of miraculous. They start out by convincing the ex-convict that he fell into crime because he was ashamed of being black, that the white man had so psychologically conditioned him that he was unable to respect himself. Then they convince the one-time prisoner that being black is a blessing, not a curse, and that in keeping with that blessing he, the ex-convict, must clean himself up and live a life of decency and respect. As a result:

You never see a Muslim without a clean shirt and tie and coat.

You never see a Muslim drink.

You never see a Muslim smoke.

You never see a Muslim dance.

You never see a Muslim use dope.

You never see a Muslim woman with an non-Muslim man.

You never see a Muslim man with a woman other than his wife.

You never see a Muslim without some means of income.

You never see a Muslim who will not stop and come to the aid of any black woman he sees in trouble.

You seldom see a Muslim lapse back into crime. (A close friend of mine is a lawyer with Muslim clients and he tells me that he has known of only four Muslims who have returned to crime in the past five years. This is remarkable when one remembers that some six hundred convicts in prison join the Black Muslims each year. The Muslim leaders arrange parole for their converts and take them in hand. Parole officers and police have told me that the Black Muslims are the best rehabilitation agency at work among Negro criminals today.)

The crucial issue is that these criminals are rehabilitated along with the other members of the group (most of the Muslims are not ex-convicts) in a faith that denies and condemns everything American. They do it by simply reciting the facts about life for the black man in America. And it is this recital that caused James Baldwin to remark that others among us have the faith but the Muslims have the facts.

Because they have the facts, and none of us can dispute them, the Black Muslims have forced every Negro spokesman in America to assume a position more extreme than that he would have assumed had the Muslims not been among us. Not that the position is false; rather that Negro spokesmen, for all their fist-pounding, are cautious fellows. But once Malcolm X makes his speech there is neither room

102 The Black Muslims

nor reason for this kind of caution, and the Negro spokesman who speaks less of the truth than Malcolm speaks simply cannot get a hearing among his own people.

The Black Muslims, like the sit-ins and the freedom rides, are part of the Negro revolt. They are not aimed in the same direction, but they stem from the same unrest: a rejection of segregation and all that it carries with it and a firm belief that the current Negro leadership organizations are not employing the proper methods to end that evil.

The Black Muslims are now accepted. Nobody bothers them much any more; they are part of the Negro community, their leaders sit on committees when community matters are being discussed. No sane man, black or white, dares plan a mass program in Harlem without including Malcolm X. For if it comes to a showdown, Malcolm can muster more people than Adam Powell, A. Philip Randolph, Martin Luther King and Roy Wilkins all put together.

The Black Muslims represent an extreme reaction to the problem of being a Negro in America today. Instead of working to improve conditions within the framework of American society, as do other Negro leadership organizations, the Black Muslims react by turning their backs on that society entirely. Their one positive aspect is that they work to make Negroes proud of being Negro.

As of now I do not feel the Black Muslims present a real threat to American society—they let off most of their steam harmlessly in their meetings and conventions, and the rituals and trappings of the faith take up much of their attention. But the Black Muslims do present a threat for the future. Should the white supremacists seem to be gaining the upper hand, if little or no progress seems to be made by the nonviolent means of CORE and the SCLC or the legalistic means of the NAACP, then the Black Muslims may grow from a curiosity on the American scene into a potent and dangerous force.

MALCOLM X

The Black Revolution*

MALCOLM X, unquestionably one of the most inspiring black leaders, was born Malcolm Little on May 19, 1925, the seventh child of his father, in Omaha, Nebraska. Malcolm's father was a Baptist preacher and a militant advocate of the black man's rights at a time when such a position was dangerous. The father was found one night with his head crushed and his body run over on a streetcar track in Lansing, Michigan, and Malcolm maintained throughout his life that his father had been assaulted by white men and placed on the tracks. The son was a dropout from school at fifteen and was convicted of burglary at twenty-one. While in prison Malcolm was converted to the Black Muslims. He quit smoking, gave up eating pork, and began his remarkable self-education in the prison library. He emerged from prison a new man with a new name, the X standing for his unknown African name lost in slavery. For twelve years, beginning in 1952 when he left prison, Malcolm X dedicated himself to being the spokesman for Elijah Muhammad and the Black Muslims, but he finally became disillusioned with the black separatists. Before he withdrew from the Black Muslims in 1964,

---

Malcolm X Speaks, copyright © 1965 by Merit Publishers and Betty Shabazz.

Malcolm considered white men to be "white devils," and he condemned whites in angry, uncompromising rhetoric. But shortly before his death he could see some hope of a "bloodless revolution" in America and he could say, "I believe in recognizing every human being as a human being . . . and when you are dealing with humanity as a family, there's no question of integration or intermarriage. It's just one human being marrying another human being or one human being living around with another human being." On February 21, 1965, about to speak to his followers, Malcolm X was shot to death by three assassins, two of whom were Black Muslims. "Whatever the future might have held for him had he lived," Robert Penn Warren has written, "his actual role was an important one, and in one sense the importance lay in his *being* rather than his *doing*. He was a man of passion, depth, and scale—and his personal story is a moving one."* "The Black Revolution" was a speech given by Malcolm X in April 1964 in New York City to an audience three-quarters white.

---

*"Malcolm X: Mission and Meaning," *The Yale Review*, December 1966. Also in my *The Way It Is: Readings in Contemporary American Prose*, Holt, Rinehart and Winston, 1970.

Friends and enemies: Tonight I hope that we can have a little fire-side chat with as few sparks as possible being tossed around. Especially because of the very explosive condition that the world is in today. Sometimes, when a person's house is on fire and someone comes in yelling fire, instead of the person who is awakened by the yell being thankful, he makes the mistake of charging the one who awakened him with having set the fire. I hope that this little conversation tonight about the black revolution won't cause many of you to accuse us of igniting it when you find it at your doorstep. . . .

During recent years there has been much talk about a population explosion. Whenever they are speaking of the population explosion, in my opinion they are referring primarily to the people of Asia or in Africa—the black, brown, red, and yellow people. It is seen by people of the West that, as soon as the standard of living is raised in Africa and Asia, automatically the people begin to reproduce abundantly. And there has been a great deal of fear engendered by this in the minds of the people of the West, who happen to be, on this earth, a very small minority.

In fact, in most of the thinking and planning of whites in the West today, it's easy to see the fear in their minds, conscious minds and subconscious minds, that the masses of dark people in the East,

105

who already outnumber them, will continue to increase and multiply and grow until they eventually overrun the people of the West like a human sea, a human tide, a human flood. And the fear of this can be seen in the minds, in the actions, of most of the people here in the West in practically everything that they do. It governs their political views and it governs their economic views and it governs most of their attitudes toward the present society.

I was listening to Dirksen, the senator from Illinois, in Washington, D.C., filibustering the civil-rights bill; and one thing that he kept stressing over and over and over was that if this bill is passed, it will change the social structure of America. Well, I know what he's getting at, and I think that most other people today, and especially our people, know what is meant when these whites, who filibuster these bills, express fears of changes in the social structure. Our people are beginning to realize what they mean.

Just as we can see that all over the world one of the main problems facing the West is race, likewise here in America today, most of your Negro leaders as well as the whites agree that 1964 itself appears to be one of the most explosive years yet in the history of America on the racial front, on the racial scene. Not only is this racial explosion probably to take place in America, but all of the ingredients for this racial explosion in America to blossom into a world-wide racial explosion present themselves right here in front of us. America's racial powder keg, in short, can actually fuse or ignite a world-wide powder keg.

There are whites in this country who are still complacent when they see the possibilities of racial strife getting out of hand. You are complacent simply because you think you outnumber the racial minority in this country; what you have to bear in mind is wherein you might outnumber us in this country, you don't outnumber us all over the earth.

Any kind of racial explosion that takes place in this country today, in 1964, is not a racial explosion that can be confined to the shores of America. It is a racial explosion that can ignite the racial powder keg that exists all over the planet that we call earth. I think that nobody would disagree that the dark masses of Africa and Asia and Latin America are already seething with bitterness, animosity, hostility, unrest, and impatience with the racial intolerance that they themselves have experienced at the hands of the white West.

And just as they have the ingredients of hostility toward the West in general, here we also have 22 million African-Americans, black, brown, red, and yellow people, in this country who are also seething with bitterness and impatience and hostility and animosity at the racial intolerance not only of the white West but of white America in particular.

And by the hundreds of thousands today we find our own people have become impatient, turning away from your white nationalism, which you call democracy, toward the militant, uncompromising policy of black nationalism. I point out right here that as soon as we announced we were going to start a black nationalist party in this country, we received mail from coast to coast, especially from young people at the college level, the university level, who expressed complete sympathy and support and a desire to take an active part in any kind of political action based on black nationalism, designed to correct or eliminate immediately evils that our people have suffered here for 400 years.

The black nationalists to many of you may represent only a minority in the community. And therefore you might have a tendency to classify them as something insignificant. But just as the fuse is the smallest part or the smallest piece in the powder keg, it is yet that little fuse that ignites the entire powder keg. The black nationalists to you may represent a small minority in the so-called Negro community. But they just happen to be composed of the type of ingredient necessary to fuse or ignite the entire black community.

And this is one thing that whites—whether you call yourselves liberals or conservatives or racists or whatever else you might choose to be—one thing that you have to realize is, where the black community is concerned, although the large majority you come in contact with may impress you as being moderate and patient and loving and long-suffering and all that kind of stuff, the minority who you consider to be Muslims or nationalists happen to be made of the type of ingredient that can easily spark the black community. This should be understood. Because to me a powder keg is nothing without a fuse.

1964 will be America's hottest year; her hottest year yet; a year of much racial violence and much racial bloodshed. But it won't be blood that's going to flow only on one side. The new generation of black people that have grown up in this country during recent years are already forming the opinion, and it's a just opinion, that if there is to be bleeding, it should be reciprocal—bleeding on both sides.

It should also be understood that the racial sparks that are ignited here in America today could easily turn into a flaming fire abroad, which means it could engulf all the people of this earth into a giant race war. You cannot confine it to one little neighborhood, or one little community, or one little country. What happens to a black man in America today happens to the black man in Africa. What happens to a black man in America and Africa happens to the black man in Asia and to the man down in Latin America. What happens to one of us today happens to all of us. And when this is realized, I think that the whites—who are intelligent even if they aren't moral or aren't just or aren't impressed by legalities—those who are intelligent will realize that when they touch this one, they are touching all of them, and this in itself will have a tendency to be a checking factor.

The seriousness of this situation must be faced up to. I was in Cleveland last night, Cleveland, Ohio. In fact I was there Friday, Saturday and yesterday. Last Friday the warning was given that this is a year of bloodshed, that the black man has ceased to turn the other cheek, that he has ceased to be nonviolent, that he has ceased to feel that he must be confined by all these restraints that are put upon him by white society in struggling for what white society says he was supposed to have had a hundred years ago.

So today, when the black man starts reaching out for what America says are his rights, the black man feels that he is within his rights—when he becomes the victim of brutality by those who are depriving him of his rights—to do whatever is necessary to protect himself. An example of this was taking place last night at this same time in Cleveland, where the police were putting water hoses on our people there and also throwing tear gas at them—and they met a hail of stones, a hail of rocks, a hail of bricks. A couple of weeks ago in Jacksonville, Florida, a young teen-age Negro was throwing Molotov cocktails.

Well, Negroes didn't do this ten years ago. But what you should learn from this is that they are waking up. It was stones yesterday, Molotov cocktails today; it will be hand grenades tomorrow and whatever else is available the next day. The seriousness of this situation must be faced up to. You should not feel that I am inciting someone to violence. I'm only warning of a powder-keg situation. You can take it or leave it. If you take the warning, perhaps you can still save yourself. But if you ignore it or ridicule it, well, death is already at your doorstep. There are 22 million African-Americans who are ready to fight for independence right here. When I say fight for independence right here, I don't mean any non-violent fight, or turn-the-other-cheek fight. Those days are gone. Those days are over.

If George Washington didn't get independence for this country nonviolently, and if Patrick Henry didn't come up with a nonviolent statement, and you taught me to look upon them as patriots and heroes, then it's time for you to realize that I have studied your books well. . . .

1964 will see the Negro revolt evolve and merge into the world-wide black revolution that has been taking place on this earth since 1945. The so-called revolt will become a real black revolution. Now the black revolution has been taking place in Africa and Asia and Latin America; when I say black, I mean non-white—black, brown, red or yellow. Our brothers and sisters in Asia, who were colonized by the Europeans, our brothers and sisters in Africa, who were colonized by the Europeans, and in Latin America, the peasants, who were colonized by the Europeans, have been involved in a struggle since 1945 to get the colonialists, or the colonizing powers, the Europeans, off their land, out of their country.

This is a real revolution. Revolution is always based on land. Revolution is never based on begging somebody for an integrated cup of coffee. Revolutions are never fought by turning the other cheek. Revolutions are never based upon love-your-enemy and pray-for-those-who-spitefully-use-you. And revolutions are never waged singing "We Shall Overcome." Revolutions are based upon bloodshed. Revolutions are never compromising. Revolutions are never based upon negotiations. Revolutions are never based upon any kind of tokenism whatsoever. Revolutions are never even based upon that which is begging a corrupt society or a corrupt system to accept us into it. Revolutions overturn systems. And there is no sytsem on this earth which has proven itself more corrupt, more criminal, than this system that in 1964 still colonizes 22 million African-Americans, still enslaves 22 million Afro-Americans.

There is no system more corrupt than a system that represents itself as the example of freedom, the example of democracy, and can go all over this earth telling other people how to straighten out their house, when you have citizens of this country who have to use bullets if they want to cast a ballot.

The greatest weapon the colonial powers have used in the past against our people has always been divide-and-conquer. America is a colonial power. She has colonized 22 million Afro-Americans by depriving us of first-class citizenship, by depriving us of civil rights, actually by depriving us of human rights. She has not only deprived us of the right to be a citizen, she has deprived us of the right to be human beings, the right to be recognized and respected as men and women. In this country the black can be fifty years old and he is still a "boy."

I grew up with white people. I was integrated before they even invented the word and I have never met white people yet—if you are around them long enough—who won't refer to you as a "boy" or a "gal," no matter how old you are or what school you came out of, no matter what your intellectual or professional level is. In this society we remain "boys."

So America's strategy is the same strategy as that which was used in the past by the colonial powers: divide and conquer. She plays one Negro leader against the other. She plays one Negro organization against the other. She makes us think we have different objectives, different goals. As soon as one Negro says something, she runs to this Negro and asks him, "What do you think about what he said?" Why, anybody can see through that today—except some of the Negro leaders.

All of our people have the same goals, the same objective. That objective is freedom, justice, equality. All of us want recognition and respect as human beings. We don't want to be integrationists. Nor do we want to be separationists. We want to be human beings. Integration is only a method that is used by some groups to obtain freedom, justice, equality and respect as human beings. Separation is only a method that is used by other groups to obtain freedom, justice, equality or human dignity.

Our people have made the mistake of confusing the methods with the objectives. As long as we agree on objectives, we should never fall out with each other just because we believe in different methods or tactics or strategy to reach a common objective.

We have to keep in mind at all times that we are not fighting for integration, nor are we fighting for separation. We are fighting for recognition as human beings. We are fighting for the right to live as free humans in this society. In fact, we are actually fighting for for rights that are even greater than civil rights and that is human rights. . . .

Among the so-called Negroes in this country, as a rule the civil-rights groups, those who believe in civil rights, spend most of their time trying to prove they are Americans. Their thinking is usually domestic, confined to the boundaries of America, and they always look upon themselves as a minority. When they look upon themselves upon the American stage, the American stage is a white stage. So a black man standing on that stage in America automatically is in the minority. He is the underdog, and in his struggle he always uses an approach that is a begging, hat-in-hand, compromising approach.

Whereas the other segment or section in America, known as the black nationalists, are more interested in human rights than they are in civil rights. And they place more stress on human rights than they do on civil rights. The difference between the thinking and the scope of the Negroes who are involved in the human-rights struggle and those who are involved in the civil-rights struggle is that those so-called Negroes involved in the human-rights struggle don't look upon themselves as Americans.

They look upon themselves as a part of dark mankind. They see the whole struggle not within the confines of the American stage, but they look upon the struggle on the world stage. And, in the world context, they see that the dark man outnumbers the white man. On the world stage the white man is just a microscopic minority.

So in this country you find two different types of Afro-Americans—the type who looks upon himself as a minority and you as the majority, because his scope is limited to the American scene; and then you have the type who looks upon himself as part of the majority and you as part of a microscopic minority. And this one uses a different approach in trying to struggle for his rights. He doesn't beg. He doesn't thank you for what you give him, because you are only giving him what he should have had a hundred years ago. He doesn't think you are doing him any favors.

He doesn't see any progress that he has made since the Civil War. He sees not one iota of progress because, number one, if the Civil War had freed him, he wouldn't need civil-rights legislation today. If the Emancipation Proclamation, issued by that great shining liberal called Lincoln, had freed him, he wouldn't be singing "We Shall Overcome" today. If the amendments to the Constitution had solved his problem, his problem wouldn't still be here today. And if the Supreme Court desegregation decision of 1954 was genuinely and sincerely designed to solve his problem, his problem wouldn't be with us today.

So this kind of black man is thinking. He can see where every maneuver that America had made, supposedly to solve this problem, has been nothing but political trickery and treachery of the worst order. Today he doesn't have any confidence in these so-called liberals. (I know that all that have come in here tonight don't call your-selves liberals. Because that's a nasty name today. It represents hypocrisy.) So these two different types of black people exist in the so-called Negro community and they are beginning to wake up and their awakening is producing a very dangerous situation.

You have whites in the community who express sincerity when they say they want to help. Well, how can they help? How can a white person help the black man solve his problem? Number one, you can't solve it for him. You can help him solve it, but you can't solve it for him today. One of the best ways that you can help him solve it is to let the so-called Negro, who has been involved in the civil-rights struggle, see that the civil-rights struggle must be ex-panded beyond the level of civil rights to human rights. Once it is expanded beyond the level of civil rights to the level of human rights, it opens the door for all of our brothers and sisters in Africa and Asia, who have their independence, to come to our rescue.

When you go to Washington, D.C., expecting those crooks down there—and that's what they are—to pass some kind of civil-rights legislation to correct a very criminal situation, what you are doing is encouraging the black man, who is the victim, to take his case into the court that's controlled by the criminal that made him the victim. It will never be solved in that way. . . .

The civil-rights struggle involves the black man taking his case to the white man's court. But when he fights it at the human-rights level, it is a different situation. It opens the door to take Uncle Sam to the world court. The black man doesn't have to go to court to be free. Uncle Sam should be taken to court and made to tell why the black man is not free in a so-called free society. Uncle Sam should be taken into the United Nations and charged with violating the UN charter of human rights.

You can forget civil rights. How are you going to get civil rights with men like Eastland and men like Dirksen and men like Johnson? It has to be taken out of their hands and taken into the hands of those whose power and authority exceed theirs. Washington has be-come too corrupt. Uncle Sam has become bankrupt when it comes to a conscience—it is impossible for Uncle Sam to solve the problem of 22 million black people in this country. It is absolutely impossible to do it in Uncle Sam's courts—whether it is the Supreme Court or any other kind of court that comes under Uncle Sam's jurisdiction.

The only alternative that the black man has in America today is to take it out of Senator Dirksen's and Senator Eastland's and President Johnson's jurisdiction and take it downtown on the East River and place it before that body of men who represent international law, and let them know that the human rights of black people are being violated in a country that professes to be the moral leader of the free world.

U.N.

Any time you have a filibuster in America, in the Senate, in 1964 over the rights of 22 million black people, over the citizenship of 22 million black people, or that will affect the freedom and justice and equality of 22 million black people, it's time for that government itself to be taken before a world court. How can you condemn South Africa? There are only 11 million of our people in South Africa, there are 22 million of them here. And we are receiving an injustice which is just as criminal as that which is being done to the black people of South Africa.

So today those whites who profess to be liberals—and as far as I am concerned it's just lip-profession—you understand why our people don't have civil rights. You're white. You can go and hang out with another white liberal and see how hypocritical they are. A lot of you sitting right here know that you've seen whites up in a Negro's face with flowery words, and as soon as that Negro walks away you listen to how your white friend talks. We have black people who can pass as white. We know how you talk.

We can see that it is nothing but a governmental conspiracy to continue to deprive the black people in this country of their rights. And the only way we will get these rights restored is by take it out of Uncle Sam's hands. Take him to court and charge him with genocide, the mass murder of millions of black people in this country—political murder, economic murder, social murder, mental murder. This is the crime that this government has committed, and if you yourself don't do something about it in time, you are going to open the doors for something to be done about it from outside forces.

I read in the paper yesterday where one of the Supreme Court justices, Goldberg, was crying about the violation of human rights of three million Jews in the Soviet Union. Imagine this. I haven't got anything against Jews, but that's their problem. How in the world are you going to cry about problems on the other side of the world when you haven't got the problems straightened out here? How can the plight of three million Jews in Russia be qualified to be taken to the United Nations by a man who is a justice in this Supreme Court, and is supposed to be a liberal, supposed to be a friend of black people, and hasn't opened up his mouth one time about taking the plight of black people down here to the United Nations? . . .

If Negroes could vote south of the—yes, if Negroes could vote south of the Canadian border—south South, if Negroes could vote in the southern part of the South, Ellender wouldn't be the head of the Agricultural and Forestry Committee, Richard Russell wouldn't be head of the Armed Services Committee, Robertson of Virginia wouldn't be head of the Banking and Currency Committee. Imagine that, all of the banking and currency of the government is in the hands of a cracker.

In fact, when you see how many of these committee men are from the South, you can see that we have nothing but a cracker government in Washington, D.C. And their head is a cracker president. I said a cracker president. Texas is just as much a cracker state as Mississippi. . . .

The first thing this man did when he came in office was invite all the big Negroes down for coffee. James Farmer was one of the first ones, the head of CORE. I have nothing against him. He's all right—Farmer, that is. But could that same President have invited James Farmer to Texas for coffee? And if James Farmer went to Texas, could he have taken his white wife with him to have coffee with the President? Any time you have a man who can't straighten out Texas, how can he straighten out the country? No, you're barking up the wrong tree.

If Negroes in the South could vote, the Dixiecrats would lose power. When the Dixiecrats lost power, the Democrats would lose power. A Dixiecrat lost is a Democrat lost. Therefore the two of them have to conspire with each other to stay in power. The Northern Dixiecrat puts all the blame on the Southern Dixiecrat. It's a con game, a giant political con game. The job of the Northern Democrat is to make the Negro think that he is our friend. He is always smiling and wagging his tail and telling us how much he can do for us if we vote for him. But at the same time that he's out in front telling us what he's going to do, behind the door he's in cahoots with the Southern Democrat setting up the machinery to make sure he'll never have to keep his promise.

This is the conspiracy that our people have faced in this country for the past hundred years. And today you have a new generation of black people who have come on the scene, who have become disenchanted with the entire system, who have become disillusioned over the system, and who are ready now and willing to do something about it.

So, in my conclusion, in speaking about the black revolution,

America today is at a time or in a day or at an hour where she is the first country on this earth that can actually have a bloodless revolution. In the past, revolutions have been bloody. Historically you just don't have a peaceful revolution. Revolutions are bloody, revolutions are violent, revolutions cause bloodshed and death follows in their paths. America is the only country in history in a position to bring about a revolution without violence and bloodshed. But America is not morally equipped to do so.

Why is America in a position to bring about a bloodless revolution? Because the Negro in this country holds the balance of power, and if the Negro in this country were given what the Constitution says he is supposed to have, the added power of the Negro in this country would sweep all of the racists and the segregationists out of office. It would change the entire political structure of the country. It would wipe out the Southern segregationism that now controls America's foreign policy, as well as America's domestic policy.

And the only way without bloodshed that this can be brought about is that the black man has to be given full use of the ballot in every one of the fifty states. But if the black man doesn't get the ballot, then you are going to be faced with another man who forgets the ballot and starts using the bullet.

Revolutions are fought to get control of land, to remove the absentee landlord and gain control of the land and the institutions that flow from that land. The black man has been in a very low condition because he has had no control whatsoever over any land. He has been a beggar economically, a beggar politically, a beggar socially, a beggar even when it comes to trying to get some education. The past type of mentality, that was developed in this colonial system among our people, today is being overcome. And as the young ones come up, they know what they want. And as they listen to your beautiful preaching about democracy and all those other flowery words, they know what they're supposed to have.

So you have a people today who not only know what they want, but also know what they are supposed to have. And they themselves are creating another generation that is coming up that not only will know what it wants and know what it should have, but also will be ready and willing to do whatever is necessary to see that what they should have materializes immediately. Thank you.

LEROI JONES

The Legacy of Malcolm X, And the Coming of the Black Nation*

LEROI JONES, the angry black poet, playwright, and social critic, was born in Newark, New Jersey, in 1934. His works include *Dutchman, Black Music, Tales,* and *Home,* from which the following essay is reprinted. Many whites will regard "The Legacy of Malcolm X" as unmitigated radicalism, but it expresses the feelings and desires of thousands of militant black Americans. LeRoi Jones uses the death of Malcolm X to explain the fallen leader's ideas and to show how they concur with his own. The essay is an attempt to arouse blacks to a sense of "National Consciousness," an awareness that blacks are a unique people or nation within the United States.

1

The reason Malik was killed (the reasons) is because he was thought dangerous by enough people to allow and sanction it. Black People and white people.

Malcolm X was killed because he was dangerous to America. He had made too great a leap, in his sudden awareness of *direction* and the possibilities he had for influencing people, anywhere.

Malcolm was killed because he wanted to become official, as, say, a statesman. Malcolm wanted an effective form in which to enrage the white man, a practical form. And he had begun to find it.

For one thing, he'd learned that Black Conquest will be a *deal*. That is, it will be achieved through deals as well as violence. (He was beginning through his African statesmanship to make deals with other nations, as statesman from a *nation*. An oppressed Black Nation "laying" in the Western Hemisphere.)

This is one reason he could use the "universal" Islam—to be at peace with all dealers. The idea was to broaden, formalize, and elevate the will of the Black Nation so that it would be able to move a great many people and resources in a direction necessary to *spring* the Black Man.

*"The Arabs must send us guns or we will accuse them of having
sold us into slavery!"* is international, and opens Black America's
ports to all comers. When the ports are open, there is an instant
brotherhood of purpose formed with most of the world.

Malcolm's legacy was his life. What he rose to be and through
what channels, e.g., Elijah Muhammad and the Nation of Islam, as
separate experiences. Malcolm changed as a minister of Islam: under
Elijah's tutelage, he was a different man—the difference being, between a man who is preaching Elijah Muhammad and a man who is
preaching political engagement and, finally, national sovereignty.
(Elijah Muhammad is now the second man, too.)

The point is that Malcolm had begun to call for Black National
Consciousness. And moved this consciousness into the broadest possible arena, operating with it as of now. We do not want a Nation,
we are a Nation. We must strengthen and formalize, and play the
world's game with what we have, from where we are, as a *truly*
separate people. America can give us nothing; all bargaining must be
done by mutual agreement. But finally, terms must be given by Black
Men *from their own shores*—which is where they live, where we all
are, now. The land is literally ours. And we must begin to act like it.

The landscape should belong to the people who see it all the
time.

We begin by being Nationalists. But a nation is land, and wars
are fought over land. The sovereignty of nations, the sovereignty of
culture, the sovereignty of race, the sovereignty of ideas and ways
"into" the world.

The world in the twentieth century, and for some centuries before, is, literally, backward. The world can be understood through
any idea. And the purely *social* condition of the world in this mil-
lennium, as, say, "compared" to other millennia, might show a far
greater loss than gain, if this were not balanced by concepts and
natural forces. That is, we think ourselves into the balance and ideas
are necessarily "advanced" of what is simply here (*what's going on,*
so to speak). And there are rockets and super cars. But, again, the
loss? What might it have been if my people were turning the
switches? I mean, these have been our White Ages, and all learning has suffered.

And so the Nationalist concept is the arrival of conceptual and
environmental strength, or the realization of it in its totality by the
Black Man in the West, *i.e.,* that he is not of the West, but even so,

like the scattered Indians after movie cavalry attacks, must regroup, and return that force on a fat, ignorant, degenerate enemy.

We are a people. We are unconscious captives unless we realize this—that we have always been separate, except in our tranced desire to be the thing that oppressed us, after some generations of having been "programmed" (a word suggested to me by Jim Campbell and Norbert Wieners) into believing that our greatest destiny was to become white people!

Malcolm's contribution

2

Malcolm X's greatest contribution, other than to propose a path *(1)* to internationalism and hence, the entrance of the American Black Man into a world-wide allegiance against the white man (in most recent times he proposed to do it using a certain kind of white liberal *(3)* as a lever), was to preach Black Consciousness to the Black Man. As a minister for the Nation of Islam, Malcolm talked about a black consciousness that took its form from religion. In his last days he talked of another black consciousness that proposed politics as its moving energy.

But one very important aspect of Malcolm's earlier counsels was his explicit call for a National Consciousness among Black People. And this aspect of Malcolm's philosophy certainly did abide throughout his days. The feeling that somehow the Black Man was different, as being, as a being, and finally, in our own time, as judge. And Malcolm propounded these differences as life anecdote and religious (political) truth and made the consideration of Nationalist ideas significant and powerful in our day.

Another very important aspect of Malcolm's earlier (or the Honorable Elijah Muhammad's) philosophy was the whole concept of *) land* land and land-control as central to any talk of "freedom" or "independence." The Muslim tack of asking for land within the continental United States in which Black People could set up their own nation, was given a special appeal by Malcolm, even though the request was seen by most people outside the movement as "just talk" or the amusing howls of a gadfly.

But the whole importance of this insistence on land is just now beginning to be understood. Malcolm said many times that when you speak about revolution you're talking about land—changing the ownership or usership of some specific land which you think is yours. But any talk of Nationalism also must take this concept of land and its primary importance into consideration because, finally, any Nationalism which is not intent on restoring or securing autonomous space for a people, *i.e.*, a nation, is at the very least short-sighted.

Elijah Muhammad has said, "We want our people in America, whose parents or grandparents were descendants from slaves, to be allowed to establish a separate state or territory of their own—either on this continent or elsewhere. We believe that our former slave-masters are obligated to provide such land and that the area must be fertile and minerally rich." And the Black Muslims seem separate from most Black People because the Muslims have a national consciousness based on their aspirations for land. Most of the Nationalist movements in this country advocate that that land is in Africa, and Black People should return there, or they propose nothing about land at all. It is impossible to be a Nationalist without talking about land. Otherwise, your Nationalism is a misnamed kind of "difficult" opposition to what the white man has done, rather than the advocation of another people becoming the rulers of themselves, and sooner or later the rest of the world.

The Muslims moved from the Back-to-Africa concept of Marcus Garvey (the first large movement by Black People back to a National Consciousness, which was, finally, only viable when the Black Man focused on Africa as literally "back home") to the concept of a Black National Consciousness existing in this land the Black captives had begun to identify as home. (Even in Garvey's time, there was not a very large percentage of Black People who really wanted to leave. Certainly, the newly emerging Black bourgeoisie would have nothing to do with "returning" to Africa. They were already created in the image of white people, as they still are, and wanted nothing to do with Black.)

What the Muslims wanted was a profound change. The National Consciousness focused on actual (nonabstract) land, identifying a people, in a land where they lived. Garvey wanted to go back to Jordan. A real one. The Nation of Islam wanted Jordan closer. Before these two thrusts, the Black Man in America, as he was Christianized, believed Jordan was in the sky, like pie, and absolutely supernatural.

Malcolm, then, wanted to give the National Consciousness its political embodiment, and send it out to influence the newly forming third world, in which this consciousness was to be included. The concept of Blackness, the concept of the National Consciousness, the proposal of a political (and diplomatic) form for this aggregate of Black spirit, these are the things given to us by Garvey, through Elijah Muhammad and finally given motion into still another area of Black response by Malcolm X.

Malcolm's legacy to Black People is what he moved toward, as the accretion of his own spiritual learning and the movement of Black People in general, through the natural hope, a rise to social understanding within the new context of the white nation and its decline under hypocrisy and natural "oppositeness" which has pushed all of us toward "new" ideas. We are all the products of national spirit and worldview. We are drawn by the vibrations of the entire nation. If there were no bourgeois Negroes, none of us would be drawn to that image. They, bourgeois Negroes, were shaped through the purposive actions of a national attitude, and finally, by the demands of a particular culture.

At which point we must consider what cultural attitudes are, what culture is, and what National Consciousness has to do with these, *i.e.,* if we want to understand what Malcolm X was pointing toward, and why the Black Man now must move in that direction since the world will not let him move any other way. The Black Man is possessed by the energies of historic necessity and the bursting into flower of a National Black Cultural Consciousness, and with that, in a living future, the shouldering to power of Black culture and, finally, Black Men . . . and then, Black ideals, which are different descriptions of a God. A righteous sanctity, out of which worlds are built.

3

What the Black Man must do now is look down at the ground upon which he stands, and claim it as his own. It is not abstract. Look down! Pick up the earth, or jab your fingernails into the concrete. It is real and it is yours, if you want it.

But to want it, as our own, is the present direction. To want what we are and where we are, but rearranged by our own consciousness. That is why it was necessary first to recrystallize national aspirations behind a Garvey. The Africans who first came here were replaced by Americans, or people responding to Western stimuli and then Americans. In order for the Americans to find out that they had come from another place, were, hence, alien, the Garvey times had to come. Elijah said we must have a place, to be, ourselves. Malcolm made it contemporarily secular.

So that now we must find the flesh of our spiritual creation. We must be *conscious.* And to be conscious is to be *cultured,* processed in specific virtues and genius. We must respond to this National Consciousness with our souls, and use the correspondence to come into our own.

The Black Man will always be frustrated until he has land (A Land!) of his own. All the thought processes and emotional orientation of "national liberation movements"—from slave uprisings onward—have always given motion to a Black National (and Cultural) Consciousness. These movements proposed that judgments were being made by Black sensibility, and that these judgments were *necessarily* different from those of the white sensibility—different, and after all is said and done, inimical.

Men are what their culture predicts (enforces). Culture is, simply, the way men live. How they have come to live. What they are formed by. Their total experience, and its implications and theories. Its paths.

The Black Man's paths are alien to the white man. Black Culture is alien to the white man. Art and religion are the results and idealized supernumeraries of culture. Culture in this sense, as Sapir said, is "The National Genius," whether it be a way of fixing rice or killing a man.

I said in *Blues People:* "Culture is simply how one lives and is connected to history by habit." Here is a graphic structure of the relationships and total context of culture:

The Axis (context and evoked relationships) of Culture.

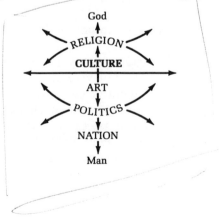

God is man idealized (humanist definition). Religion is the aspiration of man toward an idealized existence. An existence in which the functions of God and man are harmonious, even identical. Art is the movement forward, the understanding progress of man. It is feeling and making. A nation (social order) is made the way people *feel* it should be made. A race is too. Politics is man's aspiration toward an order. Religion is too. Art is an ordering as well. And all these categories are spiritual, but are also the result of the body, at one point, serving as a container of feeling. The soul is no less sensitive.

Nations are races. (In America, white people have become a nation, an identity, a race.) Political integration in America will not work because the Black Man is played on by special forces. His life, from his organs, *i.e.,* the life of the body, what it needs, what it wants, to become, is different—and for this reason racial is biological, finally. We are a different *species*. A species that is evolving to world power and philosophical domination of the world. The world will move the way Black People move!

If we take the teachings of Garvey, Elijah Muhammad and Malcolm X (as well as Frazier, DuBois and Fanon), we know for certain that the solution of the Black Man's problems will come only through Black National Consciousness. We also know that the focus of change will be racial. (If we *feel* differently, we have different *ideas*. Race is feeling. Where the body, and the organs come in. Culture is the preservation of these feelings in superrational to rational form. Art is one method of expressing these feelings and identifying the form, as an emotional phenomenon.) In order for the Black Man in the West to absolutely know himself, it is necessary for him to see himself first as culturally separate from the white man. That is, to be conscious of this separation and use the strength it proposes.

Western Culture (the way white people live and think) is passing. If the Black Man cannot identify himself as separate, and understand what this means, he will perish along with Western Culture and the white man.

What a culture produces, is, and refers to, is an image—a picture of a process, since it is a form of a process: movement seen. The changing of images, of references, is the Black Man's way back to the racial integrity of the captured African, which is where we must take ourselves, in feeling, to be truly the warriors we propose to be. To form an absolutely rational attitude toward West man, and

West thought. Which is what is needed. To see the white man as separate and as enemy. To make a fight according to the absolute realities of the world as it is.

Good-Bad, Beautiful-Ugly, are all formed as the result of image. The mores, customs, of a place are the result of experience, and a common reference for defining it—common images. The three white men in the film *Gunga Din* who kill off hundreds of Indians, Greek hero-style, are part of an image of white men. The various black porters, gigglers, ghostchumps and punkish Indians, etc., that inhabit the public image the white man has fashioned to characterize Black Men are references by Black Men to the identity of Black Men in the West, since that's what is run on them each day by white magic, *i.e.,* television, movies, radio, etc.—the Mass Media (the *Daily News* does it with flicks and adjectives).

The song title "A White Man's Heaven Is a Black Man's Hell" describes how complete an image reversal is necessary in the West. Because for many Black People, the white man has succeeded in making this hell seem like heaven. But Black youth are much better off in this regard than their parents. They are the ones who need the least image reversal.

The Black artist, in this context, is desperately needed to change the images his people identify with, by asserting Black feeling, Black mind, Black judgment. The Black intellectual, in this same context, is needed to change the interpretation of facts toward the Black Man's best interests, instead of merely tagging along reciting white judgments of the world.

Art, Religion, and Politics are impressive vectors of a culture. Art describes a culture. Black artists must have an image of what the Black sensibility is in this land. Religion elevates a culture. The Black Man must aspire to Blackness. God is man idealized. The Black Man must idealize himself as Black. And idealize and aspire to that. Politics gives a social order to the culture, *i.e.,* makes relationships within the culture definable for the functioning organism. The Black man must seek a Black politics, an ordering of the world that is beneficial to his culture, to his interiorization and judgment of the world. This is strength. And we are hordes.

4

Black People are a race, a culture, a Nation. The legacy of Malcolm X is that we know we can move from where we are. Our land is where we live. (Even the Muslims have made this statement about Harlem.) If we are a separate Nation, we must make that separateness where we are. There are Black cities all over this white nation. Nations within nations. In order for the Black Man to survive he must not only identify himself as a unique being, but take steps to insure that this being has, what the Germans call *Lebensraum* ("living room") literally space in which to exist and develop.

The concepts of National Consciousness and the Black Nation, after the death of Malik, have moved to the point where now some Black People are demanding national sovereignty as well as National (and Cultural) Consciousness. In Harlem, for instance, as director of the Black Arts Repertory Theatre School, I have issued a call for a Black Nation. In Harlem, where 600,000 Black People reside.

The first act must be the nationalization of all properties and resources belonging to white people, within the boundaries of the Black Nation. (All the large concentrations of Black People in the West are already nations. All that is missing is the consciousness of this state of affairs. All that is missing is that the Black Man take control. As Margaret Walker said in her poem "For My People": *A race of men must rise, and take control.*)

Nationalization means that all properties and resources must be harnessed to the needs of the Nation. In the case of the coming Black Nation, all these materials must be harnessed to the needs of Black People. In Harlem, it is almost common knowledge that the Jews, etc., will go the next time there's a large "disturbance," like they say. But there must be machinery set up to transfer the power potential of these retail businesses, small industries, etc., so that they may benefit Black People.

Along with nationalization of foreign-owned businesses (which includes Italian underworld businesses, some of which, like the policy racket, can be transformed into a national lottery, with the monies staying with Black People, or as in the case of heroin-selling, completely abolished) must come the nationalization of all political voices setting up to function within the community/Nation.

No white politicians can be allowed to function within the Nation. Black politicians doing funny servant business for whites, must be eliminated. Black people must have absolute political and economic control. In other words they must have absolute control over their lives and destinies.

These moves are toward the working form of any autonomous nation. And it is this that the Black Man must have. An autonomous Nation. His own forms: treaties, agreements, laws.

These are moves that the conscious Black Man (artist, intellectual, Nationalist, religious thinker, dude with "common sense") must prepare the people for. And the people must be prepared for moves they themselves are already making. And moves they have already made must be explained and analyzed. They, the people, are the bodies. . . . Where are the heads?

And it is *the heads* that are needed for the next move Black People will make. The move to Nationhood. The exact method of transformation is simple logistics.

What we are speaking about again is sovereignty. Sovereignty and independence. And when we speak of these things, we can understand just how far Malik went. The point now is to take ourselves the rest of the way.

Only a united Black Consciousness can save Black People from annihilation at the white man's hands. And no other nation on earth is safe, unless the Black Man in America is safe. Not even the Chinese can be absolutely certain of their continued sovereignty as long as the white man is alive. And there is only one people on the planet who can slay the white man. The people who know him best. His ex-slaves.

WILLIAM H. GRIER
and PRICE M. COBBS

Black Rage

WILLIAM H. GRIER and PRICE M. COBBS are practicing psychiatrists
and assistant professors of psychiatry at the University of
California Medical Center, San Francisco. In their highly acclaimed
and angry book, *Black Rage* (1968), the authors examine the
insidious effects of racial discrimination from a psychological
point of view. The following essay, which is the last chapter from
that book, is a poignant description of the hatred, frustration,
and despair which result from white racism, a description of how an
entire people may have their minds crippled because of the
thoughtless cruelty of another people. The two psychiatrists warn
that unless white Americans face the urgency of black demands, the
accumulated griefs and hatreds will inevitably explode in a
nihilistic black rage.

*Chapter X of BLACK RAGE by William H. Grier and Price M. Cobbs,
© 1968 by William H. Grier and Price M. Cobbs, Basic Books, Inc., Publishers, New York.

H istory may well show that of all the men who lived during our fateful century none illustrated the breadth or the grand potential of man so magnificently as did Malcolm X. If, in future chronicles, America is regarded as the major nation of our day, and the rise of darker people from bondage as the major event, then no figure has appeared thus far who captures the spirit of our times as does Malcolm.

Malcolm is an authentic hero, indeed the only universal black hero. In his unrelenting opposition to the viciousness in America, he fired the imagination of black men all over the world.

If this black nobleman is a hero to black people in the United States and if his life reflects their aspirations, there can be no doubt of the universality of black rage.

Malcolm responded to his position in his world and to his blackness in the manner of so many black boys. He turned to crime. He was saved by a religious sect given to a strange, unhistorical explanation of the origin of black people and even stranger solutions to their problems. He rose to power in that group and outgrew it.

Feeding on his own strength, growing in response to his own commands, limited by no creed, he became a citizen of the world and an advocate of all oppressed people no matter their color or belief. Anticipating his death by an assassin, he distilled, in a book, the essence of his genius, his life. His autobiography thus is a legacy and, together with his speeches, illustrates the thrusting growth of the man—his evolution, rapid, propulsive, toward the man he might have been had he lived.

The essence of Malcolm X was growth, change, and a seeking after truth.

Alarmed white people saw him first as an eccentric and later as a dangerous radical—a revolutionary without troops who threatened to stir black people to riot and civil disobedience. Publicly, they treated him as a joke; privately, they were afraid of him.

After his death he was recognized by black people as the "black shining prince" and recordings of his speeches became treasured things. His autobiography was studied, his life marveled at. Out of this belated admiration came the philosophical basis for black activism and indeed the thrust of Black Power itself, away from integration and civil rights and into the "black bag."

Unlike Malcolm, however, the philosophical underpinnings of the new black militancy were static. They remained encased within the ideas of revolution and black nationhood, ideas Malcolm had outgrown by the time of his death. His stature has made even his earliest statements gospel and men now find themselves willing to die for words which in retrospect are only milestones in the growth of a fantastic man.

Many black men who today preach blackness seem headed blindly toward self-destruction, uncritical of anything "black" and damning the white man for diabolical wickedness. For a philosophical base they have turned to the words of Malcolm's youth.

This perversion of Malcolm's intellectual position will not, we submit, be held against him by history.

Malcolm's meaning for us lies in his fearless demand for truth and his evolution from a petty criminal to an international statesman —accomplished by a black man against odds of terrible magnitude —in America. His message was his life, not his words, and Malcolm knew it.

Black Power activism—thrust by default temporarily at the head of a powerful movement—is a conception that contributes in a significant way to the strength and unity of that movement but is unable to provide the mature vision for the mighty works ahead. It will pass and leave black people in this country prouder, stronger, more determined, but in need of grander princes with clearer vision.

We believe that the black masses will rise with a simple and eloquent demand to which new leaders must give tongue. They will say to America simply:

"GET OFF OUR BACKS!"

The problem will be so simply defined.

What is the problem?

The white-man has crushed all but the life from blacks from the time they came to these shores to this very day.

What is the solution?

Get off their backs.

How?

By simply doing it—now.

This is no oversimplification. Greater changes than this in the relations of peoples have taken place before. The nation would benefit tremendously. Such a change might bring about a closer examination of our relations with foreign countries, a reconsideration of economic policies, and a re-examination if not a redefinition of nationhood. It might in fact be the only change which can prevent a degenerative decline from a powerful nation to a feeble, third-class, ex-colonialist country existing at the indulgence of stronger powers.

In spite of the profound shifts in power throughout the world in the past thirty years, the United States seems to have a domestic objective of "business as usual," with no change needed or in fact wanted.

All the nasty problems are overseas. At home the search is for bigger profits and smaller costs, better education and lower taxes, more vacation and less work, more for me and less for you. Problems at home are to be talked away, reasoned into nonexistence, and put to one side while we continue the great American game of greed.

There is, however, an inevitability built into the natural order of things. Cause and effect are in fact joined, and if you build a sufficient cause then not all the talk or all the tears in God's creation can prevent the effect from presenting itself one morning as the now ripened fruit of your labors.

America began building a cause when black men were first sold into bondage. When the first black mother killed her newborn rather than have him grow into a slave. When the first black man slew himself rather than submit to an organized system of man's feeding upon another's flesh. America had well begun a cause when all the rebels were either slain or broken and the nation set to the task of refining the system of slavery so that the maximum labor might be extracted from it.

The system achieved such refinement that the capital loss involved when a slave woman aborted could be set against the gain to be expected from forcing her into brutish labor while she was with child.

America began building a potent cause in its infancy as a nation.

It developed a way of life, an American ethos, a national life style which included the assumption that blacks are inferior and were born to hew wood and draw water. Newcomers to this land (if white) were immediately made to feel welcome and, among the bounty available, were given blacks to feel superior to. They were required to despise and depreciate them, abuse and exploit them, and one can only imagine how munificent this land must have seemed to the European—a land with built-in scapegoats.

The hatred of blacks has been so deeply bound up with being an American that it has been one of the first things new Americans learn and one of the last things old Americans forget. Such feelings have been elevated to a position of national character, so that individuals now no longer feel personal guilt or responsibility for the oppression of black people. The nation has incorporated this oppression into itself in the form of folkways and storied traditions, leaving the individual free to shrug his shoulders and say only: "That's our way of life."

This way of life is a heavy debt indeed, and one trembles for the debtor when payment comes due.

America has waxed rich and powerful in large measure on the backs of black laborers. It has become a violent, pitiless nation, hard and calculating, whose moments of generosity are only brief intervals in a ferocious narrative of life, bearing a ferocity and an aggression so strange in this tiny world where men die if they do not live together.

With the passing of the need for black laborers, black people have become useless; they are a drug on the market. There are not enough menial jobs. They live in a nation which has evolved a work force of skilled and semi-skilled workmen. A nation which chooses simultaneously to exclude all black men from this favored labor force and to deny them the one thing America has offered every other group—unlimited growth with a ceiling set only by one's native gifts.

The facts, however obfuscated, are simple. Since the demise of slavery black people have been expendable in a cruel and impatient land. The damage done to black people has been beyond reckoning. Only now are we beginning to sense the bridle placed on black children by a nation which does not want them to grow into mature human beings.

The most idealistic social reformer of our time, Martin Luther King, was not slain by one man; his murder grew out of that large body of violent bigotry America has always nurtured—that body of thinking which screams for the blood of the radical, or the conservative, or the villain, or the saint. To the extent that he stood in the way of bigotry, his life was in jeopardy, his saintly persuasion notwithstanding. To the extent that he was black and was calling America to account, his days were numbered by the nation he sought to save.

Men and women, even children, have been slain for no other earthly reason than their blackness. Property and goods have been stolen and the victims then harried and punished for their poverty. But such viciousness can at least be measured or counted.

Black men, however, have been so hurt in their manhood that they are now unsure and uneasy as they teach their sons to be men. Women have been so humiliated and used that they may regard womanhood as a curse and flee from it. Such pain, so deep, and such real jeopardy, that the fundamental protective function of the family has been denied. These injuries we have no way to measure.

Black men have stood so long in such peculiar jeopardy in America that a *black norm* has developed—a suspiciousness of one's environment which is necessary for survival. Black people, to a degree that approaches paranoia, must be ever alert to danger from their white fellow citizens. It is a cultural phenomenon peculiar to black Americans. And it is a posture so close to paranoid thinking that the mental disorder into which black people most frequently fall is paranoid psychosis.

Can we say that white men have driven black men mad?

An educated black woman had worked in an integrated setting for fifteen years. Compliant and deferential, she had earned promotions and pay increases by hard work and excellence. At no time had she been involved in black activism, and her only participation in the movement had been a yearly contribution to the N.A.A.C.P.

During a lull in the racial turmoil she sought psychiatric treatment. She explained that she had lately become alarmed at waves of rage that swept over her as she talked to white people or at times even as she looked at them. In view of her past history of compliance and passivity, she felt that something was wrong with her. If her controls slipped she might embarrass herself or lose her job.

A black man, a professional, had been a "nice guy" all his life. He was a hard-working non-militant who avoided discussions of race with his white colleagues. He smiled if their comments were harsh and remained unresponsive to racist statements. Lately he has experienced almost uncontrollable anger toward his white co-workers, and although he still manages to keep his feelings to himself, he confides that blacks and whites have been lying to each other. There is hatred and violence between them and he feels trapped. He too fears for himself if his controls should slip.

If these educated recipients of the white man's bounty find it hard to control their rage, what of their less fortunate kinsman who has less to protect, less to lose, and more scars to show for his journey in this land?

The tone of the preceding chapters has been mournful, painful, desolate, as we have described the psychological consequences of white oppression of blacks. The centuries of senseless cruelty and the permeation of the black man's character with the conviction of his own hatefulness and inferiority tell a sorry tale.

This dismal tone has been deliberate. It has been an attempt to evoke a certain quality of depression and hopelessness in the reader and to stir these feelings. These are the most common feelings tasted by black people in America.

The horror carries the endorsement of centuries and the entire lifespan of a nation. It is a way of life which reaches back to the beginnings of recorded time. And all the bestiality, wherever it occurs and however long it has been happening, is narrowed, focused, and refined to shine into a black child's eyes when first he views his world. All that has ever happened to black men and women he sees in the victims closest to him, his parents.

A life is an eternity and throughout all that eternity a black child has breathed the foul air of cruelty. He has grown up to find that his spirit was crushed before he knew there was need of it. His ambitions, even in their forming, showed him to have set his hand against his own. This is the desolation of black life in America.

Depression and grief are hatred turned on the self. It is instructive to pursue the relevance of this truth to the condition of black Americans.

Black people have shown a genius for surviving under the most deadly circumstances. They have survived because of their close attention to reality. A black dreamer would have a short life in Mississippi. They are of necessity bound to reality, chained to the facts of the times; historically the penalty for misjudging a situation involving white men has been death. The preoccupation with religion has been a willing adoption of fantasy to prod an otherwise reluctant mind to face another day.

We will even play tricks on ourselves if it helps us stay alive.

The psychological devices used to survive are reminiscent of the years of slavery, and it is no coincidence. The same devices are used because black men face the same danger now as then.

The grief and depression caused by the condition of black men in America is an unpopular reality to the sufferers. They would rather see themselves in a more heroic posture and chide a disconsolate brother. They would like to point to their achievements (which in fact have been staggering); they would rather point to virtue (which has been shown in magnificent form by some blacks); they would point to bravery, fidelity, prudence, brilliance, creativity, all of which dark men have shown in abundance. But the overriding experience of the black American has been grief and sorrow and no man can change that fact.

His grief has been realistic and appropriate. What people have so earned a period of mourning?

We want to emphasize yet again the depth of the grief for slain sons and ravished daughters, how deep and lingering it is.

If the depth of this sorrow is felt, we can then consider what can be made of this emotion.

As grief lifts and the sufferer moves toward health, the hatred he had turned on himself is redirected toward his tormentors, and the fury of his attack on the one who caused him pain is in direct proportion to the depth of his grief. When the mourner lashes out in anger, it is a relief to those who love him, for they know he has now returned to health.

Observe that the amount of rage the oppressed turns on his

tormentor is a direct function of the depth of his grief, and consider the intensity of black men's grief.

Slip for a moment into the soul of a black girl whose womanhood is blighted, not because she is ugly, but because she is black and by definition all blacks are ugly.

Become for a moment a black citizen of Birmingham, Alabama, and try to understand his grief and dismay when innocent children are slain while they worship, for no other reason than that they are black.

Imagine how an impoverished mother feels as she watches the light of creativity snuffed out in her children by schools which dull the mind and environs which rot the soul.

For a moment make yourself the black father whose son went innocently to war and there was slain—for whom, for what?

For a moment be any black person, anywhere, and you will feel the waves of hopelessness that engulfed black men and women when Martin Luther King was murdered. All black people understood the tide of anarchy that followed his death.

It is the transformation of *this* quantum of grief into aggression of which we now speak. As a sapling bent low stores energy for a violent backswing, blacks bent double by oppression have stored energy which will be released in the form of rage—black rage, apocalyptic and final.

White Americans have developed a high skill in the art of misunderstanding black people. It must have seemed to slaveholders that slavery would last through all eternity, for surely their misunderstanding of black bondsmen suggested it. If the slaves were eventually to be released from bondage, what could be the purpose of creating the fiction of their subhumanity?

It must have seemed to white men during the period 1865 to 1945 that black men would always be a passive, compliant lot. If not, why would they have stoked the flames of hatred with such deliberately barbarous treatment?

White Americans today deal with "racial incidents" from summer to summer as if such minor turbulence will always remain minor and one need only keep the blacks busy till fall to have made it through another troubled season.

Today it is the young men who are fighting the battles, and, for now, their elders, though they have given their approval, have not joined in. The time seems near, however, for the full range of the black masses to put down the broom and buckle on the sword.

And it grows nearer day by day. Now we see skirmishes, sputtering erratically, evidence if you will that the young men are in a warlike mood. But evidence as well that the elders are watching closely and may soon join the battle.

Even these minor flurries have alarmed the country and have resulted in a spate of generally senseless programs designed to give *temporary summer jobs!* More interesting in its long-range prospects has been the apparent eagerness to draft black men for military service. If in fact this is a deliberate design to place black men in uniform in order to get them off the street, it may be the most curious "instant cure" for a serious disease this nation has yet attempted. Young black men are learning the most modern techniques for killing —techniques which may be used against *any* enemy.

But it is all speculation. The issue finally rests with the black masses. When the servile men and women stand up, we had all better duck.

We should ask what is likely to galvanize the masses into aggression against the whites.

Will it be some grotesque atrocity against black people which at last causes one-tenth of the nation to rise up in indignation and crush the monstrosity?

Will it be the example of black people outside the United States who have gained dignity through their own liberation movement?

Will it be by the heroic action of a small group of blacks which by its wisdom and courage commands action in a way that cannot be denied?

Or will it be by blacks, finally and in an unpredictable way, simply getting fed up with the bumbling stupid racism of this country? Fired not so much by any one incident as by the gradual accretion of stupidity into fixtures of national policy.

All are possible, or any one, or something yet unthought. It seems certain only that on the course the nation now is headed it will happen.

One might consider the possibility that, if the national direction remains unchanged, such a conflagration simply might *not* come about. Might not black people remain where they are, as they did for a hundred years during slavery?

Such seems truly inconceivable. Not because blacks are so naturally warlike or rebellious, but because they are filled with such grief, such sorrow, such bitterness, and such hatred. It seems now delicately poised, not yet risen to the flash point, but rising rapidly nonetheless. No matter what repressive measures are invoked against the blacks, they will never swallow their rage and go back to blind hopelessness.

If existing oppressions and humiliating disenfranchisements are to be lifted, they will have to be lifted most speedily, or catastrophe will follow.

For there are no more psychological tricks blacks can play upon themselves to make it possible to exist in dreadful circumstances. No more lies can they tell themselves. No more dreams to fix on. No more opiates to dull the pain. No more patience. No more thought. No more reason. Only a welling tide risen out of all those terrible years of grief, now a tidal wave of fury and rage, and all black, black as night.

ELDRIDGE CLEAVER

The White Race and Its Heroes*

ELDRIDGE CLEAVER fled the United States—some say as a political fugitive—and made his way to Cuba in 1969 rather than surrender to the state of California for allegedly violating his prison parole. He was Minister of Information for the Black Panthers and a candidate in 1968 for President of the United States on the Peace and Freedom Party ticket. By invitation of the students, he was a guest lecturer at the University of California (Berkeley) to the displeasure and disapproval of state officials, including Governor Ronald Reagan. "The White Race and Its Heroes," reprinted from Mr. Cleaver's *Soul on Ice*, an outstanding collection of essays written while he was in Folsom State Prison, is a passionate but wholly reasonable essay which argues that the white race has lost its heroes, that it has begun to see through its illusions and to recognize its crimes against the colored races of the world. Unlike many other black militants, Eldridge Cleaver has high praise for some whites, especially the young, who have worked for the rights of black men.

**From SOUL ON ICE by Eldridge Cleaver. Copyright © 1968 by Eldridge Cleaver. With permission of McGraw-Hill Book Company.

> White people cannot, in the generality, be taken as models of how to
> live. Rather, the white man is himself in sore need of new standards,
> which will release him from his confusion and place him once again
> in fruitful communion with the depths of his own being.
>
> JAMES BALDWIN
> —The Fire Next Time

Right from the go, let me make one thing absolutely clear: I am not now, nor have I ever been, a white man. Nor, I hasten to add, am I now a Black Muslim—although I used to be. But I am an Ofay Watcher, a member of that unchartered, amorphous league which has members on all continents and the islands of the seas. Ofay Watchers Anonymous, we might be called, because we exist concealed in the shadows wherever colored people have known oppression by whites, by white enslavers, colonizers, imperialists, and neo-colonialists.

Did it irritate you, compatriot, for me to string those epithets out like that? Tolerate me. My intention was not necessarily to

143

sprinkle salt over anyone's wounds. I did it primarily to relieve a certain pressure on my brain. Do you cop that? If not, then we're in trouble, because we Ofay Watchers have a pronounced tendency to slip into that mood. If it is bothersome to you, it is quite a task for me because not too long ago it was my way of life to preach, as ardently as I could, that the white race is a race of devils, created by their maker to do evil, and make evil appear as good; that the white race is the natural, unchangeable enemy of the black man, who is the original man, owner, maker, cream of the planet Earth; that the white race was soon to be destroyed by Allah, and that the black man would then inherit the earth, which has always, in fact, been his.

I have, so to speak, washed my hands in the blood of the martyr, Malcohm X, whose retreat from the precipice of madness created new room for others to turn about in, and I am now caught up in that tiny space, attempting a maneuver of my own. Having renounced the teachings of Elijah Muhammad, I find that a rebirth does not follow automatically, of its own accord, that a void is left in one's vision, and this void seeks constantly to obliterate itself by pulling one back to one's former outlook. I have tried a tentative compromise by adopting a select vocabulary, so that now when I see the whites of *their* eyes, instead of saying "devil" or "beast" I say "imperialist" or "colonialist," and everyone seems to be happier.

In silence, we have spent our years watching the ofays, trying to understand them, on the principle that you have a better chance coping with the known than with the unknown. Some of us have been, and some still are, interested in learning whether it is *ultimately* possible to live in the same territory with people who seem so disagreeable to live with; still others want to get as far away from ofays as possible. What we share in common is the desire to break the ofay's power over us.

At times of fundamental social change, such as the era in which we live, it is easy to be deceived by the onrush of events, beguiled by the craving for social stability into mistaking transitory phenomena for enduring reality. The strength and permanence of "white backlash" in America is just such an illusion. However much this rearguard action might seem to grow in strength, the initiative, and the future, rest with those whites and blacks who have liberated themselves from the master/slave syndrome. And these are to be found mainly among the youth.

Over the past twelve years there has surfaced a political conflict between the generations that is deeper, even, than the struggle
between the races. Its first dramatic manifestation was within the
ranks of the Negro people, when college students in the South, fed
up with Uncle Tom's hat-in-hand approach to revolution, threw
off the yoke of the NAACP. When these students initiated the first
sit-ins, their spirit spread like a raging fire across the nation, and the
technique of non-violent direct action, constantly refined and honed
into a sharp cutting tool, swiftly matured. The older Negro "leaders," who are now all die-hard advocates of this tactic, scolded the
students for sitting-in. The students rained down contempt upon
their hoary heads. In the pre-sit-in days, these conservative leaders
had always succeeded in putting down insurgent elements among
the Negro people. (A measure of their power, prior to the students'
rebellion, is shown by their success in isolating such great black
men as the late W. E. B. DuBois and Paul Robeson, when these
stalwarts, refusing to bite their tongues, lost favor with the U.S.
government by their unstinting efforts to link up the Negro revolution with national liberation movements around the world.)

The "Negro leaders," and the whites who depended upon them
to control their people, were outraged by the impudence of the
students. Calling for a moratorium on student initiative, they were
greeted instead by an encore of sit-ins, and retired to their ivory
towers to contemplate the new phenomenon. Others, less prudent
because held on a tighter leash by the whites, had their careers
brought to an abrupt end because they thought they could lead a
black/white backlash against the students, only to find themselves
in a kind of Bay of Pigs. Negro college presidents, who expelled students from all-Negro colleges in an attempt to quash the demonstrations, ended up losing their jobs; the victorious students would no
longer allow them to preside over the campuses. The spontaneous
protests on southern campuses over the repressive measures of
their college administrations were an earnest of the Free Speech
upheaval which years later was to shake the UC campus at Berkeley.
In countless ways, the rebellion of the black students served as
catalyst for the brewing revolt of the whites.

What has suddenly happened is that the white race has lost
its heroes. Worse, its heroes have been revealed as villains and its
greatest heroes as the arch-villains. The new generations of whites,
appalled by the sanguine and despicable record carved over the
face of the globe by their race in the last five hundred years, are

rejecting the panoply of white heroes, whose heroism consisted in erecting the inglorious edifice of colonialism and imperialism; heroes whose careers rested on a system of foreign and domestic exploitation, rooted in the myth of white supremacy and the manifest destiny of the white race. The emerging shape of a new world order, and the requisites for survival in such a world, are fostering in young whites a new outlook. They recoil in shame from the spectacle of cowboys and pioneers—their heroic forefathers whose exploits filled earlier generations with pride—galloping across a movie screen shooting down Indians like Coke bottles. Even Winston Churchill, who is looked upon by older whites as perhaps the greatest hero of the twentieth century—even he, because of the system of which he was a creature and which he served, is an arch-villain in the eyes of the young white rebels.

At the close of World War Two, national liberation movements in the colonized world picked up new momentum and audacity, seeking to cash in on the democratic promises made by the Allies during the war. The Atlantic Charter, signed by President Roosevelt and Prime Minister Churchill in 1941, affirming "the right of all people to choose the form of government under which they may live," established the principle, although it took years of postwar struggle to give this piece of rhetoric even the appearance of reality. And just as world revolution has prompted the oppressed to re-evaluate their self-image in terms of the changing conditions, to slough off the servile attitudes inculcated by long years of subordination, the same dynamics of change have prompted the white people of the world to re-evaluate their self-image as well, to disabuse themselves of the Master Race psychology developed over centuries of imperial hegemony.

It is among the white youth of the world that the greatest change is taking place. It is they who are experiencing the great psychic pain of waking into consciousness to find their inherited heroes turned by events into villains. Communication and understanding between the older and younger generations of whites has entered a crisis. The elders, who, in the tradition of privileged classes or races, genuinely do not understand the youth, trapped by old ways of thinking and blind to the future, have only just begun to be vexed—because the youth have only just begun to rebel. So thoroughgoing is the revolution in the psyches of white youth that the traditional tolerance which every older generation has found it necessary to display is quickly exhausted, leaving a gulf of fear, hostility, mutual misunderstanding, and contempt.

The rebellion of the oppressed peoples of the world, along with the Negro revolution in America, have opened the way to a new evaluation of history, a re-examination of the role played by the white race since the beginning of European expansion. The positive achievements are also there in the record, and future generations will applaud them. But there can be no applause now, not while the master still holds the whip in his hand! Not even the master's own children can find it possible to applaud him—he cannot even applaud himself! The negative rings too loudly. Slave-catchers, slaveowners, murderers, butchers, invaders, oppressors— the white heroes have acquired new names. The great white states-men whom school children are taught to revere are revealed as the architects of systems of human exploitation and slavery. Reli-gious leaders are exposed as condoners and justifiers of all these evil deeds. Schoolteachers and college professors are seen as a clique of brainwashers and whitewashers.

The white youth of today are coming to see, intuitively, that to escape the onus of the history their fathers made they must face and admit the moral truth concerning the works of their fathers. That such venerated figures as George Washington and Thomas Jefferson owned hundreds of black slaves, that all of the Presidents up to Lincoln presided over a slave state, and that every President since Lincoln connived politically and cynically with the issues affecting the human rights and general welfare of the broad masses of the American people—these facts weigh heavily upon the hearts of these young people.

The elders do not like to give these youngsters credit for being able to understand what is going on and what has gone on. When speaking of juvenile delinquency, or the rebellious attitude of today's youth, the elders employ a glib rhetoric. They speak of the "alienation of youth," the desire of the young to be independent, the problems of "the father image" and "the mother image" and their effect upon growing children who lack sound models upon which to pattern themselves. But they consider it bad form to connect the problems of the youth with the central event of our era—the national liberation movements abroad and the Negro revo-lution at home. The foundations of authority have been blasted to bits in America because the whole society has been indicted, tried, and convicted of injustice. To the youth, the elders are Ugly Americans; to the elders, the youth have gone mad.

The rebellion of the white youth has gone through four broadly discernible stages. First there was an initial recoiling away, a rejection of the conformity which America expected, and had always received, sooner or later, from its youth. The disaffected youth were refusing to participate in the system, having discovered that America, far from helping the underdog, was up to its ears in the mud trying to hold the dog down. Because of the publicity and self-advertisements of the more vocal rebels, this period has come to be known as the beatnik era, although not all of the youth affected by these changes thought of themselves as beatniks. The howl of the beatniks and their scathing, outraged denunciation of the system—characterized by Ginsberg as Moloch, a bloodthirsty Semitic deity to which the ancient tribes sacrificed their firstborn children—was a serious, irrevocable declaration of war. It is revealing that the elders looked upon the beatniks as mere obscene misfits who were too lazy to take baths and too stingy to buy a haircut. The elders had eyes but couldn't see, ears but couldn't hear—not even when the message came through as clearly as in this remarkable passage from Jack Kerouac's *On the Road:*

> At lilac evening I walked with every muscle aching among the lights of 27th and Welton in the Denver colored section, wishing I were a Negro, feeling that the best the white world had offered was not enough ecstasy for me, not enough life, joy, kicks, darkness, music, not enough night. I wished I were a Denver Mexican, or even a poor overworked Jap, anything but what I so drearily was, a "white man" disillusioned. All my life I'd had white ambitions. . . . I passed the dark porches of Mexican and Negro homes; soft voices were there, occasionally the dusky knee of some mysterious sensuous gal, the dark faces of the men behind rose arbors. Little children sat like sages in ancient rocking chairs.

The second stage arrived when these young people, having decided emphatically that the world, and particularly the U.S.A., was unacceptable to them in its present form, began an active search for roles they could play in changing the society. If many of these young people were content to lay up in their cool beat pads, smoking pot and listening to jazz in a perpetual orgy of esoteric bliss, there were others, less crushed by the system, who recognized the need for positive action. Moloch could not ask for anything more than to have its disaffected victims withdraw into safe, passive, apolitical little nonparticipatory islands, in an economy less and less able to provide jobs for the growing pool of unemployed. If all the unemployed had followed the lead of the beatniks, Moloch would gladly have legalized the use of euphoric drugs and marijuana, passed out free jazz albums and sleeping bags, to all those willing to sign affidavits promising to remain "beat." The non-beat disenchanted white youth were attracted magnetically to the Negro revolution, which had begun to take on a mass, insurrectionary tone. But they had difficulty understanding their relationship to the Negro, and what role "whites" could play in a "Negro revolution." For the time being they watched the Negro activists from afar.

The third stage, which is rapidly drawing to a close, emerged when white youth started joining Negro demonstrations in large numbers. The presence of whites among the demonstrators emboldened the Negro leaders and allowed them to use tactics they never would have been able to employ with all-black troops. The racist conscience of America is such that murder does not register as murder, really, unless the victim is white. And it was only when the newspapers and magazines started carrying pictures and stories of white demonstrators being beaten and maimed by mobs and police that the public began to protest. Negroes have become so used to this double standard that they, too, react differently to the death of a white. When white freedom riders were brutalized along with blacks, a sigh of relief went up from the black masses, because the blacks knew that white blood is the coin of freedom in a land where for four hundred years black blood has been shed unremarked and with impunity. America has never truly been outraged by the murder of a black man, woman, or child. White politicians may, if Negroes are aroused by a particular murder, say with their lips what they know with their minds they should feel with their hearts —but don't.

It is a measure of what the Negro feels that when the two white and one black civil rights workers were murdered in Mississippi in 1964, the event was welcomed by Negroes on a level of understanding beyond and deeper than the grief they felt for the victims and their families. This welcoming of violence and death to whites can almost be heard—indeed it can be heard—in the inevitable words, oft repeated by Negroes, that those whites, and blacks, do not die in vain. So it was with Mrs. Viola Liuzzo. And much of the anger which Negroes felt toward Martin Luther King during the Battle of Selma stemmed from the fact that he denied history a great moment, never to be recaptured, when he turned tail on the Edmund Pettus Bridge and refused to all those whites behind him what they had traveled thousands of miles to receive. If the police had turned them back by force, all those nuns, priests, rabbis, preachers, and distinguished ladies and gentlemen old and young— as they had done the Negroes a week earlier—the violence and brutality of the system would have been ruthlessly exposed. Or if, seeing King determined to lead them on to Montgomery, the troopers had stepped aside to avoid precisely the confrontation that Washington would not have tolerated, it would have signaled the capitulation of the militant white South. As it turned out, the March on Montgomery was a show of somewhat dim luster, stage-managed by the Establishment. But by this time the young whites were already active participants in the Negro revolution. In fact they had begun to transform it into something broader, with the potential of encompassing the whole of America in a radical re-ordering of society.

The fourth stage, now in its infancy, sees these white youth taking the initiative, using techniques learned in the Negro struggle to attack problems in the general society. The classic example of this new energy in action was the student battle on the UC campus at Berkeley, California—the Free Speech Movement. Leading the revolt were veterans of the civil rights movement, some of whom spent time on the firing line in the wilderness of Mississippi/Ala-bama. Flowing from the same momentum were student demonstra-tions against U.S. interference in the internal affairs of Vietnam, Cuba, the Dominican Republic, and the Congo and U.S. aid to apartheid in South Africa. The students even aroused the intel-lectual community to actions and positions unthinkable a few years ago: witness the teach-ins. But their revolt is deeper than single-issue protest. The characteristics of the white rebels which most alarm their elders—the long hair, the new dances, their love for Negro music, their use of marijuana, their mystical attitude toward sex—are all tools of their rebellion. They have turned these tools against the totalitarian fabric of American society—and they mean to change it.

From the beginning, America has been a schizophrenic nation. Its two conflicting images of itself were never reconciled, because never before has the survival of its most cherished myths made a reconciliation mandatory. Once before, during the bitter struggle between North and South climaxed by the Civil War, the two images of America came into conflict, although whites North and South scarcely understood it. The image of America held by its most alienated citizens was advanced neither by the North nor by the South; it was perhaps best expressed by Frederick Douglass, who was born into slavery in 1817, escaped to the North, and became the greatest leader-spokesman for the blacks of his era. In words that can still, years later, arouse an audience of black Americans, Frederick Douglass delivered, in 1852, a scorching indictment in his Fourth of July oration in Rochester:

What to the American slave is your Fourth of July? I answer: a day that reveals to him, more than all other days in the year, the gross injustice and cruelty to which he is the constant victim. To him your celebration is a sham; your boasted liberty, an unholy licence; your national greatness, swelling vanity; your sounds of rejoicing are empty and heartless; your denunciation of tyrants, brass-fronted impudence; your shouts of liberty and equality, hollow mockery; your prayers and hymns, your sermons and thanksgivings, with all your religious parade and solemnity, are, to him, more bombast, fraud, deception, impiety and hypocrisy—a thin veil to cover up crimes which would disgrace a nation of savages. . . .

You boast of your love of liberty, your superior civilization, and your pure Christianity, while the whole political power of the nation (as embodied in the two great political parties) is solemnly pledged to support and perpetuate the enslavement of three millions of your countrymen. You hurl your anathemas at the crown-headed tyrants of Russia and Austria and pride yourselves on your democratic institutions, while you yourselves consent to be the mere *tools* and *bodyguards* of the tyrants of Virginia and Carolina.

You invite to your shores fugitives of oppression from abroad, honor them with banquets, greet them with ovations, cheer them, toast them, salute them, protect them, and pour out your money to them like water; but the fugitive from your own land you advertise, hunt, arrest, shoot, and kill. You glory in your refinement and your universal education; yet you maintain a system as barbarous and dreadful as ever stained the character of a nation—a system begun in avarice, supported in pride, and perpetuated in cruelty.

You shed tears over fallen Hungary, and make the sad story of her wrongs the theme of your poets, statesmen and orators, till your gallant sons are ready to fly to arms to vindicate her cause against the oppressor; but, in regard to the ten thousand wrongs of the American slave, you would enforce the strictest silence, and would hail him as an enemy of the nation who dares to make these wrongs the subject of public discourse!

This most alienated view of America was preached by the Abolitionists, and by Harriet Beecher Stowe in her *Uncle Tom's Cabin*. But such a view of America was too distasteful to receive wide attention, and serious debate about America's image and her reality was engaged in only on the fringes of society. Even when confronted with overwhelming evidence to the contrary, most white Americans have found it possible, after steadying their rattled nerves, to settle comfortably back into their vaunted belief that America is dedicated to the proposition that all men are created equal and endowed by their Creator with certain inalienable rights— life, liberty and the pursuit of happiness. With the Constitution for a rudder and the Declaration of Independence as its guiding star, the ship of state is sailing always toward a brighter vision of freedom and justice for all.

Because there is no common ground between these two contradictory images of America, they had to be kept apart. But the moment the blacks were let into the white world—let out of the voiceless and faceless cages of their ghettos, singing, walking, talking, dancing, writing, and orating *their* image of America and of Americans—the white world was suddenly challenged to match its practice to its preachments. And this is why those whites who abandon the *white* image of America and adopt the *black* are greeted with such unmitigated hostility by their elders.

For all these years whites have been taught to believe in the myth they preached, while Negroes have had to face the bitter reality of what America practiced. But without the lies and distortions, white Americans would not have been able to do the things they have done. When whites are forced to look honestly upon the objective proof of their deeds, the cement of mendacity holding white society together swiftly disintegrates. On the other hand, the core of the black world's vision remains intact, and in fact begins to expand and spread into the psychological territory vacated by the non-viable white lies, i.e., into the minds of young whites. It is remarkable how the system worked for so many years, how the majority of whites remained effectively unaware of any contradiction between their view of the world and that world itself. The mechanism by which this was rendered possible requires examination at this point.

Let us recall that the white man, in order to justify slavery and, later on, to justify segregation, elaborated a complex, all-pervasive myth which at one time classified the black man as a subhuman beast of burden. The myth was progressively modified, gradually elevating the blacks on the scale of evolution, following their slowly changing status, until the plateau of separate-but-equal was reached at the close of the nineteenth century. During slavery, the black was seen as a mindless Supermasculine Menial. Forced to do the backbreaking work, he was conceived in terms of his ability to do such work—"field niggers," etc. The white man administered the plantation, doing all the thinking, exercising omnipotent power over the slaves. He had little difficulty dissociating himself from the black slaves, and he could not conceive of their positions being reversed or even reversible.

Blacks and whites being conceived as mutually exclusive types, those attributes imputed to the blacks could not also be imputed to the whites—at least not in equal degree—without blurring the line separating the races. These images were based upon the social function of the two races, the work they performed. The ideal white man was one who knew how to use his head, who knew how to manage and control things and get things done. Those whites who were not in a position to perform these functions nevertheless aspired to them. The ideal black man was one who did exactly as he was told, and did it efficiently and cheerfully. "Slaves," said Frederick Douglass, "are generally expected to sing as well as to work." As the black man's position and function became more varied, the images of white and black, having become stereotypes, lagged behind.

The separate-but-equal doctrine was promulgated by the Supreme Court in 1896. It had the same purpose domestically as the Open Door Policy toward China in the international arena: to stabilize a situation and subordinate a non-white population so that racist exploiters could manipulate those people according to their

Supreme Ct 1896

own selfish interests. These doctrines were foisted off as *the epitome of enlightened justice, the highest expression of morality.* Sanctified by religion, justified by philosophy and legalized by the Supreme Court, separate-but-equal was enforced by day by agencies of the law, and by the KKK & Co. under cover of night. Booker T. Washington, the Martin Luther King of his day, accepted separate-but-equal in the name of all Negroes. W. E. B. DuBois denounced it.

Separate-but-equal marked the last stage of the white man's flight into cultural neurosis, and the beginning of the black man's frantic striving to assert his humanity and equalize his position with the white. Blacks ventured into all fields of endeavor to which they could gain entrance. Their goal was to present in all fields a performance that would equal or surpass that of the whites. It was long axiomatic among blacks that a black had to be twice as competent as a white in any field in order to win grudging recognition from the whites. This produced a pathological motivation in the blacks to equal or surpass the whites, and a pathological motivation in the whites to maintain a distance from the blacks. This is the rack on which black and white Americans receive their delicious torture! At first there was the color bar, flatly denying the blacks entrance to certain spheres of activity. When this no longer worked, and blacks invaded sector after sector of American life and economy, the whites evolved other methods of keeping their distance. The illusion of the Negro's inferior nature had to be maintained.

One device evolved by the whites was to tab whatever the blacks did with the prefix "Negro." We had *Negro* literature, *Negro* athletes, *Negro* music, *Negro* doctors, *Negro* politicians, *Negro* workers. The malignant ingeniousness of this device is that although it accurately describes an objective biological fact—or, at least, a sociological fact in America—it concealed the paramount psychological fact: that to the white mind, prefixing anything with "Negro" automatically consigned it to an inferior category. A well-known example of the white necessity to deny due credit to blacks is in the realm of music. White musicians were famous for going to Harlem and other Negro cultural centers literally to steal the black man's music, carrying it back across the color line into the Great White World and passing off the watered-down loot as their own original creations. Blacks, meanwhile, were ridiculed as *Negro* musicians playing inferior coon music.

The Negro revolution at home and national liberation movements abroad have unceremoniously shattered the world of fantasy in which the whites have been living. It is painful that many do not yet see that their fantasy world has been rendered uninhabitable in the last half of the twentieth century. But it is away from this world that the white youth of today are turning. The "paper tiger" hero, James Bond, offering the whites a triumphant image of themselves, is saying what many whites want desperately to hear reaffirmed: *I am still the White man, lord of the land, licensed to kill, and the world is still an empire at my feet.* James Bond feeds on that secret little anxiety, the psychological white backlash, felt in some degree by most whites alive. It is exasperating to see little brown men and little yellow men from the mysterious Orient, and the opaque black men of Africa (to say nothing of these impudent American Negroes!) who come to the UN and talk smart to us, who are scurrying all over our globe in their strange modes of dress—much as if they were new, unpleasant arrivals from another planet. Many whites believe in their ulcers that it is only a matter of time before the Marines get the signal to round up these truants and put them back securely in their cages. But it is away from this fantasy world that the white youth of today are turning.

In the world revolution now under way, the initiative rests with people of color. That growing numbers of white youth are repudiating their heritage of blood and taking people of color as their heroes and models is a tribute not only to their insight but to the resilience of the human spirit. For today the heroes of the initiative are people not usually thought of as white: Fidel Castro, Che Guevara, Kwame Nkrumah, Mao Tse-tung, Gamal Abdel Nasser, Robert F. Williams, Malcolm X, Ben Bella, John Lewis, Martin Luther King, Jr., Robert Parris Moses, Ho Chi Minh, Stokely Carmichael, W. E. B. DuBois, James Forman, Chou En-lai.

The white youth of today have begun to react to the fact that the "American Way of Life" is a fossil of history. What do they care if their old baldheaded and crew-cut elders don't dig their caveman mops? They couldn't care less about the old, stiffassed honkies who don't like their new dances: Frug, Monkey, Jerk, Swim, Watusi. All they know is that it feels good to swing to way-out body-rhythms instead of dragassing across the dance floor like zombies to the dead beat of mind-smothered Mickey Mouse music. Is it any wonder that the youth have lost all respect for their elders, for law and order, when for as long as they can remember all they've witnessed is a monumental bickering over the Negro's place in American society and the right of people around the world to be left alone by outside powers? They have witnessed the law, both domestic and international, being spat upon by those who do not like its terms. Is it any wonder, then, that they feel justified, by sitting-in and freedom riding, in breaking laws made by lawless men? Old funny-styled, zipper-mouthed political night riders know nothing but to haul out an investigating committee *to look into the disturbance* to find the cause of the unrest among the youth. Look into a mirror! The cause is you, Mr. and Mrs. Yesterday, you with your forked tongues.

A young white today cannot help but recoil from the base deeds of his people. On every side, on every continent, he sees racial arrogance, savage brutality toward the conquered and subjugated people, genocide; he sees the human cargo of the slave trade; he sees the systematic extermination of American Indians; he sees the civilized nations of Europe fighting in imperial depravity over the lands of other people—and over possession of the very people themselves. There seems to be no end to the ghastly deeds of which his people are guilty. *GUILTY.* The slaughter of the Jews by the Germans, the dropping of atomic bombs on the Japanese people—these deeds weigh heavily upon the prostrate souls and tumultuous consciences of the white youth. The white heroes, their hands dripping with blood, are dead.

The young whites know that the colored people of the world, Afro-Americans included, do not seek revenge for their suffering. They seek the same things the white rebel wants: an end to war and exploitation. Black and white, the young rebels are free people, free in a way that Americans have never been before in the history of their country. And they are outraged.

There is in America today a generation of white youth that is truly worthy of a black man's respect, and this is a rare event in the foul annals of American history. From the beginning of the contact between black and whites, there has been very little reason for a black man to respect a white, with such exceptions as John Brown and others lesser known. But respect commands itself and it can neither be given nor withheld when it is due. If a man like Malcolm X could change and repudiate racism, if I myself and other former Muslims can change, if young whites can change, then there is hope for America. It was certainly strange to find myself, while steeped in the doctrine that all whites were devils by nature, commanded by the heart to applaud and acknowledge respect for these young whites—despite the fact that they are descendants of the masters and I the descendant of slave. The sins of the fathers are visited upon the heads of the children—but only if the children continue in the evil deeds of the fathers.

DICK GREGORY

You Will Know the Truth*

DICK GREGORY, the topical standup comedian and satirist of
segregation, was born in 1932 in St. Louis, Missouri. A track star in
high school, Dick Gregory was awarded an athletic scholarship
to Southern Illinois University and was named the school's
outstanding athlete in 1953. He dropped out of the University after
two years, served in the Army, and then drifted to Chicago, where
he worked in the post office. He was fired from the post office
for impersonating his co-workers and for sorting all mail addressed
to the state of Mississippi into the overseas slot. After a few lean
years of telling jokes in local bars, Dick Gregory came to be
recognized as one of America's freshest, wittiest comics, a black
Mark Twain or Will Rogers. His humor is often directed at the
insanity of racial prejudice and though it may sting, his humor is
never bitter. Dick Gregory is a truly gentle, compassionate man.
During the 1960s he not only spoke out against social injustices but
gave time and money to the civil rights movement. While running

---

*From THE SHADOW THAT SCARES ME, copyright © 1968 by Dick
Gregory. Reprinted by permission of Doubleday & Company, Inc.

unsuccessfully for mayor of Chicago and President of the
United States (1968), he bore witness for millions of suffering and
dispossessed Americans by focusing on the inequities and
iniquities which are part of our society. In "You Will Know the
Truth," Dick Gregory writes, "There is a great social revolution going
on in America today. And the wonderful thing about this revolution
is that it is not black against white. It is simply right against wrong."
The essay, taken from *The Shadow That Scares Me* (1968), is
concerned with what that revolution is all about.

You will know the truth, and the truth will make you free.

JOHN 8:32

When I stand in the pulpit to speak and look out into the faces
of those good church folks, I am always reminded of the old
spiritual, "Were you there when they crucified my Lord?" When
church people sing those words, they have an expression on their
faces which suggests they *would* have been there—on the Hill of
the Skull standing at the foot of the cross—if they had the chance.
But it is so cheap and easy to sing about what you *would* do two
thousand years too late. It is time to talk about what you *will* do
and *are* doing right now.

God is nothing more, or less, than truth. So let us being to tell
the truth, especially in church. The Gospel of John suggests that
telling the truth is the way to really worship God. And Jesus said
that the truth will make us free. Not until we are willing to tell the
whole truth can we expect to be free. When we were marching nonviolently and the truth was being crucified in the streets of this

161

nation today, were you there? When your children and grandchildren read about the current struggle for human dignity in their history books, what will be your answer when they look into your eyes and ask, "Were you there?"

And if the Russians or the Chinese took over this country in the morning and issued a decree that anyone attending religious services would be mowed down with a machine gun, would you be there in church? Perhaps you would. I believe many Negroes would lay down their lives for their church. But there is one thing those same Negroes would *not* do. They would not wear a freedom button on their jobs in front of white folks!

As long as we are telling the truth about freedom, let me make an honest confession. I am almost beginning to love George Wallace. He is a man who came up North and proved to northerners what Negroes have known all their lives and been afraid to say. He proved to the nation that the system of oppression over black people does not begin south of the Mason-Dixon line. It really begins south of the Canadian border. George Wallace sat on national television, on *Face the Nation,* and showed pictures of police brutality; of cops riding horses into crowds of teenage demonstrators; of nightsticks being used to break up demonstrations. And all of these pictures were taken in northern cities. For more than a hundred years it has been popular to put the blame for the racial situation in the country on the southern white brother. The southerner has been accused over and over again in all sorts of heinous ways.

But let us tell the truth long enough to realize who sold the black man into slavery. Northerners controlled the ships which were used to bring us to these shores from Africa. We were sold by a northern white man to a southern white man. Then the northern white man got slick one day and turned to his southern brother, after he had pocketed the money, and said, "Ged rid of your slaves." The southerner should have said, "Do I get a refund?" The storekeeper will give you two cents back on a Coke bottle, if the bottle belongs to you!

We have been so unfair to that southerner. When the federal government finally decides that the Mississippi schools must be integrated, we stand by and watch them send a gun and a soldier to the South to force Mississippi to integrate. When we get ready to try to integrate the schools in Chicago or New York City, they give us a bus to transport a few children from one segregated neighborhood to another. If a gun and a soldier are appropriate for the southern white brother, the same standard should apply to the North.

On the opening day of school in the fall of 1964, school after school was integrated in Jackson, Mississippi, without any kind of incident. The same day in Jackson Heights, Queens, in liberal old New York City, sixty-five screaming white mothers, with their babies in their arms, were arrested for opposing the new school integration plan. For too long the South has been viewed as the garbage can of race relations. No matter what happened to point out northern injustices, people have always looked to the South and said, "See how much worse it is down there." But now the brother in the South is putting the lid tightly on that racial garbage can and there is no place for northerners to dump their garbage except in their own backyard. And the stink is beginning to spread all over the North.

Once when I was in Selma, Alabama, a colored cat called me up and asked, "Would you come over to the station and be on my television show?" In Selma, Alabama, in 1964, a Negro had his own television show from eight o'clock in the morning until twelve noon. How many Negroes have their own television shows on stations in the North? Mississippi radio stations have colored disc jockeys playing soul music. And these are major network stations. In the North, if you hear a colored disc jockey, you can bet it is an all-colored station and you are not going to hear the stock market report on that same station.

Over the past fifty years, most of the top athletes in northern colleges have been Negroes; in the Big Ten, the Ivy League, and the West Coast Conference. Yet there has not been one Negro head coach or one Negro referee in those conferences. That is a disgrace. If you drew up a list of the outstanding Negroes in this country, you would find that 98 percent have been educated in southern segregated schools. For when that southern white brother gave the Negro an all-black school, he also gave him black teachers and a black principal. At a very early age, the southern Negro student was able to see black folks in authority and could identify with achievement. Up North 99.9 percent of the schools have white principals and the Negro student must identify with the colored janitor.

THE REVOLUTION OF RIGHT AGAINST WRONG

There is a great social revolution going on in America today. And the wonderful thing about this revolution is that it is not black against white. It is simply right against wrong. You only realize this truth when you are on the front line of the struggle for human dignity. There are many white folks who hate civil rights demonstrators. But if they really knew the truth, they would love those of us on the front line. White folks should really dislike the Negroes who sit back and do nothing but tell them what they want to hear, while all the time hating white folks' guts.

If the closest you ever get to the front line struggle is the Huntley-Brinkley Report on television, you will never know the truth. On that television news report, the Negro who is not on the front line sees a dog biting his little black cousin or a white cop knocking his grandma down to the ground. Quite naturally his invisible hatred for white folks comes boiling to the surface. But the cameras fail to show all those white kids getting knocked down also. The television cameras were not around to show that white sheriff who came into the jail, tore off his badge and threw it to the ground, with tears in his eyes, because he just couldn't stand being wrong any longer. You only see these beautiful sights on the front line of action, but this is the truth about freedom and dignity in this social revolution.

The television cameras are not able to portray the *real* truth. They cannot capture the strange truth that ten minutes after we are arrested and thrown into the jail, we *own* that jail. When a man is jailed for doing right, suddenly the jail becomes the prisoner. The people behind the bars are in control and the prison guards are the slaves of wrongdoing. This is a revolution of right against wrong. And wrong has never ultimately won out against right in the history of the world.

The day you join the revolution is the day you will quit hating. The only people who hate the Germans or the Japanese today are those who stayed home during the war. The soldiers on the front line married the "enemy" after the war was over, because there is no hatred on the front line. And Negroes who never joined the struggle for human dignity are the ones who will be shooting white folks in the streets, because they are hating more and more every day. I know this truth because I have been physically beaten by Negroes who tell me that I have been bought by the white man because I preach non-violence.

We have gone into towns to demonstrate and Negro ministers have refused to let us use their churches as freedom schools. I have to wonder how we can go downtown to picket the white brother when there are so many of our own brothers who are wrong. A man does not have to be white to wear a sheet or black to wear a freedom button. It is time to expose Negroes who are holding us back and put a sheet over their heads. Ours is not a struggle of black against white, but of right against wrong. When we know this truth, we are on our way to freedom.

THE SOLDIERS AND THE 4-F's

What is hurting this revolution most of all is the 4-F's who sit back and do nothing. Then when the struggle is over, the 4-F's receive the GI Bill. Never before in the history of revolutions has this happened, but it is happening to us. The Negro attorney who says, "Demonstrations are hurting our cause," becomes the first Negro prosecuting attorney, after the suffering and the bleeding are over. The Negro doctor who tells white folks what they want to hear, who says we should not be extreme in demonstrating, becomes the first colored public health commissioner, after his brothers on the front line have been jailed and beaten.

I went to the Auto Show in Chicago in 1964 and it brought tears to my eyes. It was the biggest Auto Show of the year anywhere in the country. And many of the fashion models were Negro! The year before there were no Negro models. Seeing all of those beautiful black models made me sick to my stomach. Because I knew who had gotten them their job. It was the sister on the front line. You saw her in every demonstration that was covered by the television camera crews. She was that short, black, nappy-haired girl being bitten by the dogs. She couldn't win a beauty contest in her own living room with her momma as the judge! But she got those Negro models their jobs at the Auto Show. And yet if you asked one of those models to come out to the front line of action, or even to pick up a picket sign, she would look at you as if you were a fool. The 4-F's are getting all of the GI Bill.

I remember demonstrating in Atlanta, Georgia, in 1963. It was a long hard struggle, with minimum participation by local Negroes, but we finally integrated seventeen restaurants. After the struggle was over, I looked so disgusted that the white restaurant owner asked me, "What's wrong, Gregory?" And I told him, "I just wish I could give you a picture of each one of us demonstrators who faced the dogs, had hot water thrown on us, and went to jail to force you to open your doors to everyone. I would ask you to hang those pictures over your cash register. And if a Negro walked into your restaurant whose picture was not on the wall, I would ask you not to serve him. Tell him to integrate a restaurant for himself."

This is the greatest revolution in history because of the soldiers fighting the battle. They are like no other soldiers who ever fought. There are Negroes on the front line who will lay down their lives demonstrating in front of a new housing development. Yet they know that after the victory is won, the only person who can move into that new development is Ralph Bunche. That front line soldier in the battle for human dignity will demonstrate in front of a hospital to get more Negro doctors on the staff. If the administrator of the hospital came out to the picket line and offered that soldier a job, he couldn't take it; because he didn't even finish grade school. But he is laying down his life for his brother. This front line soldier in the battle for right lives by the true spirit of God, "I am my brother's keeper." Beyond that, the front line soldier in the struggle for human dignity is trying to create a nation where each man is his brother's brother. This struggle is not black against white.

We were demonstrating in Chicago in 1964 and the cops started pushing and shoving. After I walked off the front line of demonstration, a Negro cop followed me, winking and blinking, and said, "Hey, brother, I didn't mean to shove you just now, but my job is at stake. I'm a colored cop." Not until he said he was a "colored cop" did I get mad. I told him, "I defy you to make this revolution black against white. When you shoved us on the steps of city hall just now, you were a cop like all the rest of them. But since you want to be a colored cop, let me tell you why you cannot mess up our revolution. I have seen the white sheriff throw down his badge because he couldn't take any more. I saw the white farmer in Birmingham, Alabama, throw down his hose rather than spray little black kids. He was arrested by his racist brothers. I had some respect for you when you were just a cop. But when you try to beg off because of being a colored cop, I have no respect at all. Because you are trying to inject racism into our revolution."

THE BLACK RACISTS

If we are going to *know* the truth which makes us free, we must *tell* the truth about racism. White folks are not the only racists in the country today. Black folks are racist also. And their racism is not only directed toward white folks, but also against other Negroes. I do a comedy routine about moving into a white neighborhood. The first day I receive some callers on my front porch. Not the white racists, but the colored delegation. Dr. Jones standing there with his lips tucked in. The delegation has come by to make sure I act right and don't embarrass them in this white neighborhood. Dr. Jones says, "You have to watch yourself out here and remember the white folks are watching us." And I say, "What are you doin', stealin' or something?"

Sophisticated Negroes are embarrassed by the actions of their poor black brother in the ghetto, but are not embarrassed by the actions of poor whites in their ghetto. That is racism. But it is not a Negroid characteristic. It is the normal result of living under a system of oppression. After a period of time, the oppressed man begins imitating the behavior of the oppressor. It was not uncommon in the concentration camps of World War II for the Jewish prisoners to imitate the Nazi soldiers when their backs were turned. Some of the Jewish prisoners would cut their clothes in the same way the German uniforms were fashioned. They would misuse fellow prisoners in the manner of their Nazi oppressors. Imitating the behavior of the oppressor is a way of escaping one's own oppression. Negroes who have made a few advances within the system of oppression are frequently prejudiced toward other Negroes whose behavior reminds them of the worst the oppressive system has to offer.

If I had to choose between losing my wife to a white man and losing her to a black man, I would choose the black man, because I would not want to face the embarrassment of my friends reminding me that a white man stole my wife. Yet I know I am making a racist choice. A simple illustration will show the extent to which unconscious racism victimizes every human being in this country. My secretary and I boarded a plane in Chicago on our way to Newark. The plane was crowded and there were no two seats together available. My secretary took one single seat and I took another. I happened to be sitting next to a white woman and we began talking about the social problems of America. I mentioned that I thought the number one problem in America was racism. She was visibly relieved to hear me say this and she said, "You are so right. You know, I wanted to get up and give the young lady who is with you my seat. But I was afraid you would think I didn't want to sit next to you."

Suppose two airplanes took off at the same time; one filled with white passengers and the other filled with black passengers. If you had to decide which plane would crash, what would your choice be? Most white folks will choose the all-black plane and mosts Negroes will choose the all-white plane. That is racism. If it is not possible to save the good Negroes and the good white folks in each plane, then they should both go down. Whenever a man's color becomes the basic factor in the choices of life, it is racism.

There are many critics of the struggle for human dignity, both black and white. These critics are fond of saying that certain kinds of demonstrations only hurt the Negro's cause. Such a statement is like saying you are giving too much medicine to a dead man. Even President Johnson has criticized certain forms of protest. But if he and Lady Bird woke up one morning as black as my wife and me, they would both sign up for the next demonstration!

So many people criticized the stall-in in New York City on the opening day of the World's Fair. They said we were going too far. People used to ask me, "Where did they ever get such a crazy, wild idea of running out of gas on the expressways?" The answer is simple; from watching all those cars run of gas on that TV commercial. I can easily justify the stall-in. If the senior citizens of this country, our Senators and Congressmen, can hold a stall-in in the sacred halls of Congress debating civil right legislation, and call it a "filibuster," we second class citizens can hold a stall-in on a dirty American highway.

The critics also say we should take our problem to court and fight the battle legally. I tried that and it didn't work. How can I get justice in a court where the judge is an elected official whose votes come out of an all-white neighborhood? When the judge knows he will have to have voter approval to get reelected, he cannot have an open and sympathetic ear for my problem.

And how can I get justice from a judge who honestly does not know that he is prejudiced? For example, many rich Negroes have gotten divorces in northern courts, but you have never read where a colored woman has gotten a large settlement from her rich colored husband. Yet the rich white man better not lose his wife or she gets all his money. So how is this judge going to give me justice when he can't even treat my woman right?

The court and society have never treated my woman right. If my wife goes downtown and steals something, when she is caught she is called a hoodlum. If a white celebrity's wife gets caught stealing, she is a kleptomaniac. The black woman is listed with the crime rate and the white woman is placed on the sick list.

A white man and his wife can go to court and get a divorce. Say he is making fifty thousand dollars a year and they have three children. The court grants the wife custody of the children. If she marries another white man who is making fifty thousand dollars a year, do you think the father could go back into court and get custody of his children because his wife married again? Not a chance. But if I married her he could do just that. Such is the racism of the American court. I cannot take my problem there.

HOW FAIR CAN THE BLACK MAN BE?

The critics say that the Negro is expecting too much too fast. Extreme demonstrations involving civil disobedience are condemned as an example of how unfair the Negro is being. He cannot expect freedom overnight. The history of the Negro in America is a study in patience and trying to be fair. Negroes did not want to get out into the streets to demonstrate their problem. They were so busy trying to be fair. For over a hundred years white America told the Negro to try to raise himself up to the white man's standards and he would get his freedom. And in fairness the Negro tried. Slaves didn't wear good clothes or shoes, but we tried to meet that standard. We put on the white man's shoes, his socks, his underwear, his shirt and his tie. But that wasn't enough and we still didn't get our freedom.

In our effort to be fair, we thought the problem must be our physical appearance. So we grew a mustache and tried to cover up our thick lips. Still no freedom. We thought nappy hair must be the hang-up. So we got processes and straightened out the hair problem. Over a hundred-year period, we have gone from the bottom of our feet to the top of our heads trying to be fair. Finally we ran out of things to do to try to please white America and we were driven into the streets.

How fair can the black man be? Think about all those black women in the South who raised those white boys who ended up lynching their sons. And still they cooked and cared for their son's murderers, taking comfort only in the thought, "The Lord will take care of them. Vengeance is mine saith the Lord." A person cannot be any more fair than that. When you stop to consider how long Negroes have been controlling the white folks' kitchen, you realize how fair we have been. Negroes have prepared every bite white America put into its mouth. If Negroes had wanted to be vicious enough to seek revenge, one well-organized poison campaign would have drastically altered the ethnic balance.

Think about that slave couple, especially those of you who have children. Close your eyes and imagine yourself a slave. Your wife comes to you and tells you she is pregnant. Visualize the slave couple falling to their knees in prayer, begging God Almighty that their child be born deformed so that he might be free from being sold on the slave block. Imagine being the victim of a society so vicious that your child could be sold not only to another slave master but taken to another state. How would you feel?

The slave couple would pitifully petition the Lord God to grant that their baby be born without an arm or a leg, so that he could escape the labor of the fields. Sometimes the prayer was answered and the baby was born deformed. And the black woman would look at the black man, with tears of joy streaming down her face, and exclaim, "Our prayer has been answered. Our baby was born deformed." Can you see both of them falling to their knees in a prayer of thanks; thanking their God for blessing them with a deformed child? How fair can the black man be? It is an unwritten law that a man who destroys another man's home shall inherit the wind.

I remember when we were demonstrating to integrate public accommodations, the restaurant owner told us to be fair. He said his place of business belonged to him; he opened it with his hard-earned money and he insisted he had the right to serve anyone he chose to serve. I was glad to tell that white restaurant owner, "Good brother, you don't have to serve me." But I had to remind him also that it is my tax money which pays the public health commissioner to license his restaurant. My tax dollars are used to pay the fireman who comes to protect his establishment when the skillet gets too hot. My tax dollars pay the cop who guards the restaurant while the day's receipts are being counted. If a man wants a restaurant to himself and his friends, let him hire his own health commissioner, his own cop, and his own fireman. Then he can have his crummy joint. But the day is over when I will allow my tax money to be spent protecting a place which will not serve me, but any non-tax-paying white foreigner can come in and use the air conditioning while sipping a mint julep out of a glass I made sure was inspected. That is how fair I am willing to be.

THE TRUTH ABOUT FREEDOM

In fairness to America, we must tell the truth about freedom. White and black youth are drafted into the armed services to be the defenders of truth and freedom in Vietnam. But the truth about freedom must be told in this country before it can be represented on foreign shores. How can I be asked to go to Vietnam to fight for the "instant freedom" of the Vietnamese, when my own black kids at home must get their freedom on the installment plan? It does not make sense to require a black youth to sacrifice his life to guarantee a foreigner a better way of life than his own parents have in America. Back home the black soldier's parents will hear people say, "Education is the problem. Freedom for the Negro in America depends upon raising his educational standard." But no one has ever questioned the Vietnamese educational standard. If the educational standard is not a question in granting freedom to the Vietnamese, America had better stop questioning mine.

America requires a Negro soldier from Mississippi to go to Vietnam and chase a Vietcong through the bushes trying to kill him. Yet it is a crime in America for that same Negro to chase a Mississippi Ku Klux Klaner through the swamps of Mississippi trying to kill him. On the battlefield of Vietnam, the Negro soldier only has to worry about losing his own life; the fight is between himself and the Vietcong. Back home, the racist in America will not only kill that Negro soldier, but wipe out his whole family and blow up his church. Yet it is a crime *not* to go to Vietnam and kill the Vietcong and also a crime *to* kill the racist in America who will wipe out a whole family. That is the insane truth about freedom.

It is not only the black soldier who sees the contradictions about freedom displayed on the Vietnam battlefield. Eighteen- and nineteen-year-old young men, white and black, are required to go to Vietnam to lay down their lives to secure the right to vote for the Vietnamese. When those soldiers return to their America, they must wait two or three years before they can exercise their own right to vote. They are old enough to die for another man's right to vote, but too young to vote themselves.

The white soldier will suffer, bleed, and die for the rights of a colored Vietnamese. Then the soldier comes home to Cicero, Philadelphia, or Memphis. If the same colored Vietnamese, whom the white soldier was willing to die for, tried to move next door to him in America, many white veterans would point the gun at their would-be colored neighbors. A nation this sick cannot survive.

When America admits the truth about freedom at home, she will begin to understand her image abroad. If I were a known child molester and had served time in jail for that crime, you would not hire me to be your baby-sitter. You would know the history of my past performance when I get around children and you would not want to take a chance. Because of my record, you would not trust me. People all over the world know America's record. They know the history of America looting her land from the original native inhabitants. They continue to see the atrocities committed upon the Indian. In the eyes of the world, America has been convicted over and over again of molesting her black children, by permitting Negroes to be lynched and civil rights workers to be gunned down in the streets. Is it any wonder that countries all over the world do not trust America, with her record of man's inhumanity to man, to baby-sit for their freedom?

Those who are opposed to freedom always resist the truth. Consider the number of churches that have been blown up or burned to the ground in the South. Negroes and liberal-minded white folks consider such acts terrible atrocities. When human lives are lost in the destruction of a church, it is a tragedy. But the destruction of the church itself is not tragic. When the church building is destroyed, religion is forced out into the street where it should have been all along!

THE SYNDICATE AND THE KU KLUX KLAN

The reason why churches were destroyed in the South is because ministers finally started telling the truth about freedom. For years southern ministers have been afraid to speak out. The Ku Klux Klan has always been able to terrify and intimidate the southern Negro. One day the minister developed enough backbone to overcome his fear, climb into his pulpit, and tell the truth about the Klan. He called the names of Klan members and openly identified the law-enforcement officers and the businessmen hiding under those hoods. The minister traced the route of Klan violence. As a result, his church was destroyed the next morning. Those who are opposed to freedom always resist the truth.

But this is not a southern phenomenon. If the northern minister, priest or rabbi would stand in his pulpit one morning and call the names of the top men in the crime syndicate; if he would trace the syndicate's reefer route and tell the truth about dope traffic, violence, and prostitution, that northern clergyman's church would be destroyed also.

The syndicate has the same grip of fear on the North as the Klan has always had on the South. The syndicate has burned more restaurants in Chicago than the Klan has burned churches in Mississippi. The syndicate killed more people in Chicago in eighteen months than the Klan lynched in Mississippi in two years. These acts of violence go unnoticed by the same people who decry southern atrocities.

People in the North will see a man shot down in the street with a machine gun. If they know the syndicate is behind the killing, they are afraid to appear in court as a witness. They know what the reprisals will be. Yet those same fear-ridden people cannot understand how the Klan gets by with their acts of violence. Opponents of truth use fear to create a climate of silence. Until that silence is shattered by the open and fearless speaking of the truth all over this country, no man is free.

THE WHITE MAN'S SLAVERY

The free man is the man with no fears. The strange truth in America today is that the Negro has become the psychological master and the white man the psychological slave. It is the mark of the slave to be afraid. Since he is not a free man, he is the victim of fear. The master has no fears. The slave runs and hides.

When a Negro family moves into an all-white neighborhood, white residents begin running. Immediately the "For Sale" signs appear in the front lawn of every house on the block. Who is free? If I went on the Ed Sullivan Show tonight and spoke in favor of integrated marriages, nothing would happen to me. If Ed Sullivan spoke in favor of the same thing, he would lose his rating and his job. Who is free?

If I have a white friend who needs a place to stay, I can give him my keys and let him use my apartment as long as he likes. My neighbors will think nothing of his being in my home, even if my wife and kids are home and I am away. The white man in America today cannot give me his keys or let me use his apartment without every white neighbor in the block being outraged. If he is away from the apartment and I am alone with his wife, the neighbors will automatically assume I am doing something sexually with her. Who is free?

I was on a radio show not long ago. It was one of those talk shows which encouraged listeners to telephone in their opinions. A lady phoned to speak with me while I was on the air. She identified herself as being white and said, "I am sorry I can't give you my name. I just wanted you to know that I agree with you." She agreed with me; but her color and the reactions of her friends and neighbors who might be listening to the same program kept her from mentioning her own name. Who is free? Only the psychological slave hides from his own name!

One of my white neighbors revealed his psychological slavery to me one day. We live in the same apartment building and have daughters the same age. We send our children to the University of Chicago Lab School. My white neighbor came to me one day mentally upset and said, "Greg, I have to talk to you." He told me that he had gone to pick up his little four-year-old daughter at school. She came out of the school with her arm around a little Negro boy. When my neighbor saw this, all of a sudden it dawned on him that he did not want his daughter to marry a Negro. This sudden realization upset him and he wanted to talk to me about it.

I looked into that white man's eyes and said, "My little daughter is freer than your daughter. She can marry a gorilla if she wants to." But the frightening recognition was that this white man, with all of his education and wealth, was such a psychological slave that he could look at a little four-year-old child and worry about whom she will be having sexual intercourse with one day. What kind of mental slavery will cause a man to rob his own daughter of her childhood? Who can think of a four-year-old kid being married? I would never consider worrying about whom my daughter will marry until she is close to marriageable age. The only thing I worry about now is how much money I am paying for those funny-looking pictures she draws in Lab School.

The psychological slave has allowed himself to be mentally victimized by his own fears. Does it not seem strange that after all these years of being called "nigger" Negroes have never developed a word just as vicious for white folks? In most cases the white man will not be hit by a Negro if he calls him "nigger." If the white man calls the Negro a "bastard," he might have a fight on his hands. But he will usually get no physical reaction from "nigger." Somehow Nature instinctively teaches you who to hit and who to feel sorry for.

The Negro has refused to allow himself to be psychologically enslaved. I am Dick Gregory; I live in America; I am a Negro. I am an individual first, an American second, and a Negro third. If a man calls me a nigger, he is calling me something I am not. The nigger exists only in his own mind; therefore his mind is the nigger. I must feel sorry for such a man.

If I looked at a television set and called it an ice-cream cone, the ice-cream cone would exist only in my own mind. My mind becomes the ice-cream cone. A white sheriff called me a "monkey" one day. A monkey has straight hair, thin lips, and blue eyes. Anyone can look at me and tell I don't fit that description. The sheriff is the monkey because "monkey-image" exists only in his own mind. He has become the psychological slave; the victim of his own fears.

Only the truth will make men free. The psychological slave will never be free until he knows the truth about his fears. The Negro in America will never be free until he tells white America the absolute truth, however painful that truth might be for both whites and blacks. There is one way the truth could create instant freedom for all people. If some strange, stubborn, many-headed creature from outer space landed on this earth one day and addressed us all as "Earth People," he would be speaking the truth. For we are *all* earth people. Nations all over the world would set aside their petty differences and sit down at the conference table to decide how to deal with this strange creature from outer space; this creature who has spoken the truth about us all. World cooperation and universal brotherhood would become an instantaneous reality.

THE WINTERTIME SOLDIER

Today the truth is being spoken and lived by the wintertime soldier in the great moral revolution for human dignity. The wintertime soldier is the man who struggles for truth and freedom when all the odds are against him. George Washington headed a band of wintertime soldiers. He inspired them to march on Christmas Eve against the British in spite of overwhelming odds. George Washington used the words of Tom Paine to give strength and courage to his wintertime soldiers. And those words echo today as an ode to freedom and truth for all men everywhere. Tom Paine said: "These are times that try men's souls. The summer soldier and the sunshine patriot will, in this crisis, shrink from the service of their country; but he that stands it *now*, deserves the love and thanks of man and woman. Tyranny, like hell, is not easily conquered; yet we have this consolation with us, that the harder the conflict, the more glorious the triumph. What we obtain too cheap, we esteem too lightly. If there be trouble, let it be in my day that my children may have peace. It is dearness only that gives everything its value. Heaven knows how to put a proper price upon its goods; and it would be strange indeed if so celestial an article as *freedom* should not be highly rated."

JAMES FARMER

Integration or Desegregation*

JAMES FARMER, one of the most influential civil rights leaders in the
1960s, was born in 1920 in Marshall, Texas. He was one of the
founders of the Congress of Racial Equality (CORE) in 1942 and
became the organization's national director in 1961. CORE has long
been in the front line of the civil rights struggle and the
organization pioneered Freedom Rides and sit-ins. In the 1968
election Mr. Farmer ran unsuccessfully for Congress from Brooklyn,
but President Nixon subsequently appointed him to his
Administration to work on urban and racial problems. In
"Integration or Desegregation," reprinted from his book
Freedom—When? (1965), Mr. Farmer discusses the difference
between separation, which some black men would *choose*, and
segregation, which all black men loathe. The essay also examines
other questions, including whether the black man deserves
preferential, compensatory treatment and whether there should
be interracial marriage.

*From FREEDOM—WHEN? by James Farmer. © Copyright 1965 by
The Congress of Racial Equality. Reprinted by permission of Random
House, Inc.

One feels his two-ness—An American, a Negro, two souls, two
thoughts, two unreconciled strivings, two warring ideals, in one
dark body. . . .

The history of the American Negro is the history of this strife—
this longing to attain self-conscious manhood, to merge his double
self into a better and truer self. . . . He would not Africanize
America, for America has too much to teach the world and Africa.
He would not bleach the Negro soul in a flood of white Americanism,
for he knows that Negro blood has a message for the world. He
simply wishes to make it possible for a man to be both a Negro and
an American without being cursed and spit upon. . . .

—W. E. B. DU BOIS, 1903

No word has served to epitomize the movement's goals for these
last ten years as well as "integration." We would be integrated
into America and destroy "segregation," the hated opposite of this
new concept. So we demanded integrated schools and housing and
employment, and integrated commercial messages on television, and

integrated casts on opera and dramatic stages, and integrated movies, and mayors' committees, and civic-planning boards, etc. The value of integration took on the status of a self-evident truth.

Today, however, many Negroes, gripped by a new wave of self-pride and group-pride, are beginning to ask critical questions of the integrationist creed: How can we be prideful without advocating an inverted form of "separate but equal"? Is self-pride another term for self-segregation? Must we renounce ourselves and our community for the sake of integration?

Let me say immediately that much of "integration" remains valid for us and, in our view, for America, but with somewhat altered emphasis and meaning.

What do we mean by "integration"? For some the term means complete assimilation, a kind of random dispersal of Negroes throughout the society and the economy. There would be no Negro neighborhoods, no Negro schools, no jobs reserved for Negroes. America would be a land of individuals who were American and nothing else, and Negro individuals would differ from their fellow Americans only in their skin color—that most insignificant of human differences. Some of us even dreamed that differences of color too would soon melt away when love and colorblindness permeated the land. As I have said, no one can question the ultimate goodness of this ideal. The question is: Is it too good to be true?

Integration has been the nation's implicit ideal since America was a glint in Jefferson's eye. It is nothing but Jeffersonian individualism extended to all people. But it did not become a practical political goal until quite recently, and the reasons for this make an important story. Like most Americans, Negroes were still accepting "separate but equal" as the law of the land as late as the mid-forties, and our major efforts were expended in making the "equal" of "separate but equal" a reality. In the decades before the 1954 Supreme Court decision desegregating schools the NAACP brought to the court cases treating discrimination in education, voting, interstate and intrastate travel, public facilities, and selection of juries. The court in those years invariably found that Negro facilities were palpably unequal and ruled that segregation was constitutional only if facilities and accommodations were truly equal. In other words, the whole burden of the civil rights movement's case then was: if facilities are going to be separate, at least make them equal. Separate but equal was reaffirmed.

Toward the end of the forties NAACP lawyers and strategists

began to argue that in certain respects separate facilities could never be equal. For example, a Negro relegated to a Negro law school could not hope to make professional contacts that would enable him to swim in the main stream of the profession as readily as someone at a white law school—and this was true no matter how beautiful the buildings and how well-stocked the library at the Negro law school was. A Pullman seat in a car reserved for Negroes could not be the equal of a seat in the white car because the manifest intention of "for Negroes only" was to convey inferiority. By a natural process of evolution the demand for what we might term equal-if-separate turned into a demand for desegregation.

To argue that a beautiful Negro law school or a plush seat in a Negro Pullman was inferior to its white counterpart demanded some subtlety. To argue that the segregated public school system treated Negroes as second-class citizens demanded no subtlety at all. Comparison of expenditures per student, school plant, teachers' salaries, experience and training of teachers, books and supplies, and other measurable factors, made it clear that throughout the country, and in the South particularly, the Negro, forced by law and fact into segregated schools, was being deprived of equality under law. The 1954 Supreme Court decision attempted to correct this intolerable inequity in the only way practical and intelligent men could—by eliminating the dual school systems.

But the court added a theoretical dimension to its factual and practical findings: "Separate educational facilities," it said, "are *inherently* unequal" [emphasis added] and it cited as evidence certain psychological data—principally those of Professor Kenneth Clark—which document the serious psychological damage race separation causes in Negro youngsters. Now, I am not certain what "inherently unequal" or even "separate educational facilities" mean in this context, and I will want to return to these phrases shortly; but first I would like to explain how we interpreted the court's decision. For us it was a recognition of what every Negro knows: that the system of segregation was mounted and perpetuated for the purpose of keeping the black man down; that it was and is a conspiracy to instill in the Negro *and the white* a sense of Negro inferiority. Segregation is slavery made legal. Segregation *means* inferiority, as indelibly as the scarlet letter meant adulteress to the New England Puritans. The Negro knows this; it was intended that he know this, and so too must any American with the most rudimentary sense of history know it. And now the court was saying that this country would segregate no more.

So we began to protest against segregated schools of all kinds, *de facto* and *de jure,* demanding quality integrated education, knowing all the time that we were combating and helping eliminate the hated *meaning* which had been assigned to our lives.

As separate schools were inferior, so too were separate neighborhoods (quite obviously the *meaning* of segregated neighborhoods is simply that the great white world doesn't want black folk living next to it; anyone who doubts this need only observe the hysteria and violence which ensue when a Negro family moves into a white neighborhood). The effect of living in an enforced ghetto is conveyed graphically in the desolation and wreckage, human and material, in which most Negroes live today. So we moved to desegregated housing and some aimed at dismantling the ghetto.

Indeed, every instance and symbol of segregation and every invidious discrimination could now be legitimately challenged. There are millions, and we took them on one by one, case by case. At lunch counters, restaurants, rest rooms, swimming pools, amusement parks, beaches, labor unions, banks, factories, offices, department stores, professional societies, churches, colleges. To the most rabid integrationists even the institutions of Negro communal life were implicated. They saw no reason for a Negro Medical Society; all energies must be directed to breaking down the AMA. Negro colleges, Negro churches, Negro newspapers were at best tolerated as unnecessary anachronisms.

Integration was a white man's cause as well as a black man's, and the literally thousands of interracial organizations which came into being to fight the good fight became themselves temporary models of integrated living. CORE was one, and remains one. Many whites recognize the superiority complex demanded of the white man in a segregated system to be as harmful in its way as the inferiority complex demanded of Negroes. Many quite sincerely set about curing themselves and their neighborhoods and schools of this affliction.

The rabid integrationist aims at mixing every unit of society in "ideal" proportions. In middle-class neighborhoods housing committees were formed to persuade reluctant white homeowners to accept respectable Negroes, and courageous and well-to-do Negroes were sought who would brave white wrath. And when one or two Negroes had entered a neighborhood, the same committees, now with the eager help of the Negroes, organized to keep other Negroes out. We mustn't let the neighborhood tip, they said. Housing developments adopted informal quotas to help engineer integrated living. Dedicated builders, like Morris Milgrim of Philadelphia, began to persuade investors that quality housing projects, open to all, could return a modest profit, and integrated oases soon sprang up in several previously all-white deserts. Many liberals grew uncomfortable with the irony that in order to achieve integration they had to adopt racial quotas of various sorts, designating Negroes in order to eliminate racial designations, as it were, and some became discouraged at the solemn spectacle of Negroes chasing whites from suburb to suburb—in quest of integration. But among white liberals and some black liberals the dream of complete integration persisted.

Almost imperceptibly the demand for desegregation had shaded into a demand for black dispersal and assimilation. We were told, and for a while told ourselves, that *all* Negro separation was inherently inferior, and some folk began to think that Negroes couldn't be fully human in the presence of other Negroes. But what of Africa? Was separation inferior there too? And what of the *de facto* separation of other minority groups, the Jews and Chinese, for example. Was separation so self-evidently inferior for them as it was for us?

I am not a lawyer, but I think that the phrase "separate educational facilities are inherently unequal," which supports the philosophy of total integration, invites some misinterpretation. Separation need not be inferior in all cases and places. What is crucial is the meaning the culture places upon the separation. Separation, in other words, is not necessarily segregation, *though in America, Negro separation in fact and in law means segregation*. This is the crucial insight. The separation of Negroes in America *means* segregation—slavery. In its decision the Supreme Court was offering a particular and indisputable reading of the meaning of American history. In the context of our civilization with its history of racism, the court said, separate educational institutions are inherently inferior.

When a Negro child goes through the doors of a segregated school, he knows implicitly that his culture is telling him to go there because he is not fit to be with others, and every time a Negro child hears of a white parent who becomes hysterical at the thought that his child will have to endure the likes of him, he feels the pressure of his inferiority a little more firmly. As a result he is damaged. And this too the Supreme Court saw. As long as the ideology of racial inferiority persists, segregation will be an insult and blackness a stigma.

One does not undo the accumulated meanings of centuries by waving a magic wand: "*Abracadabra!* Once you were segregation. Now you are separation." This is tokenism: the belief by one gesture, one concession, yes, even one sincere cry of the heart, one moment of honest compassion, the country will transform the manifest meaning of historic life-ways. The desegregation fight is crucial to all Americans. What we are attempting is nothing less than to reverse the latent *meaning* of our lives and practices. For a civilization to do this takes remarkable strength of purpose, time, persistence, and most of all, honesty. Because the foot is on his neck, Negroes have been much more honest about America than the whites. We know this civilization is still segregated in its heart of hearts. We test the spirit of its ways, and white Americans who would be honest about America listen attentively when we tell them about their country.

Now, this distinction between separation and segregation was often made by Malcolm X. Time and again, he denied that the Black Muslims were segregationists. We are separationists, he said, not segregationists. Without qualification all American Negroes hate segregation. Some Negroes, however, would choose to live separately, and Malcolm saw this and tried to make it a legitimate desire. But in one very essential respect I differ strongly with Malcolm. He believed that Negroes can change the manifest meaning of their separated existence solely by the force of their own wills. I believe that there is much Negroes can do for themselves, but I do not believe they can separate truly if the nation does not simultaneously desegregate.

Culturally we are Americans, and like all men we know ourselves, in part, by what our culture tells us about ourselves. The fact is that American segregationists take delight in the Black Muslims' program. I do not believe the rumor that the Ku Klux Klan and some Texas millionaires support the Muslims, but I do know that they take no small comfort from Muslim activities. Even CORE's decision to emphasize self-help in the Negro community succeeds in making Parents and Taxpayers Associations breathe easier. And Negroes know this. In other words, there is a certain validity to the integrationist insight that separate Negro efforts and institutions simply perpetuate segregation. If, in his heart of hearts, the Negro believes that self-separation is only a rationalization for cowardly acceptance of segregation, then separation will fail.

The only way Negro separation would not mean segregation is if the Negro has the sense that he chooses to live separately, and this will happen only when total freedom of choice is a reality in America. Desegregation and the development of Negro self-pride work side by side. Desegregation makes separation possible.*

---

*Of course, Negroes do not have the right to exclude whites who choose to live among them.

What we wish is the freedom of choice which will cause any choice we make to seem truly our own. That freedom of choice must apply throughout American society and American life. A person should be able to choose where he wants to live and live there. If he chooses to live in Lovely Lane in Orchard Gardens, he should be able to, if he has the money to swing it. He should be able to work at any job for which he is qualified and equipped, regardless of his color. Jim Brown, a thoughtful man and pretty good fullback, offended some people when he said that he personally wouldn't want to live with whites but that he damned well wanted to know that he could if he did want to. I think he represents the thinking of many Negroes.

But many other Negroes will choose to integrate; they should be permitted to. James Baldwin asks whether it is worth integrating into a sinking ship. Many middle-class Negroes, whose spines are straighter than Baldwin and others suppose, would answer, "You're damned right it is." Many will buy their twenty- or thirty-thousand-dollar homes and move into neighborhoods which suit them culturally and financially. Indeed, most Negroes integrating such a neighborhood will probably have a higher educational level than their white neighbors, prejudice being what it is. It is easy to scoff at the spectacle of a middle-class Negro shoving his way into a white enclave. Some say, "Does white approval mean that much? Why go where you're not wanted?" But I have known many of these men. They brave abuse nobly and stand tough witness to noble ideals. Their acts shake the system of segregation and for that reason their efforts are more closely connected to efforts to eliminate the psychological ghetto than is commonly granted.

We must not forget that there are solid, perhaps incomparable, values in truly integrated living. W. E. B. Du Bois, a proud black man, once said that the real tragedy in our world today is not that men are poor; all men know something of poverty. Nor that men are ignorant; what is truth? Nor that men are wicked; who is good? But that men know so little of men.

It is important for Negroes to know white men and for white men to know Negroes. I might add that white men should insist that we live among them for their own sakes. And if some Negroes resist white blandishments, they will be fuller men for having resisted a valuable temptation.

Those who glibly abuse "middle-class" Negroes often commit the racist fallacy of demanding that black men behave according to their definition of him. If a black man wants to skip five thousand lunches, as Dick Gregory says, in order to buy a Cadillac, then he should. At CORE we have come to believe that in a free society many Negroes will choose to live and work separately, *although not in total isolation.* They will cultivate the pride in themselves which comes in part from their efforts to make this a free land. Even those living and working in "racially balanced" situations will value their Negro identity more than before. In helping themselves, they will come to love themselves. From loving themselves, they will determine to help themselves. They will be Americans and Negroes. They will be free to pick and choose from several rich traditions. They may thrill to the example of modern Africa and search out the richness of Africa's past as Du Bois did. Or they may as Americans and Westerners seize as models such great American cultural heroes as Lincoln or Hemingway or Duke Ellington. They will be as American as St. Patrick's Day and Columbus Day and Rosh Hashanah.

We are beginning now to see a more ideal division of effort within CORE and among the groups comprising the entire civil rights movement. Clearly the desegregation movement must continue unabated. We must demand that segregation end. Tokenism of all kinds must be rejected. We shall demand quality integrated education, now definitely adding to it the demand that Negro history be taught in the public schools so that our youngsters can learn that they are ancient citizens of this land. There must be open housing and fair employment practices, in law and in fact. And we will still demand preferential, compensatory treatment (I shall discuss this more fully later). In brief, there should be no abatement in the efforts of the last years. At the same time we will enter the Negro community, working with those masses who couldn't care less about integrating and couldn't afford it if they did care. Our efforts in the ghettos to help the people build a community life and a community spirit will be spurred by the knowledge that desegregation is taking place simultaneously. In this way segregation will be transformed into separation. Perhaps "independence" is a better term than separation. We shall become independent men. We will accept, in other words, part of Malcolm's insight that segregation will become separation only with a separate effort of Negro heart and soul rejecting the notion of some of the older civil rights organizations (and of the original CORE) that desegregation and integration *in itself* will accomplish miracles. But we will correct the Muslims' belief that the Negro can do all things alone. There must be simultaneous desegregation and we must demand it. By this amendment we will affirm that we are Americans and that the civil rights movement is an American movement.

It is clear from this summary that there is something for everyone to do. How often I have been asked by white middle-class liberals, "But what can I do?" The answer is simple. You can integrate your neighborhoods and schools as purely and diligently as ever. You are responsible for segregation and only you can end it. The white man should be an integrationist. And the fact that some Negroes now build their own lives independently without apology has no bearing upon this white responsibility. Nor, I think, should whites advise Negroes to separate themselves, for that always sounds suspiciously like a demand for segregation. Separation, independence, must be our choice to make and our program to achieve. It should affect the traditional integrationist efforts of civil rights and civil liberties groups, church and labor groups, fair housing and fair employment committees not a jot.

Is it divisive of me to suggest that all parties to the movement will not share identical perspectives? Some think so. But I believe that one cannot be all men at all times and remain himself. There is a two-ness, to use Du Bois's term, in the movement as there is in the Negro, and no synthesis, as far as I can see now, is possible. Perhaps ultimately, God willing. We should not be frightened by slight ambivalences. They are a sign that we are becoming free, for freedom eludes simple definitions.

II

We might now look into two sensitive issues. One has been urgently debated for several years; the other is relegated to a limbo of silence, perhaps out of fear of the repercussions open advocacy would cause. I speak of our demands for special, "preferential," compensatory treatment for Negroes and, of course, of interracial marriage.

Admittedly there is something startling about any demand that a whole ethnic group receive special attention. It seems to go in the teeth of our belief in individual fair play. "Are all Negroes disadvantaged?" critics ask. "Should we assume that a black skin is itself sufficient proof that the bearer deserves special consideration?" When other "minorities" devised a strategy to get a fair shake, they were "content"—the argument against us goes—to achieve immunity as individuals from group discrimination. Indeed, Negro organizations have been partners for years in a broad civil rights alliance which produced legislation in many Northern states attempting to establish non-discriminatory employment and home occupancy and in general seeking to obtain equal opportunity for all individuals (I say "attempting," because the states have moved to execute these laws with the speed of a glacier). So when an organization like CORE or Urban League demands special group attention—in education, job training, and employment—many sense a thief afoot in the liberal house, trying to steal advantages he doesn't individually deserve.

Now, as I have pointed out, the aim of treating each individual as an individual and nothing more—which is the premise underlying the philosophy of integration—is undeniably sound. The idea is to give everyone an equal start for equal opportunities. But the simple truth is that the Negro does not start on the same line as whites, nor is the economy he enters today the same as that which the immigrants entered—individually, they say—over the last half century. The reasons for this are historical and have to do, as I have said, with the meaning and impact of segregation. But the fact of it is crystal clear. Tom Kahn, Executive Secretary of the League for Industrial Democracy, has graphically described the economics of American racism in *The Economics of Equality*. The median income of Negro families, says Kahn, is $3,233—54 per cent of the white family's median income. And in the last ten years the Negro's position, relative to the white, has actually declined. Unemployment is twice as high among Negroes as among whites, and among the young, eighteen to twenty-six years old, the disproportion is far greater. Ominously, most of the job classifications in which Negro participation has increased in the last decade are in those unskilled and semiskilled areas which are today being eliminated by automation and cybernetics. Considering how poorly the Negro is being educated today in comparison to whites (who aren't being educated too well either) and considering the skills and training which more than ever will be necessary in the new economy, we can confidently predict that Negro unemployment and general economic depression will increase in the coming years. Unless something is done about it.

It is cruel nonsense in this new mass age of super technology to speak of equal opportunity in individualistic terms; the back wheels of the car never catch the front. The Negro community constitutes an economic disaster area. And it was with this in mind that CORE supported the Urban League's call for a domestic Marshall Plan which would offer the same kind of special and concerted attention in employment, education, and welfare that America gave to Hungarian and Cuban refugees, or that we gave to the G.I. after World War II, or that we give to Appalachia today.

We recommend a crash program in education and in job training, stressing that the Negro be trained to enter the new technological economy. We emphasized that he be trained in these emerging job categories because there is some tendency in technical high schools and some of the programs developed in the anti-poverty program to train the Negro for jobs which are either nonexistent or fast disappearing from the economy. And we recommend this to all institutions and agencies in American life—government (federal, state, and local) as well as private corporations, businesses, labor unions, and service organizations.*

It is important to emphasize that we make these recommendations not only in the name of equity but in the name of historical justice. The integrationists fear that by demanding special help for the Negro, we will make him more Negro than ever and compound his disabilities. It is a class problem, they will say, not a race problem. Well, it is that too. But we must call injustice by its given name. America is racist and it is a man called Negro who is specially victimized beyond his class and beyond any other formal classifications one might coin. And he knows he is. He will not cease to be victimized nor will he cease to victimize himself until segregation

---

*In some respects the Urban League and CORE place different emphasis on various aspects of compensation. The ten-point program which Whitney Young formulated in 1963 centers its fire on the business community—corporations and foundations. While we second Young's motion—and are grateful that he is so influential with American businessmen—we have worked on smaller units in the economy: labor unions, small and middle-sized businesses. Both Urban League and CORE have pressed for vigorous and expensive government programs.

I think it should be pointed out, too, that in some degree our demands for special attention have been fully accepted and applied—albeit under a different rubric. Opportunities for talented and obviously promising young Negroes to attend choice universities and get lucrative and satisfying work have increased markedly. Unfortunately, these opportunities are still reserved for a talented twentieth of our people. We must now apply our special effort where it is most needed.

of mind and spirit ends. And to end segregation this nation must turn directly to the Negro and undo what is has done. We are not so worried if we get to be known as Negroes in the process. We rather like the name these days. Again, we are desegregationists, not necessarily integrationists.

As for interracial marriage, it is, of course, the touchiest of subjects. Perhaps, as James Baldwin and others have finally said, *sex* is at the bottom of the race problem. Well we know how irrepressibly those dreadful words drift to the lips of whites: "Would you want your daughter. . . ." In ten years the civil rights movement has forced this nation to tear down numerous symbols of Negro degradation: separate waiting rooms and rest rooms; separate laws and regulations; separate gestures; separate vocabulary and manners—we challenged them all. And yet we have tip-toed around what a man from Mars might objectively call the most degrading and revealingly racist symbols of American public life. As I write this some nineteen states, mainly in the South, have "anti-miscegenation laws," prohibiting marriage between the races. In these states, even those "mixed" couples which have legally married in other states cannot live or even travel together as man and wife. Constitutional lawyers tell me that these statutes are indubitably unconstitutional, and though in 1965 the Supreme Court was preparing to rule on these laws, it is still a fact of history, to be recorded, that until recently the court, with full permission of our Negro organizations, has avoided the issue. Jewish friends tell me that the first clue of what was to happen in Germany was the infamous Nuremberg Laws prohibiting sexual intercourse between Aryans and Jews. From that brutish moment, they say, all things followed. Yet we have had Nuremberg Laws for almost a century here. And remained silent.

We Negroes have made something of an art of detecting hypocrisy lately, yet what hypocrisy is so overt as this one? As Lillian Smith has shown so eloquently in *Killers of the Dream,* and as any Negro anywhere knows, Southerners do not believe in sexual segregation; they believe in sexual exploitation. In no respect are we so exploited as in this. Black women are for white men to have; white women are for no one to have. In a typical Southern town, every Negro knows of the whites who are kin to him. Miscegenation, so-called, is an established practice, in one direction. But the Negro male in the South cannot look upon a white woman or even seem to be looking upon her without literally inviting slaughter. And we know it. And in the law it says in effect that we are not fit to be loved in the light of day.*

And yet how tenderly we have treated this issue. Reasons are not difficult to cite. Clearly, we cannot even broach the topic without throwing whites into apoplectic resistance. Why risk losing other goals? How do you say to people who are literally insane on the subject, "We are not advocating anything, we are only saying the prohibition is insulting"?

And we are *not* advocating interracial marriage. I believe that such advocacy is as dirty-minded as the prohibition. One simply must not dictate to the human heart this way. (As Eleanor Roosevelt said, marriage is not a social matter with private implications, it is a private matter with social implications.) Those few who advocate amalgamation and those who would prohibit it—as many black nationalists would—are equally guilty of tampering. All we can do is try to make men believe they are free by leaving them to their choices.

Should I now rush, as many commentators do, to assure the reader that interracial marriage couldn't be further from the mind of most Negroes? Indeed, from the description of growing pride in the Negro community which I have offered in this book, many may draw this conclusion. If I were asked, Do you expect a significant increase in interracial marriages as desegregation progresses? I would answer: No, I do not foresee a significant increase. Asked if I believe in such marriages, I would answer that what I believe or what anyone believes should not matter. Free men who care about the freedom of others should keep their counsel in these matters.

CORE will not make an issue of the question, and that itself is something of a commentary on this country. We are normally a fairly aggressive bunch. Yet in our hearts we know that desegregation will not be complete until America is cleansed of the filth of legislating whom one may not marry.

---

*A young Negro was convicted in North Carolina a while back for "reckless eyeballing." "Rape by leer" was another term used to describe this "crime."

CLAUDE M. LIGHTFOOT

The Struggle for Black Power*

IT IS REMARKABLE that few black Americans have turned to Communist ideology in their exasperation with American society. Claude Lightfoot is one black man who, years ago, believed he discerned in Marxist-Leninist philosophy the promise of a better life for his people. In the essay that follows, Mr. Lightfoot examines, without ideological jargon, the goals and obstacles of the black revolution.

Black America is like a ball of fire. Its revolts spread over the land leaving hardly any Northern city unscathed, and the end is nowhere in sight. Starting out as civil rights struggles, the movement now takes on the aspects of a social revolution, a black revolution, a revolt of the poor.

Where is this revolt heading?

How can its goals be obtained?

The answers to questions like these require clear knowledge of the roots and causes, and of the dynamic forces which are accelerating the pace.

The revolt rests on four principal developments. It is occasioned by the necessity for black people to have a substantial share of power over decisions affecting their welfare. It is an outgrowth of the terrible conditions in the ghettos. It is aggravated by the problems in the rural areas of the South. It is compounded by the intensification of racism in the white community.

The black power slogan has come to symbolize the end of an era. A new one is being born with the usual birth pains that accompany the emergence of the new. The slogan has been used by the white power structure to break up old alignments between black and white and among blacks themselves. When it was projected, white liberals in large numbers fled from the civil rights movement as if a deadly plague had hit it. The more conservative Negro leaders rushed to assure their white bosses that the black power advocates did not speak for them.

The purpose of this attack was to destroy the younger militants and to arrest trends toward greater radicalism in the black community. Thus, the pressures of the white-led power structure have helped to provoke sharp cleavages between the various civil rights organizations and leaders.

There are also material factors within the Negro community which often engender clashes. Black people are not a homogeneous group. Although oppressed, like other peoples they consist of various class strata. But in one way or another, since Jim Crow policies affect all Negroes, the community often finds common denominators which unite all. However, there are times when collisions between classes come to the forefront.

In the previous period they did not come too sharply into view because of the nature of the demands and of the struggles being waged. Civil rights battles during that period took place primarily in the South, where the social aspects of discrimination dominated the picture. The economic aspects of the struggle against Jim Crow had not yet come forward prominently. Also, the dominant leadership in the civil rights movement consisted of middle-class or middle-class-oriented people who gave priority to the social and civil aspects, and the promotion of individual Negroes, as against the alleviation of the rotten economic conditions of the broad masses.

In 1964, after the March on Washington, civil rights struggles became more broadly distributed. Tremendous mass actions took place in the Negro ghettos—especially in Chicago, New York and Cleveland—against discrimination in the school systems. The masses of black people supported these initiatives because to them the struggle for the specific demand, no matter what it is, carries within it struggle against the whole system of Jim Crow and segregation. But while they supported the school boycott movements, these were not necessarily the issues to which they gave priority.

They were primarily concerned with those aspects of Jim Crow which keep them in a state of permanent impoverishment. But the problems of the black people on the lowest rung of the economic ladder received little or no attention. As a consequence, when the outbursts took place in Harlem in 1964, we saw revealed for the first time the sharp cleavages between leaders who had been prominent in civil rights circles and the masses of the people. Thus, the problem of what issues are to have priority carries within it the seeds of cleavages within the movement.

These problems were portrayed with great clarity by the Harlem Council for Jobs and Freedom in its Prospectus:

"Construction of new and better housing which the poor can afford is an important objective; but without any change in the tenant's income, without better jobs, the life-style of poverty is perpetuated and the 'project' may become a new, somewhat less . . . ugly, but equally degrading slum. . . .

"Likewise, more and better education is meaningless without more and better job opportunities. The converse is also true, of course, but the shameful fact remains that job opportunities have seriously lagged behind educational opportunities for decades. Average Negro incomes at every level of education are notoriously lower than those of whites. Negroes are still virtually—in some cases entirely—excluded from whole industries and job classifications quite arbitrarily and without regard for qualifications."

The problems posed here apply to the entire country.

The position taken by the Jobs Council in Harlem does not overlook the struggle for better housing or better education; on the contrary, it encompasses such struggles. But it places the economic questions right in the center of things. The course of events has already put the economic problems of the Negro masses at the center of the struggle in the coming period. Not all Negro leaders see this problem clearly. Not all of them, including many of the younger militants and radicals, understand what is going to be required to achieve goals along this line. Nonetheless, there are many hopeful signs that most black people are beginning to see the primacy of the struggle on the economic and political fronts, and it is in the context of such a growing awareness that we can hopefully look forward to the reemergence of Negro unity on a higher level. There will still be many struggles between classes, trends and tendencies, but the movement will continue to find common interests which can unite all strata of the Negro people.

At the present moment, most civil rights organizations, including the more radical ones, seem to be in a period of decline. This gives rise to questions such as these:

Have organizations like the National Association for the Advancement of Colored People (NAACP) and the Urban League outlived their usefulness?

Did the withdrawal of funds by white liberals leave such organizations as the Student Nonviolent Coordinating Committee (SNCC) and the Congress on Racial Equality (CORE) stranded with no place to go?

I believe this is not the case. Of course, all civil rights movements and organizations, conservative and radical, are called upon to make adjustments to the needs of this period. But there is no reason to believe that most of them will not readjust and continue to make vital contributions.

The new period will have a logic of its own. It will call for emphasis on new techniques of struggle, new priorities on issues, and new class alignments. Some of the older civil rights organizations may not be able to do what is required. The position of the top leaders of the NAACP on the black power issue and on the removal of Congressman Adam Clayton Powell, as well as their efforts to keep the Negro out of the peace movement, shows how difficult it will be for this organization to adjust to the requirements of the new period.

The civil rights movement in the last 15 years has passed through various phases of development. Each one required new organizations and leaders as a supplement to the old. During the period from 1948 to 1954, the NAACP dominated the scene. It was geared mainly to the legal aspects of the struggle. It led most of the court battles which eventually resulted in the Supreme Court decision on school desegregation. However, it was not equipped or oriented to do what was required following the Court's rulings. Especially was this true when the center of gravity of the struggle shifted from the courts to mass action. The inadequacies of the Association left a void which was filled by the Southern Christian Leadership Conference (SCLC) and the emergence of new leaders like Dr. Martin Luther King, Rev. Ralph Abernathy and Rev. Fred Shuttlesworth. Later, the youth sit-in movement in the South produced a new organization, SNCC, and invigorated CORE. These organizations also produced new leaders who reflected more fully the mass aspects of the problem. This was the period which brought to prominence John Lewis, James Foreman, Stokeley Carmichael and Julian Bond. Now, with the economic and political aspects of the struggle, as well as the fight for peace, becoming the dominant themes, new organizations and new leaders will come to the fore who will reflect the realities of this period.

The present is like a twilight zone. The new has not yet arrived fully and the old has not yet made the needed adjustments; however, there are hopeful signs in both directions.

Black power means many things to different people. It has many positive values ranging from the psychological to the political. As a slogan, it encompasses practically every phase of the black man's struggle in the United States. But the central reason why the slogan has been embraced by most people is the recognition of the necessity for black people to have a greater share of economic and political power.

The problem of power comes into greater focus now because we have reached a point where *enforcement* of the law has become the key aspect of the struggle. Insofar as civil rights are concerned, there are adequate laws to meet the problems. We have passed through a period beginning with the establishment of FEPC by the Roosevelt Administration in World War II, through the Supreme Court ruling on desegregation of the schools in 1954, and the passage of the civil rights and voter registration bills in 1964–65, in which enabling legislation was secured to deal with all the practices of Jim Crow and segregation.

Significant advances were made on all levels of government. On the federal level, all three branches took a position on these matters, in the form of judicial rulings, executive orders and new laws. Most state and city governments in the North did likewise. Laws prohibiting discrimination in hiring practices, were enacted in over 30 states. Other civil rights laws and ordinances prohibiting discrimination in public places were passed in all major Northern cities and states.

Of course, it could be argued that all these court rulings, executive orders and laws were unnecessary. The citizenship rights of black people had already been established in the 13th and 14th Amendments to the Constitution. And during the Reconstruction period civil rights laws and codes were established which provided the legal means to prevent discrimination against people of color. For example, the Civil Rights Law of 1871 proclaimed: "Whenever insurrection, domestic violence, unlawful combinations or conspiracies in any state so hinders the execution of the laws thereof and of the United States . . . it shall be lawful for the President and *it shall be his duty* to take such measures . . . or any other means he may deem necessary." (Emphasis added.)

On the basis of this law, which has never been rescinded, every President since then has had the power to put an end to the violations of the citizenship rights of black people. That they did not do so means that every one of them has been holding office illegally. The law states, "It shall be his duty."

On this basis the Presidents have been just as guilty of malfeasance in office as all Southern Congressmen. It might be said that in a basic sense, all the enabling acts of the last 20 years were unnecessary. However, the struggle to secure them represented progress, and to some extent has helped to lessen the blight of Jim Crow. The main problem now is not enabling legislation, but law enforcement.

Everyone with an ounce of common sense or honesty realizes that despite all the court rulings, executive orders and laws, the Negro in many areas of our national life is almost as much a second-class citizen as he was a hundred years ago. It should also be noted that whatever the progress, it was the result of actions initiated by Negroes themselves. In this respect their path was illuminated by Frederick Douglass who once pointed out, "He who would be free must himself strike the first blow."

Today, as when Douglass wrote, the role Negroes themselves must play is highlighted by the black power concept. This proposition does not deny the necessity for allies. Nor is it necessarily divisive. There are those, white and black, who seek to make it so, but "it ain't necessarily so."

The Negro seeks a share of governmental power now to help enforce the laws which his own actions helped to bring into existence.

An examination of his position in the power structure of the country illustrates the enormous tasks that must be carried out. Since the close of the Reconstruction period, he has been forced to live in the blighted areas of the cities and on the plantations of the rural South. Based upon this enforced segregation, the Negro is preyed upon by every exploitative element in our society. He is exploited as a worker, but in addition his color has made it easier to set him aside from the rest of the people for super-exploitation. As a consequence, he constitutes not only a class but also a people without money. And since money in our society is a major source of power, Negroes are a people without power.

Thus, the struggle to obtain black power and "green power" are important changes in the on-going black revolt. The black revolt, therefore, is not only violence in the streets in response to provocations, but a revolt at the polls, a revolt to change the composition of government and to enforce the laws involving the rights of black people.

JULIUS LESTER

Look Out, Whitey!...Black Power's Gon' Get Your Mama*

J ULIUS LESTER was born in St. Louis in 1939. He was graduated
from Fisk University in 1960 and became a field secretary
for the Student Non-Violent Coordinating Committee. He has written
articles for *The Village Voice, The National Guardian,* and
Liberator. The following essay is reprinted from the last chapter of
Mr. Lester's book, *Look Out, Whitey! Black Power's Gon' Get Your
Mama* (1968). The essay is a strong, threatening discussion of
black power and the need to destroy the present white racist society
in America.

*Reprinted from LOOK OUT, WHITEY! BLACK POWER'S GON' GET
YOUR MAMA by Julius Lester. Copyright © 1968 by Julius Lester and
used by permission of the publisher, The Dial Press, Inc.

It is clear that America as it now exists must be destroyed. There is no other way. It is impossible to live within this country and not become a thief or a murderer. Young blacks and young whites are beginning to say NO to thievery and murder. Black power confronts White Power openly, and as the SNCC poet Worth Long cried: "We have found you out, false-faced America. We have found you out!"

Having "found you out," we will destroy you or die in the act of destroying. That much seems inevitable. To those who fearfully wonder if America has come to the point of a race war, the answer is not certain. However, all signs would seem to say yes. Perhaps the only way that it might be avoided would be through the ability of young white radicals to convince blacks, through their actions, that they are ready to do whatever is necessary to change America.

The race war, if it comes, will come partly from the necessity for revenge. You can't do what has been done to blacks and not expect retribution. The very act of retribution is liberating, and perhaps it is no accident that the symbolism of Christianity speaks of being washed in Blood as an act of purification. Psychologically, blacks have always found an outlet for their revenge whenever planes have fallen, autos have collided, or just every day when white folks die. One old black woman in Atlanta, Georgia, calmly reads through her paper each day counting the number of white people killed the previous day in wrecks, storms, and by natural causes. When the three astronauts were killed in February, 1967, black people did not join the nation in mourning. They were white and were spending money that blacks needed. White folks trying to get to the moon, 'cause it's there. Poverty's here! Now get to that! Malcolm X spoke for all black people when a plane full of Georgians crashed in France: "Allah has blessed us. He has destroyed twenty-two of our enemies."

It is clearly written that the victim must become the executioner. The executioner preordains it when all attempts to stop the continual executions fail. To those who point to numbers and say that black people are only ten percent, it must be said as Brother Malcolm said: "It only takes a spark to light the fuse. We are that spark."

Black Power is not an isolated phenomenon. It is only another manifestation of what is transpiring in Latin America, Asia, and Africa. People are reclaiming their lives on those three continents and blacks in America are reclaiming theirs. These liberation movements are not saying give us a share; they are saying we want it all! The existence of the present system in the United States depends upon the United States taking all. This system is threatened more and more each day by the refusal of those in the Third World to be exploited. They are colonial people outside the United States; blacks are a colonial people within. Thus, we have a common enemy. As the Black Power movement becomes more politically conscious, the spiritual coalition that exists between blacks in America and the Third World will become more evident. The spiritual coalition is not new. When Italy invaded Ethiopia in 1938, blacks in Harlem held large demonstrations protesting this. During World War II, many blacks were rooting for the Japanese. Blacks cannot overlook the fact that it was the Japanese who were the guinea pigs for the atomic bomb, not the Germans. They know, too, that if the U.S. were fighting a European country, it would not use napalm, phosphorus and steel-pellet bombs, just as they know that if there had been over one hundred-thousand blacks massed before the Pentagon on October 21, 1967, they would not have been met by soldiers with unloaded guns. In fact, they know they would never have been allowed to even reach the Pentagon.

The struggle of blacks in America is inseparable from the

struggle of the Third World. This is a natural coalition—a coalition of those who know that they are dispossessed. Whites in America are dispossessed also, but the difference is that they will not recognize the fact as yet. Until they do, it will not be possible to have coalitions with them, even the most radical. They must recognize the nature and character of their own oppression. At present, too many of them recognize only that they are white and identify with whites, not with the oppressed, the dispossessed. They react against being called "honky" and thereby establish the fact that they are. It is absolutely necessary for blacks to identify as blacks to win liberation. It is not necessary for whites. White radicals must learn to nonidentify as whites. White is not in the color of the skin. It is a condition of the mind: a condition that will be destroyed. It should be possible for any white radical to yell "honky" as loud as a black radical. "Honky" is a beautiful word that destroys the mystique surrounding whiteness. It is like throwing mud on a sheet. Whiteness has been used as an instrument of oppression; no white radical can identify himself by the color of his skin and expect to fight alongside blacks. Black Power liberates whites also, but they have refused to recognize this, preferring to defend their whiteness.

Black Power is not anti-white people, but is anti anything and everything that serves to oppress. If whites align themselves on the side of oppression, then Black Power must be antiwhite. That, however, is not the decision of Black Power.

For blacks, Black Power is the microscope and telescope through which they look at themselves and the world. It has enabled them to focus their energies while preparing for the day of reckoning. That day of reckoning is anticipated with eagerness by many, because it is on that day that they will truly come alive. The concept of the black man as a nation, which is only being talked about now, will become reality when violence comes. Out of the violence will come the new nation (if the violence is successful) and the new man. Frantz Fanon wrote that "For the colonised people this violence, because it constitutes their only work, invests their characters with positive and creative qualities. The practice of violence binds them together as a whole, since each individual forms a violent link in the great chain, a part of the great organism of violence which has surged upwards in reaction to the settler's violence in the beginning. The group recognize each other and the future nation is already indivisible. The armed struggle mobilises the people; that is to say, it throws them in one way and in one direction."

It is obvious, of course, that White Power will not allow Black Power to evolve without trying to first subvert it. This is being attempted, as was mentioned in the previous chapter. This attempt will fail and White Power will have no choice but to attempt to physically crush Black Power. This is being prepared for, with intensive riot-control training for the National Guard, chemicals for the control of large crowds, and concentration camps. It is to be expected that eventually black communities across the country will be cordoned off and a South African passbook system introduced to control the comings and goings of blacks.

At the moment, though (but, oh, how short a moment is), the tactic is one of subversion. Particular attention and energy is being given toward the subversion of SNCC. An inordinate number of SNCC men have received draft notices since January of 1967. Another tactic has been the calling of court cases to trial that have lain dormant for two or three years, cases that in many instances had been forgotten by SNCC. The most sophisticated tactic has been the legal maneuvers the government has used to keep SNCC's chairman, H. Rap Brown, confined to Manhattan Island, thus preventing him from traveling around the country and speaking. Having accomplished that, the government now seems content to take its own good time about bringing Brown's cases up for trial.

Black Power, however, will not be denied. America's time is not long and the odds are on our side.

Black Power seeks to destroy what now is, but what does it offer in replacement? Black Power is a highly moral point of view, but its morality is one that sees that a way of life flows from the economic and political realities of life. It is these that must be changed. Mrs. Ida Mae Lawrence of Rosedale, Mississippi, put it beautifully when she said, "You know, we ain't dumb, even if we are poor. We need jobs. We need houses. But even with the poverty program we ain't got nothin' but needs. . . . We is ignored by the government. The thing about property upset them, but the things about poor people don't. So there's no way out, but to begin your own beginning, whatever way you can. So far as I'm concerned, that's all I got to say about the past. We're beginning a new future."

In his 1966 Berkeley speech, Stokely Carmichael put it another way. ". . . our vision is not merely of a society in which all black men have enough to buy the good things of life. When we urge that black money go into black pockets, we mean the communal pocket. We want to see money go back into the community and used to benefit it. We want to see the cooperative concept applied in business and banking. . . . The society we seek to build among black people is not a capitalistic one. It is a society in which the spirit of community and humanistic love prevail. The word love is suspect; black expectations of what it might produce have been betrayed too often. But those were expectations of a response from the white community, which failed us. The love we seek to encourage is within the black community, the only American community where men call each other 'brother' when they meet. We can build a community of love only where we have the ability and power to do so; among blacks.''

Those whites who have a similar vision and want to be a part of this new world must cast down their bucket where they are. If this kind of a world is as important and as necessary for them as it is for us, they must evolve an approach to their own communities. We must organize around blackness, because it is with the fact of our blackness that we have been clubbed. We therefore turn our blackness into a club. When this new world is as totally necessary for whites as it is for blacks, then maybe we can come together and work on some things side by side. However, we will always want to preserve our ethnicity, our community. We are a distinct cultural group, proud of our culture and our institutions, and simply want to be left alone to lead our good, black lives. In the new world, as in this one, I want to be known, not as a man who happens to be black, but as a black man. With that knowledge I can visit the graves of my slave foreparents and say, "I didn't forget about you . . . those hot days you worked in the fields, those beatings, all that shit you took and just grew stronger on. I'm still singing those songs you sang and telling those tales and passing on to the young ones so they will know you, also. We will never forget, for your lives were lived on a spider web stretched over the mouth of hell and yet, you walked that walk and talked that talk and told it like it is. You can rest easy now. Everything's up-tight.''

The old order passes away. Like the black riderless horse, boots turned the wrong way in the stirrups, following the coffin down the boulevard, it passes away. But there are no crowds to watch as it passes. There are no crowds, to mourn, to weep. No eulogies to read and no eternal flame is lit over the grave. There is no time, for there are streets to be cleaned, houses painted, and clothes washed. Everything must be scoured clean. Trash has to be thrown out. Garbage dumped and everything unfit, burned.

> The new order is coming, child.
> The old is passing away.

DEVERE E. PENTONY

The Case for Black Studies*

D EVERE E. PENTONY is a professor of international relations and
Dean of the School of Behavioral and Social Sciences at
San Francisco State College. The following essay examines the
promise and perils of black studies programs.

The history of the development of various American groups into an integrated culture is a complex story, but there is one simple fact that seems germane to the problems of black-white integration in the United States. This obvious fact is that almost every immigrant group with the major exception of the blacks came to these shores because they wanted to come. America was to be the land of opportunity, the land where the rigidities for social mobility would be relaxed, and the land where a man could be free. That these expectations were not quickly fulfilled is a cloudy part of the political and social history of the United States, but in retrospect the members of most of these groups, the Irish, the Germans, the Dutch, the Scotch, the Italians now view the story of their ethnic past in the United States as a reasonably successful one.

No similar memories have been available to the black man and woman. Brought to this country in chains, torn from family and tribal past, physically and psychologically enslaved, taught by lash and example to be subservient, forced to suffer indignities to their basic humanity, and instantly categorized by the accident of color, black people have all too often found the American dream a nightmare. Instead of joining the dominant culture, many have learned to exist in the psychologically bewildering atmosphere neither slave

211

nor free. That they have survived at all is tribute to their magnificent resiliency and basic toughness; but that some carry with them a heavy baggage of hate and rage is not surprising.

While many whites in America have congratulated themselves upon the progress toward freedom and equality that has recently been made, a number of black intellectuals are eloquently questioning whether, indeed, meaningful progress has been made. Perhaps blacks are all too familiar with the ability of white people to dash black hopes for freedom and dignity on rocks of intransigence and patience. Witness the rise and fall of hope in the story of black men in America: in the aftermath of the Civil War they were told that they were freed from slavery only to find that they were not free— not free to be treated as individuals, not free to eat, or sleep, or live, or go to school, or drink from the same fountain, or ride the same conveyance, or enjoy the same political and economic privileges as people of "white" skin. And when in the twentieth century they had their hopes raised by long overdue court decisions and civil rights legislation finally demanding integration, these hopes were once again shattered as blacks found that significant segments of the white culture often lagged far behind the basic justice of these acts. This had led some of the black community to question whether integration was not just another scheme to preserve the dominance of the whites, seducing blacks to give up their black identities and to copy the speech, manner, hair, dress, and style of the whites, and to accept the myths, heroes, and historical judgment of white America without reciprocity or without appreciation of, or respect for, black experience. Moreover, this estimate has been coupled with the hunch that in any significant way, only the "talented tenth" of the black community could really hope to overcome the monetary, social, and psychological barriers to true integration with whites. The remaining 90 percent would, therefore, be left in poverty and psychological degradation, doomed to an almost motiveless, hopeless existence, forever on the dole, forever caught in hate of self and of others. Thus has been posed a transcendent dilemma for the black man and woman: to succeed in the white world is to fail, to overcome the outrageous obstacles thrown in their way by white society seems partially to deny their black experience. Above all, to integrate on an individual basis in a society that makes this increasingly possible for the fortunate may well mean an exodus of the talented tenth from the black community, with the consequent decimation of the ranks of potential leaders whose commitment to the whole community could help set their people free.

Seen in this light, the demand for black studies is a call for black leadership. The argument is that if there is to be an exodus from the land of physical and psychological bondage, an informed and dedicated leadership is needed to help bring about individual and group pride and a sense of cohesive community. To accomplish this, black people, like all people, need to know that they are not alone. They need to know that their ancestors were not just slaves laboring under the white man's sun but that their lineage can be traced to important kingdoms and significant civilizations. They need to be familiar with the black man's contribution to the arts and sciences. They need to know of black heroes and of the noble deeds of black men. They need to know that black, too, is beautiful, and that under the African sky people are at proud ease with their blackness. In historical perspective they need to know the whole story of white oppression and of the struggle of some blacks, and some whites too, to overcome that oppression. They need to find sympathetic encouragement to move successfully into the socio-economic arenas of American life.

To help fulfill all these needs, the contention is, a black studies effort must be launched. At the beginning, it must be staffed by black faculty, who must have the time and resources to prepare a solid curriculum for college students and to get the new knowledge and new perspectives into the community as quickly as possible. In a situation somewhat similar to the tremendous efforts at adult education in some of the less developed societies, the advocates of black studies press to get on with the urgent tasks.

It is in this context that a basic challenge is made to many of the traditional values of the college or university. Important critical questions arise: Will black studies be merely an exchange of old lies for new myths? Is it the work of the college to provide an ideological underpinning for social movement? Will the traditional search for the truth be subordinated to the goal of building a particular group identity? Is the ideal of the brotherhood of all men to be sacrificed to the brotherhood of some men and the hatred of others? Can the college teach group solidarity for some groups and not for others? Will the results of separatist studies be a heightening of group tensions and a reactive enlarging of the forces of racism? Will standards of excellence for students and faculty alike be cast aside in the interest of meeting student and community needs? Will anti-intellectualism run rampant? Will constitutional and other legal provisions be violated by this new version of "separate if not equal"?

A REMEDY FOR WHITE STUDIES

It seems clear that the advocates of a black studies program see it as a remedy for "white studies" programs that they have been subjected to all their lives and as a way to bring pride, dignity, and community to black people. They are questioning the relevance of the style and content of education designed to meet the needs and expectations of the dominant white culture, and some seem to be suggesting that the life-styles and ways of perceiving the world in much of the black community are sufficiently different to justify a new, almost bicultural approach to educating the members of the community who are at once a part of, yet apart from, the general American culture. While they hope that this effort will range over the whole educational experience from childhood through adulthood, they seem to view the college or university as the place where talents can be gathered and resources mobilized to provide intellectual leadership and academic respectability to their efforts. The college is to be the place for the writing of books, the providing of information, and the training of students to help with the critical tasks. It is to be one of the testing grounds for the idea that black people need to have control of their own destiny.

But what of the outcome? There is obvious concern that efforts to focus on blackness as one of the answers to white racism will result in an equally virulent black racism. Black "nationalism," with its glorifying of the black ingroup, may have powerful meaning only when it focuses on the hate object of whiteness. Indeed, it is painfully true that whites through their words and deeds over many generations have provided the black nationalists with all the bitter evidence they need for building a negative nationalism based mainly on hatred and rage. Thus we should expect that a significant ingredient in constructing black unity and group dignity would be an antiwhiteness.

Increasingly, the black intellectual is drawing a colonial analogy to the situation of the black community in the United States. Like people in the colonized lands of Asia, Africa, and Latin America, some black men look at their rather systematic exclusion from first-class citizenship in the United States as a close parallel to the exploitation and subjugation perpetrated by those who shouldered the "white man's burden" during the high tide of imperialism. Thus the focus on black culture and black history is to prepare the black community to be as free and proud as anyone in the newly emerging states. And the outcome of that may be the growth of the self-confidence and sense of personal dignity that pave the way for an easier integration into a common culture on the basis of feelings of real equality.

While it would be foolish to deny that ugly and self-defeating racism may be the fruits of the black studies movement, we should not forget that a sense of deep compassion and intense concern for all humanity has often shone through the rage and hate of such prophets of the movement as Malcolm X, Stokely Carmichael, and W. E. B. Dubois. Whether that hopeful strain of compassion and human concern will gain the upper hand in the days that lie ahead may well depend on the degree of understanding and tenderness with which the white community is able to react to these efforts.

There is the possibility that an emphasis on blackness, black dignity, black contributions, and black history will provide whites with new perspectives about the black man and woman. In turn, these new perspectives may indicate what clues of behavior and guides to proper responsiveness are necessary to enable whites to relate to blacks in something other than a patronizing or deprecating fashion. Through black studies there may be opportunities for whites to enrich their understanding of the black man and thus, perhaps, to help build more meaningful bridges of mutual respect and obligation. Moreover, if the truth can make blacks free and open, it may also free the whites from their ignorant stereotypes of the black man and his culture. Unfortunately, it may also be possible for those who teach black studies to reinforce those stereotypes by aping the worst features of the white society and becoming merely a mirror image of that aspect of white society that is insensitive and inhuman.

STANDARDS AND SCHOLARSHIP

Will accepted standards and scholarship be maintained in the black studies program? When any new program is proposed, a question of this sort is certainly appropriate for members of the academic community. However, it is an extremely difficult one to answer for a black studies program or for any other new program. All that can be safely said is that the pressures for respectable scholarly performance and for recognized achievements will be at least as great for black studies as for any other new program.

In the performance and evaluation of students, we can probably expect the same ferment over learning, grading, and evaluative practices that perturbs the rest of the academic world. But academicians who are pushing the black studies idea give no indication that they will be content with a half-hearted, sloppy, shoddy intellectual effort on the part of themselves or their students. Indeed, one of the underlying assumptions of black studies seems to be that students who become involved in it will become highly motivated toward academic success not only in black studies but in the rest of the curriculum as well. Out of the black studies experience are to come black students, committed, socially aware, ambitious, devoted to the welfare of black people, and equipped for helping the black community assume its rightful place in American society. These are high ambitions which are not likely to be fulfilled immediately by a black studies program, but which deserve to be given the same benefit of doubt and the same opportunities for growth by trial and error that most new programs are given.

Will black studies scholars manipulate data, bias their studies, and create towering myths which bear little resemblance to the shifting realities of human existence? The answer is difficult to assess.

In one respect the quest for pristine outside objectivity may miss the point. A distinguished philosopher has argued that the search for intergroup accommodation must be based upon what he terms the discovery of the normative inner order—that is, the values, assumptions, and world views or images of various societies or cultures. It may be that one of the most important roles that the black scholar can play is to share in the discovery and articulation of this normative inner order of the black community, with the possible result of improving the chances for mutually beneficial black-white interaction.

In this process we should expect that there will be black professors who profess a certain "ideology" just as white professors do. We can even expect a case for racial superiority of blacks, but surely this is not a reason for opposing black studies. To do so on those grounds would be analogous to opposing the teaching of biology because a certain biologist has attempted to make a case for a black inferiority based on some of his genetic investigations, or of economics because certain economists continue to adhere to pre-Keynesian economic principles.

Moreover, the ideology argument may mean no more than that black scholars will attempt to emphasize common assumptions about American society from the perspective of the black experience. But this kind of "indoctrination" is not essentially different from what is found, for example, in many college textbooks in American government which rest on some value-laden assumptions about the American political system. A more serious charge would be that black professors may insist that their students follow some "party line" as they examine the various facets of the black situation. But students are not as gullible as we sometimes imagine and are generally quite capable of resisting efforts at indoctrination.

Closely allied to the questions of standards and scholarship are questions of curriculum. What is an appropriate beginning curriculum for a black studies effort? The unspoken consensus seems to be that an area studies program should dig as deeply as possible into the history, the culture, the language, the politics, the economics, the geography, the literature, the arts, the life-styles, and the world views of the people in the area concerned. How this is all put together in a way that students will understand and benefit from is a significant organizing problem for all area studies programs, including black studies. But it would be foolish to expect those problems to be creatively attacked before a working faculty is on the scene. The first efforts to establish a satisfactory curriculum in black studies will be experimental in many ways and as such subject to more rapid change than our established curricula.

ARE BLACK STUDIES LEGAL AND PROPER?

The question of legality of a black studies program requires examination. Like the closely related area studies program, the curriculum would seem to face no legal questions from federal or state law. However, it is in the realm of staffing and student access that the most serious questions arise. For example, can tests of color be applied for hiring faculty members in the black studies program? Posed in this sharp way, the answer to the question is probably no. The equal protection of the laws section of the United

States Constitution and various state legal requirements about non-discrimination in employment could very likely be interpreted to preclude the hiring of faculty simple because they are black. However, if the qualifications for hiring are put on a broader experiential basis than color alone, then the questions and answers may change. Already factors of ethnic background and experience play a role in hiring at the colleges and universities in the United States. While this is particularly obvious in the hiring of teachers in foreign languages and literature—note, for example, the number of people teaching Chinese language and literature who are Chinese—ethnic background has often been considered in other aspects of area studies and other programs from the Peace Corps to social work.

The question of hiring black faculty is probably not a legal question at all. Rather the critical focal point for the black studies program would seem to be, on the one hand, whether the particular experiences gained from a black ethnic background tend to make the faculty member a better scholar and teacher or, on the other hand, whether the ethnic emotional involvement will permit a useful scholarly detachment in the evaluation and presentation of data. Completely satisfactory answers to this dilemma are not likely to be found. A short-run solution to the dilemma may rest on the ability of black studies programs to attract black faculty with a passion for the truth as well as an emotional identification with the subject of blackness, and on the certainty that nonblack scholars will continue to view, comment upon, and analyze the black experience in various parts of the academic community. Enough flexibility and openness should exist for students majoring in black studies to encounter the views of nonblack scholars. Similarly, the educational experiences of the rest of the academic community would undoubtedly be enriched by the participation of black studies faculty in the general intellectual life of the college. It would be tragic if the black studies faculty were to be prevented from commentary on the general questions of man in society by their own preoccupation with black studies. Few would argue that the infusion of an increasing number of black faculty into the academic community is not desirable. The black studies program would speed the process and provide the black community with incentives and opportunities for greater participation in the education of youth. The institutions of higher education cannot rely on narrow legal interpretation and conventional dogmas as trustworthy guidelines to hiring faculty in programs like black studies.

A second serious question about the legality of the black studies program is the question of student access to it. Can an academic institution worthy of the name deny access to any of its academic programs on the basis of color or ethnic background? The answer is no. Here the legal answer and the moral answer would seem to reinforce one another. If one of the purposes of the black studies program is to tell it as it really is, then the message should go out to students regardless of color even though it is likely to have a particular additional value to the black student. The college cannot be a place where knowledge is developed and subjects taught in semisecret. Just as any college contracting to the government for secret research would be open to serious charges of violation of the traditional ethics of scholarship, so would any academic program that excluded students solely on the basis of ethnic background raise serious questions of propriety and legality.

However, even in this connection a dilemma remains. As anyone who has participated in an area program in a Peace Corps training effort knows, the things that can be easily said about one's own culture and about another culture tend to be modified when there are members of another culture in attendance. It seems to become more difficult to tell it "as it really is" or at least as it "really is perceived" when the outsiders are in. This is a significant problem that will have to be faced by the black studies program. The fortunate thing about many of those who are advocating black studies is that they want to tell it as it really is to anyone who will listen. They have been shielding their feelings, perceptions, and analyses so long that it will probably be refreshing for them to speak honestly with nonblack students as well as blacks. Nonetheless, they may feel that the first efforts to get their programs established will be so overrun by well-meaning whites anxious to gain new perspectives that black students will not have access to the courses.

In practice, the problem may not be so great, especially since courses about various ethnic communities will continue to be offered in the existing departments, with even the possibility of exchange of faculty on occasion. Nonetheless, the colleges must make every effort within the budgetary limitations imposed upon them to accommodate as many students as possible. No black student who enters the college should be denied an opportunity to take black studies courses; neither, of course, should he be forced to do so. In this connection, the attractiveness of the course offerings to whites as well as blacks may be important in the effort to sustain enrollments in a fledgling program, and thus help provide the necessary resources which are closely tied to the level of student demand for courses. So, the question of student access seems to be not so much a question of legality as of the availability of faculty and other resources.

A sometime country lawyer once said: "The dogmas of the quiet past are inadequate to the stormy present. The occasion is piled high with difficulty, and we must rise to the occasion. As our case is new, so we must think anew and act anew. We must disenthrall ourselves, and then we shall save the country" (Abraham Lincoln). The time is now for higher education to show that it can disenthrall itself and become relevant to the problems of social change highlighted by the call for black studies. If a black studies program serves only to awaken whites to the desperate need to change themselves, it will have been worth the effort.

JULIAN BOND

A New Vision, A Better Tomorrow*

JULIAN BOND is a member of the Georgia House of Representatives
and an active civil rights worker. Because of his allegedly unpatriotic
views—now shared by most Americans—on the war in Vietnam,
he was temporarily denied his seat in the legislature. A leader of a
dissident group of state delegates to the 1968 National Democratic
Convention in Chicago, Mr. Bond was symbolically nominated
as a candidate for Vice President, but he had his name withdrawn
because he was too young for the office. However, there are those,
including Professor Kenneth B. Clark, who believe this young man
may be the first black man to run for the office of Vice President in
the not-too-distant future. Mr. Bond's essay is a brief discussion
of the condition of the black man today. Although economic and
social conditions have improved in the last decade for blacks,
Mr. Bond suggests that it may be necessary to restructure American
society if more far-reaching improvements are to be made.

---

*Reprinted from THE HUMANIST, with permission.

The greatest change in the lives of most black people in the 1960's has occurred because we have become, with the rest of the United States, an urban population. We have moved from the country to the city. In Richmond, Nashville, New Orleans, Jacksonville, and Birmingham we are over 40 per cent of the population. In addition to having gone through that geographical change, black people in this country have gone through another change as well. For some of us, a great number of things have got better. We can now eat in places we could not eat in before. We can go to school at places we could not before. We can get jobs in places we could not get jobs in before. We can vote in places where we could not vote before; we can hold elective offices in places where we couldn't hold elective offices before.

But in many ways, a lot of things have got much worse—and to substantiate this statement let me cite a speech by America's greatest authority on race relations, Lyndon B. Johnson. Johnson said in this speech, delivered at Howard University a little over two years ago, that in 1948 the 8 per cent unemployment rate for Negro teen-age boys was less than that of the whites. By 1964 the rate had grown to 23 per cent as against 13 per cent for whites. Between 1949 and 1959 the income of Negro men relative to white men declined in every section of the country. From 1952 to 1963 the median income of Negro families as compared to whites actually dropped from 57 per cent to 53 per cent. Since 1947 the number of white families living in poverty has decreased 27 per cent, while the number of nonwhite families living in poverty has decreased only 3 per cent. The infant mortality rate for nonwhites in 1940 was 70 per cent greater than for whites. In 1962 the infant mortality rate for nonwhite children was 90 per cent greater than for whites.

When you discuss poverty in the United States, you have to be honest and admit that not all poor people are black people. There are lots of poor white people as well. Poor white people, however, enjoy the dubious distinction of knowing that they are not poor because they are white but are poor in spite of their whiteness. From this we have to assume that there are two kinds of problems in this country; there are problems of race and problems of class. There are 357,000 black men and 419,000 black women who to-morrow morning will be looking for jobs they can't find. There are another 300,000 to 400,000 black women and men who have given up looking for work and are therefore no longer counted as being unemployed by the Labor Department. Unemployment among young black people between the ages of 16 and 21 runs six times as high as that for white people in the same age group.

If you were to take all those statistics and mold an average black man in this country, this would be what you would find: First, there is better than a 50 per cent chance he would have dropped out of high school. He would not only be unemployed but by current standards would be unemployable. He would have no saleable skill. Neither of his parents would have gone beyond the eighth grade. He would have entered school at six but because of overcrowding would have had to attend halfday sessions. During his six years in elementary school he would have attended four different schools.

In discussing this average young slum dweller one has to ask oneself what kind of efforts were made in his past and what efforts will be made in his future to improve his life. Since 1954 there have been various sorts of methods and techniques directed at solving the race problems. These have included the sit-in demonstration and the nonviolent march, the pursuit of education as a barrier breaker, the use of violence as an inducement to change, the challenge in the courts of segregation by law, and the thrust for power through political action. Each of these very obviously has its own successes and its own failures, its own strengths and its own weaknesses. Legal action, for instance, brought black people one of the greatest legal victories of the 20th century—a statement from the Supreme Court in 1954 that segregation in the public schools was illegal. But 15 years later, in 1969, there are more black children attending more black schools north of the Mason-Dixon line than there were in 1954. The sit-in demonstrations and nonviolent marches have obviously had their successes also. They won for southern black people the integrated lunch counter, the integrated bus and train station, the integrated toilet, and the right to vote. Now these first victories, integration of places of public accommodation, have had little meaning for most black people; and the last victory, the right to vote, has yet to win a bread-and-butter victory for them.

A great many people seem to think that education is the answer to the problems of race in this country, but education as a means of breaking down racial barriers dies as an effective means of social change every day that black ghetto children are taught that whiteness is rightness. The young slum dweller was told that poverty would be defeated, diminished, and finally removed from the United States. But by 1967 it had become obvious that the war in Vietnam had rendered that promise almost useless, if it ever was really meant. Violence has been the offical policy of the United States Government in settling her disputes with other nations, and that belief has seeped into the police stations and the slums across the land. War has brewed anger in the black community and has given birth to the belief that nonviolence is only a joke.

There are some people still who believe that nonviolence and nonviolent confrontation will force this government to turn its attention towards a real solution of the race problem in America. There are those who believe that progress of a sort is being made today, and who believe like Scarlett O'Hara that tomorrow will be another day. There are those who are convinced that nothing good will come tomorrow until the structure of today is changed; and there are those who believe that giving small amounts of power, like control of neighborhood schools, will hold off the day of judgment. Now all of these sorts of things have their place, nonviolent confrontation among them, but one ought to remember that the success of nonviolence in India depended on the English having a conscience, while this government is thought to have none. A measure of the amount of conscience in the United States Congress was that only 36 out of all the congressmen could be found to support the recommendations of President Johnson's Committee on Civil Disorder. Now it is true that better days have come for some black people and that perhaps in some far distant future true equality is coming for us. We have to be careful what kind of equality it will be, however, because we may be winning an equal chance to be poor instead of the more than equal chance we have now. If that is democracy, I would suggest that it is a little too much of a good thing. We need to examine and dissect the democratic system, and discover ways of directing it towards benefiting those who are presently its victims. We need to examine and change the job system, the welfare system, the police system, the housing system, the education system, and the health system. These systems need to be controlled by those who are now controlled by them and need to be responsive to the needs and desires of people whose needs and desires are presently now being recorded. President Johnson's Commission on Civil Disorders asked for 500,000 new jobs for blacks. His Administration responded by requesting only 100,000 new jobs. The Commission on Disorders asked for 6 million new housing units for low- and moderate-income families. The Administration responded by asking for only 2^1/$_2$ million. The Commission said that unemployment was the major cause of summer disorder. The Administration responded by cutting 35 million dollars from the emergency summer programs of 1968. Poor education, the Commission said, is a persistent source of grievance and resentment in the black community. President Johnson responded by cutting Federal aid to education. Now if that's the kind of response that we can expect from government, then quite obviously changes must be made. We await with anticipation the programs of the new Congress and the Nixon Administration to see if our expectations can be realized—though at this moment we are dubious. Our decision is between allowing America to continue as she does now, continuing racism, continuing poverty, continuing despair, continuing war, or having the country adopt a new vision of a better tomorrow.

MARTIN LUTHER KING, JR.

A Testament of Hope*

WHEN MARTIN LUTHER KING, JR., was murdered in Memphis the
evening of April 4, 1968, America was deprived of more than
a moderate but effective civil rights leader. It lost a great and good
man and an irreplaceable spiritual force. Unlike many Christians,
Dr. King emulated Christ in his life and work, combining gentleness
and strength with patience. Born in Georgia in 1929, he became
a Baptist minister in Montgomery, Alabama, in 1954 after studying
at Morehouse College, Crozer Theological Seminary, and Boston
University. By organizing and leading the successful bus boycott in
Montgomery in 1956, Dr. King emerged as an important black
spokesman. He founded the Southern Christian Leadership
Conference (SCLC) which was dedicated to winning human rights
for blacks by means of non-violent agitation and confrontation.
Although attacked verbally and physically and periodically jailed,
Martin Luther King worked selflessly for deprived and despairing
blacks in the North as well as the South—and he was intensely

*From A TESTAMENT OF HOPE Copyright © 1968 by the estate of
Martin Luther King, Jr., by permission of Joan Daves.

loved and hated. In 1963 he led the famous March on Washington by thousands of blacks and whites to dramatize the need for broader civil rights legislation. On the steps of the Lincoln Memorial he gave, in his deep and moving voice, an unforgettable speech, in which he said: "I say to you today, my friends, that in spite of the difficulties and frustrations of the moment I still have a dream. It is a dream deeply rooted in the American dream. I have a dream that one day this nation will rise up and live out the true meaning of its creed: 'We hold these truths to be self-evident; that all men are created equal.' "

More celebrated abroad than in his own country, at least during his lifetime, Dr. King was awarded the Nobel Peace Prize in 1964. His books include *Stride Toward Freedom* (1958), *Strength of Love* (1963), *Why We Can't Wait* (1964), and *Where Do We Go From Here: Chaos or Community?* (1967). "A Testament of Hope," the last essay he wrote before his death, was published in *Playboy* magazine in January 1969. The essay ranges widely over the frightening social problems facing America today, focusing on the problem of race. In the essay Dr. King reiterates his belief that the civil rights movement cannot be divorced from the insane war in South Vietnam, an idea which was greeted with derision by many persons who have since changed their minds. Although the title of the essay indicates that Dr. King still had hope for America and for racial harmony, one senses a recurring note of pessimism. Perhaps this hint of pessimism will strike the reader today as a realistic glimpse at the social situation. But pessimism is not despair, which literally means being without hope.

W henever I am asked my opinion of the current state of the civil
rights movement, I am forced to pause; it is not easy to describe a crisis so profound that it has caused the most powerful
nation in the world to stagger in confusion and bewilderment. Today's problems are so acute because the tragic evasions and defaults
of several centuries have accumulated to disaster proportions. The
luxury of a leisurely approach to urgent solutions—the ease of
gradualism—was forfeited by ignoring the issues for too long. The
nation waited until the black man was explosive with fury before
stirring itself even to partial concern. Confronted now with the
interrelated problems of war, inflation, urban decay, white backlash
and a climate of violence, it is now *forced* to address itself to race
relations and poverty, and it is tragically unprepared. What might
once have been a series of separate problems now merge into a
social crisis of almost stupefying complexity.

I am not sad that black Americans are rebelling; this was not
only inevitable but eminently desirable. Without this magnificent
ferment among Negroes, the old evasions and procrastinations would
have continued indefinitely. Black men have slammed the door shut
on a past of deadening passivity. Except for the Reconstruction
years, they have never in their long history on American soil strug-

gled with such creativity and courage for their freedom. These are our bright years of emergence; though they are painful ones, they cannot be avoided.

Yet despite the widening of our stride, history is racing forward so rapidly that the Negro's inherited and imposed disadvantages slow him down to an infuriating crawl. Lack of education, the dislocations of recent urbanization and the hardening of white resistance loom as such tormenting roadblocks that the goal sometimes appears not as a fixed point in the future but as a receding point never to be reached. Still, when doubts emerge, we can remember that only yesterday Negroes were not only grossly exploited but negated as human beings. They were invisible in their misery. But the sullen and silent slave of 110 years ago, an object of scorn at worst or of pity at best, is today's angry man. He is vibrantly on the move; he is forcing change, rather than waiting for it in pathetic futility. In less than two decades, he has roared out of slumber to change so many of his life's conditions that he may yet find the means to accelerate his march forward and overtake the racing locomotive of history.

These words may have an unexpectedly optimistic ring at a time when pessimism is the prevailing mood. People are often surprised to learn that I am an optimist. They know how often I have been jailed, how frequently the days and nights have been filled with frustration and sorrow, how bitter and dangerous are my adversaries. They expect these experiences to harden me into a grim and desperate man. They fail, however, to perceive the sense of affirmation generated by the challenge of embracing struggle and surmounting obstacles. They have no comprehension of the strength that comes from faith in God and man. It is possible for me to falter, but I am profoundly secure in my knowledge that God loves us; He has not worked out a design for our failure. Man has the capacity to do right as well as wrong, and his history is a path upward, not downward. The past is strewn with the ruins of the empires of tyranny, and each is a monument not merely to man's blunders but to his capacity to overcome them. While it is a bitter fact that in America in 1968, I am denied equality solely because I am black, yet I am not a chattel slave. Millions of people have fought thousands of battles to enlarge my freedom; restricted as it still is, progress has been made. This is why I remain an optimist, though I am also a realist, about the barriers before us. Why is the issue of equality still so far from solution in America, a nation that professes itself to be democratic, inventive, hospitable to new ideas, rich, productive and awesomely powerful? The problem is so tenacious because, despite its virtues and attributes, America is deeply racist and its democracy is flawed both economically and socially. All too many Americans believe justice will unfold painlessly or that its absence for black people will be tolerated tranquilly.

Justice for black people will not flow into society merely from court decisions nor from fountains of political oratory. Nor will a few token changes quell all the tempestuous yearnings of millions of disadvantaged black people. White America must recognize that justice for black people cannot be achieved without radical changes in the structure of our society. The comfortable, the entrenched, the privileged cannot continue to tremble at the prospect of change in the *status quo*.

Stephen Vincent Benét had a message for both white and black Americans in the title of a story, *Freedom Is a Hard Bought Thing*. When millions of people have been cheated for centuries, restitution is a costly process. Inferior education, poor housing, unemployment, inadequate health care—each is a bitter component of the oppression that has been our heritage. Each will require billions of dollars to correct. Justice so long deferred has accumulated interest and its cost for this society will be substantial in financial as well as human terms. This fact has not been fully grasped, because most of the gains of the past decade were obtained at bargain rates. The desegregation of public facilities cost nothing; neither did the election and appointment of a few black public officals.

The price of progress would have been high enough at the best of times, but we are in an agonizing national crisis because a complex of profound problems has intersected in an explosive mixture. The black surge toward freedom has raised justifiable demands for racial justice in our major cities at a time when all the problems of city life have simultaneously erupted. Schools, transportation, water supply, traffic and crime would have been municipal agonies whether or not Negroes lived in our cities. The anarchy of unplanned city growth was destined to confound our confidence. What is unique to this period is our inability to arrange an order of priorities that promises solutions that are decent and just.

Millions of Americans are coming to see that we are fighting an immoral war that costs nearly 30 billion dollars a year, that we are perpetuating racism, that we are tolerating almost 40,000,000 poor during an overflowing material abundance. Yet, they remain helpless to end the war, to feed the hungry, to make brotherhood a reality; this has to shake our faith in ourselves. If we look honestly at the realities of our national life, it is clear that we are not marching forward; we are groping and stumbling; we are divided and confused. Our moral values and our spiritual confidence sink, even as our material wealth ascends. In these trying circumstances, the black revolution is much more than a struggle for the right of Negroes. It is forcing America to face all its interrelated flaws—racism, poverty, militarism and materialism. It is exposing evils that are rooted deeply in the whole structure of our society. It reveals systemic rather than superficial flaws and suggests that radical reconstruction of society itself is the real issue to be faced.

It is time that we stopped our blithe lip service to the guarantees of life, liberty and pursuit of happiness. These fine sentiments are embodied in the Declaration of Independence, but that document was always a declaration of intent rather than of reality. There were slaves when it was written; there were still slaves when it was adopted; and to this day, black Americans have not life, liberty nor the privilege of pursuing happiness, and millions of poor white Americans are in economic bondage that is scarcely less oppressive. Americans who genuinely treasure our national ideals, who know they are still elusive dreams for all too many, should welcome the stirring of Negro demands. They are shattering the complacency that allowed a multitude of social evils to accumulate. Negro agitation is requiring America to re-examine its comforting myths and may yet catalyze the drastic reforms that will save us from social catastrophe.

In indicting white America for its ingrained and tenacious racism, I am using the term "white" to describe the majority, not *all* who are white. We have found that there are many white people who clearly perceive the justice of the Negro struggle for human dignity. Many of them joined our struggle and displayed heroism no less inspiring than that of black people. More than a few died by our side; their memories are cherished and are undimmed by time.

Yet the largest part of white America is still poisoned by racism, which is as native to our soil as pine trees, sagebrush and buffalo grass. Equally native to us is the concept that gross exploitation of the Negro is acceptable, if not commendable. Many whites who concede that Negroes should have equal access to public facilities and the untrammeled right to vote cannot understand that we do not intend to remain in the basement of the economic structure; they cannot understand why a porter or a housemaid would dare dream of a day when his work will be more useful, more remunerative and a pathway to rising opportunity. This incomprehension is a heavy burden in our efforts to win white allies for the long struggle.

But the American Negro has in his nature the spiritual and worldly fortitude to eventually win his struggle for justice and freedom. It is a moral fortitude that has been forged by centuries of oppression. In their sorrow and their hardship, Negroes have become almost instinctively cohesive. We band together readily; and against white hostility, we have an intense and wholesome loyalty to one another. But we cannot win our struggle for justice all alone, nor do I think that most Negroes want to exclude well-intentioned whites from participation in the black revolution. I believe there is an important place in our struggle for white liberals and I hope that their present estrangement from our movement is only temporary. But many white people in the past joined our movement with a kind of messianic faith that they were going to save the Negro and solve all of his problems very quickly. They tended, in some instances, to be rather aggressive and insensitive to the opinions and abilities of the black people with whom they were working; this has been especially true of students. In many cases, they simply did not know how to work in a supporting secondary role. I think this problem became most evident when young men and women from elite Northern universities came down to Mississippi to work with the black students at Tougaloo and Rust Colleges, who were not quite as articulate, didn't type quite as fast and were not as sophisticated. Inevitably, feeling of white paternalism and black inferiority became exaggerated. The Negroes who rebelled against white liberals were trying to assert their own equality and to cast off the mantle of paternalism.

Fortunately, we haven't had this problem in the Southern Christian Leadership Conference. Most of the white people who were working with us in 1962 and 1963 are still with us. We have always enjoyed a relationship of mutual respect. But I think a great many white liberals, outside S.C.L.C. also have learned this basic lesson in human relations, thanks largely to Jimmy Baldwin and others who have articulated some of the problems of being black in a multiracial society. And I am happy to report that relationships between whites and Negroes in the human rights movement are now on a much healthier basis.

In society at large, abrasion between the races is far more evident—but the hostility was always there. Relations today are different only in the sense that Negroes are expressing the feelings that were so long muted. The constructive achievements of the decade 1955 to 1965 deceived us. Everyone underestimated the amount of violence and rage Negroes were suppressing and the vast amount of bigotry the white majority was disguising. All-black organizations are a reflection of that alienation—but they are only a contemporary [sic] way station on the road to freedom. They are a product of this period of identity crisis and directionless confusion. As the human rights movement becomes more confident and aggressive, more nonviolently active, many of these emotional and intellectual problems will be resolved in the heat of battle, and we will not ask what is our neighbor's color but whether he is a brother in the pursuit of racial justice. For much of the fervent idealism of the white liberals has been supplemented recently by a dispassionate recognition of some of the cold realities of the struggle for that justice.

One of the most basic of these realities was pointed out by the President's Riot Commission, which observed that the nature of the American economy in the late 19th and early 20th Centuries made it possible for the European immigrants of that time to escape from poverty. It was an economy that had room for—even a great need for—unskilled manual labor. Jobs were available for willing workers, even those with the educational and language liabilities they had brought with them. But the American economy today is radically different. There are fewer and fewer jobs for the culturally and educationally deprived; thus does present-day poverty feed upon and perpetuate itself. The Negro today cannot escape from his ghetto in the way that Irish, Italian, Jewish and Polish immigrants escaped from their ghettos 50 years ago. New methods of escape must be found. And one of these roads to escape will be a more equitable sharing of political power between Negroes and whites. Integration is meaningless without the sharing of power. When I speak of integration, I don't mean a romantic mixing of colors, I mean a real sharing of power and responsibility. We will eventually achieve this, but it is going to be much more difficult for us than for any other minority. After all, no other minority has been so constantly, brutally and deliberately exploited. But because of this very exploitation, Negroes bring a special spiritual and moral contribution to American life—a contribution without which America could not survive.

The implications of true racial integration are more than just national in scope. I don't believe we can have world peace until America has an "integrated" foreign policy. Our disastrous experiences in Vietnam and the Dominican Republic have been, in one sense, a result of racist decision making. Men of the white West, whether or not they like it, have grown up in a racist culture, and their thinking is colored by that fact. They have been fed on a false mythology and tradition that blinds them to the aspirations and talents of other men. They don't really respect anyone who is not white. But we simply cannot have peace in the world without mutual respect. I honestly feel that a man without racial blinders–or, even better, a man with personal experience of racial discrimination— would be in a much better position to make policy decisions and to conduct negotiations with the underprivileged and emerging nations of the world (or even with Castro, for that matter) than would an Eisenhower or a Dulles.

The American Marines might not even have been needed in Santo Dominigo, had the American ambassador there been a man who was sensitive to the color dynamics that pervade the national life of the Dominican Republic. Black men in positions of power in the business world would not be so unconscionable as to trade or traffic with the Union of South Africa, nor would they be so insensitive to the problems and needs of Latin America that they would continue the patterns of America exploitation that now prevail there. When we replace the rabidly segregationist chairman of the Armed Services Committee with a man of good will, when our ambassadors reflect a creative and wholesome interracial background, rather than a cultural heritage that is a conglomeration of Texas and Georgia politics, then we will be able to bring about a qualitative difference in the nature of American foreign policy. This is what we mean when we talk about redeeming the soul of America. Let me make it clear that I don't think white men have a monopoly on sin or greed. But I think there has been a kind of collective experience—a kind of shared misery in the black community—that makes it a little harder for us to exploit other people.

I have come to hope that American Negroes can be a bridge between white civilization and the nonwhite nations of the world, because we have roots in both. Spiritually, Negroes identify understandably with Africa, an identification that is rooted largely in our color; but all of us are a part of the white-American world, too. Our education has been Western and our language, our attitudes—though we sometimes tend to deny it—are very much influenced by Western civilization. Even our emotional life has been disciplined and some-times stifled and inhibited by an essentially European upbringing. So, although in one sense we are neither, in another sense we are both American and Africans. Our very bloodlines are a mixture. I hope and feel that out of the universality of our experience, we can help make peace and harmony in this world more possible.

Although American Negroes could, if they were in decision-making positions, give aid and encouragement to the underprivileged and disenfranchised people in other lands, I don't think it can work the other way around. I don't think the nonwhites in other parts of the world can really be of any concrete help to us, given their own problems of development and self-determination. In fact, American Negroes have greater collective buying power than Canada, greater than all four of the Scandinavian countries combined. American Negroes have greater economic potential than most of the nations—perhaps even more than *all* of the nations—of Africa. We don't *need* to look for help from some power outside the boundaries of our country, except in the sense of sympathy and identification. Our challenge, rather, is to organize the power we already have in our midst. The Newark riots, for example, could certainly have been prevented by a more aggressive political involvement on the part of that city's Negroes. There is utterly no reason Addonizio should be the mayor of Newark, with the Negro majority that exists in that city. Gary, Indiana, is another tinderbox city; but its black mayor, Richard Hatcher, has given Negroes a new faith in the effectiveness of the political process.

One of the most basic weapons in the fight for social justice will be the cumulative political power of the Negro. I can foresee the Negro vote becoming consistently the decisive vote in national elections. It is already decisive in states that have large numbers of electoral votes. Even today, the Negroes in New York City strongly influence how New York State will go in national elections, and the Negroes of Chicago have a similar leverage in Illinois. Negroes are even the decisive balance of power in the elections in Georgia, South Carolina and Virginia. So the party and the candidate that get the support of the Negro voter in national elections have a very definite edge, and we intend to use this fact to win advances in the struggle for human rights. I have every confidence that the black vote will ultimately help unseat the diehard opponents of equal rights in Congress—who are, incidentally, reactionary on all issues. But the Negro community cannot win this victory alone; indeed, it would be an empty victory even if the Negroes *could* win it alone. Intelligent men of good will everywhere must see this as their task and contribute to its support.

The election of Negro mayors, such as Hatcher, in some of the nation's larger cities has also had a tremendous psychological impact upon the Negro. It has shown him that he has the potential to participate in the determination of his own destiny—and that of society. We will see more Negro mayors in major cities in the next ten years, but this is not the ultimate answer. Mayors are relatively impotent figures in the scheme of national politics. Even a white mayor such as John Lindsay of New York simply does not have the money and resources to deal with the problems of his city. The necessary money to deal with urban problems must come from the Federal Government, and this money is ultimately controlled by the Congress of the United States. The success of these enlightened mayors is entirely dependent upon the financial support made available by Washington.

The past record of the Federal Government, however, has not been encouraging. No President has really done very much for the American Negro, though the past two Presidents have received much undeserved credit for helping us. This credit has accrued to Lyndon Johnson and John Kennedy only because it was during their Administrations that Negroes began doing more for themselves. Kennedy didn't voluntarily submit a civil rights bill, nor did Lyndon Johnson. In fact, both told us at one time that such legislation was impossible. President Johnson did respond realistically to the signs of the times and used his skills as a legislator to get bills through Congress that other men might not have gotten through. I must point out, in all honesty, however, that President Johnson has not been nearly so diligent in *implementing* the bills he has helped shepherd through Congress.

Of the ten titles of the 1964 Civil Rights Act, probably only the one concerning public accommodations—the most bitterly contested section—has been meaningfully enforced and implemented. Most of the other sections have been deliberately ignored. The same is true of the 1965 Voting Rights Act, which provides for Federal referees to monitor the registration of voters in counties where Negroes have systematically been denied the right to vote. Yet of the some 900 counties that are eligible for Federal referees, only 58 counties to date have had them. The 842 other counties remain essentially just as they were before the march on Selma. Look at the pattern of Federal referees in Mississippi, for example. They are dispersed in a manner that gives the appearance of change without any real prospect of actually shifting political power or giving Negroes a genuine opportunity to be represented in the government of their state. There is a similar pattern in Alabama, even though that state is currently at odds with the Democratic Administration in Washington because of George Wallace. Georgia, until just recently, had no Federal referees at all, not even in the hard-core black-belt counties. I think it is significant that there are no Federal referees at all in the home districts of the most powerful Southern Senators—particularly Senators Russell, Eastland and Talmadge. The power and moral corruption of these Senators remain unchallenged, despite the weapon for change the legislation promised to be. Reform was thwarted when the legislation was inadequately enforced.

But not all is bad in the South, by any means. Though the fruits of our struggle have sometimes been nothing more than bitter despair, I must admit there have been some hopeful signs, some meaningful successes. One of the most hopeful of these changes is the attitude of the Southern Negro himself. Benign acceptance of second-class citizensip has been displaced by vigorous demands for full citizenship rights and opportunities. In fact, most of our concrete accomplishments have been limited largely to the South. We have put an end to racial segregation in the South; we have brought about the beginning of reform in the political system; and, as incongruous as it may seem, a Negro is probably safer in most Southern cities than he is in the cities of the North. We have confronted the racist policemen of the South and demanded reforms in the police departments. We have confronted the Southern racist power structure and we have elected Negro and liberal white candidates through much of the South in the past ten years. George Wallace is certainly an exception, and Lester Maddox is a sociological fossil. But despite these anachronisms, at the city and county level, there is a new respect for black votes and black citizenship that just did not exist ten years ago. Though school integration has moved at a depressingly slow rate in the South, it *has* moved. Of far more significance is the fact that we have learned that the integration of schools does not necessarily solve the inadequacy of schools. White schools are often just about as bad as black schools, and integrated schools sometimes tend to merge the problems of the two without solving either of them.

There *is* progress in the South, however—progress expressed by the presence of Negroes in the Georgia House of Representatives, in the election of a Negro to the Mississippi House of Representatives, in the election of a black sheriff in Tuskegee, Alabama, and, most especially, in the integration of police forces throughout the Southern states. There are now even Negro deputy sheriffs in such black-belt areas as Dallas County, Alabama. Just three years ago, a Negro could be beaten for going into the county courthouse in Dallas County; now Negroes share in running it. So there *are* some changes. But the changes are basically in the social and political areas; the problems we now face–providing jobs, better housing and better education for the poor throughout the country—will require money for their solution, a fact that makes those solutions all the more difficult.

The need for solutions, meanwhile, becomes more urgent every day, because these problems are far more serious now than they were just a few years ago. Before 1964, things were getting better economically for the Negro; but after that year, things began to take a turn for the worse. In particular, automation began to cut into our jobs very badly, and this snuffed out the few sparks of hope the black people had begun to nurture. As long as there was some measurable and steady economic progress, Negroes were willing and able to press harder and work harder and hope for something better. But when the door began to close on the few avenues of progress, the hopeless despair began to set in.

The fact that most white people do not comprehend this situation—which prevails in the North as well as in the South—is due largely to the press, which molds the opinions of the white community. Many whites hasten to congratulate themselves on what little progress we Negroes have made. I'm sure that most whites felt that with the passage of the 1964 Civil Rights Act, all race problems were automatically solved. Because most white people are so far removed from the life of the average Negro, there has been little to challenge this assumption. Yet Negroes continue to live with racism every day. It doesn't matter where we are individually in the scheme of things, how near we may be either to the top or to the bottom of society; the cold facts of racism slap each one of us in the face. A friend of mine is a lawyer, one of the most brilliant young men I know. Were he a white lawyer, I have no doubt that he would be in a $100,000 job with a major corporation or heading his own independent firm. As it is, he makes a mere $20,000 a year. This may seem like a lot of money and, to most of us, it is; but the point is that this young man's background and abilities would, if his skin color were different, entitle him to an income many times that amount.

I don't think there is a single major insurance company that hires Negro lawyers. Even within the agencies of the Federal Government, most Negro employees are in the lower echelons; only a handful of Negroes in Federal employment are in upper-income brackets. This is a situation that cuts across this country's economic spectrum. The Chicago Urban League recently conducted a research project in the Kenwood community on the South Side. They discovered that the average educational grade level of Negroes in that community was 10.6 years and the median income was about $4200 a year. In nearby Gage Park, the median educational grade level of the whites was 8.6 years, but the median income was $9600 per year. In fact, the average white high school dropout makes as much as, if not more than, the average Negro college graduate.

Solutions for these problems, urgent as they are, must be constructive and rational. Rioting and violence provide no solutions for economic problems. Much of the justification for rioting has come from the thesis—originally set forth by Franz Fanon—that violence has a certain cleansing effect. Perhaps, in a special psychological sense, he may have had a point. But we have seen a better and more constructive cleansing process in our nonviolent demonstrations. Another theory to justify violent revolution is that rioting enables Negroes to overcome their fear of the white man. But they are just as afraid of the power structure after a riot as before. I remember that was true when our staff went into Rochester, New York, after the riot of 1964. When we discussed the possibility of going down to talk with the police, the people who had been most aggressive in the violence were afraid to talk. They still had a sense of inferiority; and not until they were bolstered by the presence of our staff and given reassurance of their political power and the rightness of their cause and the justness of their grievances were they able and willing to sit down and talk to the police chief and the city manager about the conditions that had produced the riot.

As a matter of fact, I think the aura of paramilitarism among the black militant groups speaks much more of fear than it does of confidence. I know, in my own experience, that I was much more afraid in Montgomery when I had a gun in my house. When I decided that, as a teacher of the philosophy of nonviolence, I couldn't keep a gun, I came face to face with the question of death and I dealt with it. And from that point on, I no longer needed a gun nor have I been afraid. Ultimately, one's sense of manhood must come from within him.

The riots in Negro ghettos have been, in one sense, merely another expression of the growing climate of violence in America. When a culture begins to feel threatened by its own inadequacies, the majority of men tend to prop themselves up by artificial means, rather than dig down deep into their spiritual and cultural wellsprings. America seems to have reached this point. Americans as a whole feel threatened by communism on one hand and, on the other, by the rising tide of aspirations among the undeveloped nations. I think most Americans know in their hearts that their country has been terribly wrong in its dealings with other peoples around the world. When Rome began to disintegrate from within, it turned to a strengthening of the military establishment, rather than to a correction of the corruption within the society. We are doing the same thing in this country and the result will probably be the same— unless, and here I admit to a bit of chauvinism, the black man in America can provide a new soul force for all Americans, a new expression of the American dream that need not be realized at the expense of other men around the world, but a dream of opportunity and life that can be shared with the rest of the world.

It seems glaringly obvious to me that the development of a humanitarian means of dealing with some of the social problems of the world—and the correlative revolution in American values that this will entail—is a much better way of protecting ourselves against the threat of violence than the military means we have chosen. On these grounds, I must indict the Johnson Administration. It has seemed amazingly devoid of statesmanship; and when creative statesmanship wanes, irrational militarism increases. In this sense, President Kennedy was far more of a statesman than President Johnson. He was a man who was big enough to admit when he was wrong—as he did after the Bay of Pigs incident. But Lyndon Johnson seems to be unable to make this kind of statesmanlike gesture in connection with Vietnam. And I think that this has led, as Senator Fulbright has said, to such a strengthening of the military-industrial complex of this country that the President now finds himself almost totally trapped by it. Even at this point, when he can readily summon popular support to end the bombing in Vietnam, he persists. Yet bombs in Vietnam also explode at home; they destroy the hopes and possibilities for a decent America.

In our effort to dispel this atmosphere of violence in this country, we cannot afford to overlook the root cause of the riots. The President's Riot Commission concluded that most violence-prone Negroes are teenagers or young adults who, almost invariably, are underemployed ("underemployed" means working every day but earning an income below the poverty level) or who are employed in menial jobs. And according to a recent Department of Labor statistical report, 24.8 percent of Negro youth are currently unemployed, a statistic that does not include the drifters who avoid the census takers. Actually, it's my guess that the statistics are very, very conservative in this area. The Bureau of the Census has admitted a ten-percent error in this age group, and the unemployment statistics are based on those who are actually applying for jobs.

But it isn't just a lack of work; it's also a lack of *meaningful* work. In Cleveland, 58 percent of the young men between the ages of 16 and 25 were estimated to be either unemployed or underemployed. This appalling situation is probably 90 percent of the root cause of the Negro riots. A Negro who has finished high school often watches his white classmates go out into the job market and earn $100 a week, while he, because he is black, is expected to work for $40 a week. Hence, there is a tremendous hostility and resentment that only a difference in race keeps him out of an adequate job. This situation is social dynamite. When you add the lack of recreational facilities and adequate job counseling, and the continuation of an aggressively hostile police environment, you have a truly explosive situation. Any night on any street corner in any Negro ghetto of the country, a nervous policeman can start a riot simply by being impolite or by expressing racial prejudice. And white people are sadly unaware how routinely and frequently this occurs.

It hardly needs to be said that solutions to these critical problems are overwhelmingly urgent. The President's Riot Commission recommended that funds for summer programs aimed at young Negroes should be increased. New York is already spending more on its special summer programs than on its year-round poverty efforts, but these are only tentative and emergency steps toward a truly meaningful and permanent solution. And the negative thinking in this area voiced by many whites does not help the situation. Unfortunately, many white people think that we merely "reward" a rioter by taking positive action to better his situation. What these white people do not realize is that the Negroes who riot have given up on America. When nothing is done to alleviate their plight, this merely confirms the Negroes' conviction that America is a hopelessly decadent society. When something positive is done, however, when constructive action follows a riot, a rioter's despair is allayed and he is forced to re-evaluate America and to consider whether some good might eventually come from our society after all.

But, I repeat, the recent curative steps that have been taken are, at best, inadequate. The summer poverty programs, like most other Government projects, function well in some places and are totally ineffective in others. The difference, in large measure, is one of citizen participation; that is the key to success or failure. In cases such as the Farmers' Marketing Cooperative Association in the black belt of Alabama and the Child Development Group in Mississippi, where the people were really involved in the planning and action of the program, it was one of the best experiences in self-help and grass-roots initiative. But in places like Chicago, where poverty programs are used strictly as a tool of the political machinery and for dispensing party patronage, the very concept of helping the poor is defiled and the poverty program becomes just another form of enslavement. I still wouldn't want to do away with it, though, even in Chicago. We must simply fight at both the local and the national levels to gain as much community control as possible over the poverty program.

But there is no single answer to the plight of the American Negro. Conditions and needs vary greatly in different sections of the country. I think that the place to start, however, is in the area of human relations, and especially in the area of community-police relations. This is a sensitive and touchy problem that has rarely been adequately emphasized. Virtually every riot has begun from some police action. If you try to tell the people in most Negro communities that the police are their friends, they just laugh at you. Obviously, something desperately needs to be done to correct this. I have been particularly impressed by the fact that even in the state of Mississippi, where the FBI did a significant training job with the Mississippi police, the police are much more courteous to Negroes than they are in Chicago or New York. Our police forces simply must develop an attitude of courtesy and respect for the ordinary citizen. If we can just stop policemen from using profanity in their

(handwritten margin note: Police Occupation Troops)

encounters with black people, we will have accomplished a lot. In the larger sense, police must cease being occupation troops in the ghetto and start protecting its residents. Yet very few cities have really faced up to this problem and tried to do something about it. It is the most abrasive element in Negro-white relations, but it is the last to be scientifically and objectively appraised.

When you go beyond a relatively simple though serious problem such as police racism, however, you begin to get into all the complexities of the modern American economy. Urban transit systems in most American cities, for example, have become a genuine civil rights issue—and a valid one—because the layout of rapid-transit systems determines the accessibility of jobs to the black community. If transportation systems in American cities could be laid out so as to provide an opportunity for poor people to get meaningful employment, then they could begin to move into the mainstream of American life. A good example of this problem is my home city of Atlanta, where the rapid-transit system has been laid out for the convenience of the white upper-middle-class suburbanites who commute to their jobs downtown. The system has virtually no consideration for connecting the poor people with their jobs. There is only one possible explanation for this situation, and that is the racist blindness of city planners.

The same problems are to be found in the areas of rent supplement and low-income housing. The relevance of these issues to human relations and human rights cannot be overemphasized. The kind of house a man lives in, along with the quality of his employment, determines, to a large degree, the quality of his family life. I have known too many people in my own parish in Atlanta who, because they were living in overcrowded apartments, were constantly bickering with other members of their families—a situation that produced many kinds of severe dysfunctions in family relations. And yet I have seen these same families achieve harmony when they were able to afford a house allowing for a little personal privacy and freedom of movement.

All these human-relations problems are complex and related, and it's very difficult to assign priorities—especially as long as the Vietnam war continues. The Great Society has become a victim of the war. I think there was a sincere desire in this country four or five years ago to move toward a genuinely great society, and I have little doubt that there would have been a gradual increase in Federal expenditures in this direction, rather than the gradual decline that has occurred, if the war in Vietnam had been avoided.

One of the incongruities of this situation is the fact that such a large number of the soldiers in the Armed Forces in Vietnam—especially the front-line soldiers who are actually doing the fighting—are Negroes. Negroes have always held the hope that if they really demonstrate that they are great soldiers and if they really fight for America and help save American democracy then when they come back home, America will treat them better. This has not been the case. Negro soldiers returning from World War One were met with race riots, job discrimination and continuation of the bigotry that they had experienced before. After World War Two, the GI Bill did offer some hope for a better life to those who had the educational background to take advantage of it, and there was proportionately less turmoil. But for the Negro GI, military service still represents a means of escape from the oppressive ghettos of the rural South and the urban North. He often sees the Army as an avenue for educational opportunities and job training. He sees in the military uniform a symbol of dignity that has long been denied him by society. The tragedy in this is that military service is probably the only possible escape for most young Negro men. Many of them go into the Army, risking death, in order that they might have a few of the human possibilities of life. They know that life in the city ghetto or life in the rural South almost certainly means jail or death or humiliation. And so, by comparison, military service is really the lesser risk.

One young man on our staff, Hosea Williams, returned from the foxholes of Germany a 60-percent-disabled veteran. After 13 months in a veterans' hospital, he went back to his home town of Attapulgus, Georgia. On his way home, he went into a bus station at Americus, Georgia, to get a drink of water while waiting for his next bus. And while he stood there on his crutches, drinking from the fountain, he was beaten savagely by white hoodlums. This pathetic incident is all too typical of the treatment received by Negroes in this country—not only physical brutality but brutal discrimination when a Negro tries to buy a house, and brutal violence against the Negro's soul when he finds himself denied a job that he knows he is qualified for.

There is also the violence of having to live in a community and pay higher consumer prices for goods or higher rent for equivalent housing than are charged in the white areas of the city. Do you know that a can of beans almost always costs a few cents more in grocery chain stores located in the Negro ghetto than in a store of that same chain located in the upper-middle-class suburbs, where the median income is five times as high? The Negro knows it, because he works in the white man's house as a cook or a gardener. And what do you think this knowledge does to his soul? How do you think it affects his views of the society he lives in? How can you expect anything but disillusionment and bitterness? The question that now faces us is whether we can turn the Negro's disillusionment and bitterness into hope and faith in the essential goodness of the American system. If we don't, our society will crumble.

It is a paradox that those Negroes who have given up on America are doing more to improve it than are its professional patriots. They are stirring the mass of smug, somnolent citizens, who are neither evil nor good, to an awareness of crisis. The confrontation involves not only their morality but their self-interest, and that combination promises to evoke positive action. This is not a nation of venal people. It is a land of individuals who, in the majority, have not cared, who have been heartless about their black neighbors because their ears are blocked and their eyes blinded by the tragic myth that Negroes endure abuse without pain or complaint. Even when protest flared and denied the myth, they were fed new doctrines of inhumanity that argued that Negroes were arrogant, lawless and ungrateful. Habitual white discrimination was transformed into white backlash. But for some, the lies had lost their grip and an internal disquiet grew. Poverty and discrimination were undeniably real; they scarred the nation; they dirtied our honor and diminished our pride. An insistent question defied evasion: Was security for some being purchased at the price of degradation for others? Everything in our traditions said this kind of injustice was the system of the past or of other nations. And yet there it was, abroad in our own land.

Thus was born—particularly in the young generation—a spirit of dissent that ranged from superficial disavowal of the old values to total commitment to wholesale, drastic and immediate social reform. Yet all of it was dissent. Their voice is still a minority; but united with millions of black protesting voices, it has become a sound of distant thunder increasing in volume with the gathering of storm clouds. This dissent is America's hope. It shines in the long tradition of American ideals that began with courageous minutemen in New England, that continued in the Abolitionist movement, that re-emerged in the Populist revolt and, decades later, that burst forth to elect Franklin Roosevelt and John F. Kennedy. Today's dissenters tell the complacement majority that the time has come when further evasion of social responsibility in a turbulent world will court disaster and death. America has not yet changed because so many think it need not change, but this is the illusion of the damned. America must change because 23,000,000 black citizens will no longer live supinely in a wretched past. They have left the valley of despair; they have found strength in struggle; and whether they live or die, they shall never crawl nor retreat again. Joined by white allies, they will shake the prison walls until they fall. America must change.

A voice out of Bethlehem 2000 years ago said that all men are equal. It said right would triumph. Jesus of Nazareth wrote no books; he owned no property to endow him with influence. He had no friends in the courts of the powerful. But he changed the course of mankind with only the poor and the despised. Naïve and unsophisticated though we may be, the poor and despised of the 20th Century will revolutionize this era. In our "arrogance, lawlessness and ingratitude," we will fight for human justice, brotherhood, secure peace and abundance for all. When we have won these—in a spirit of unshakable nonviolence—then, in luminous splendor, the Christian era will truly begin.